Eighteenth Century Chemistry as it Relates to Alchemy

Encyclopedia Brittania (1771)

ISBN 1-56459-304-5

Kessinger Publishing's Rare Reprints
Thousands of Scarce and Hard-to-Find Books!

.
.
.
.
.
.
.
.
.
.
.
.
.
.
.
.
.
.

We kindly invite you to view our extensive catalog list at:
http://www.kessinger.net

TABLE OF CONTENTS

TABLE OF CONTENTS

ii

TABLE OF CONTENTS

iii

TABLE OF CONTENTS

TABLE OF CONTENTS

PREFACE

I was naturally elated about six months ago when I received a long distance telephone call from Curt Kobylarz, saying he had located the Encyclopedia Britannia for 1771 containing the article on CHEMISTRY, which, on the saying of the Rocky Mountain Alchemist, contains the process for obtaining the Philosopher's Mercury. When he offered to send me a zerox copy of the article I was overjoyed. On receiving the material and going over it, it rang a bell in my mind. I felt almost as though I were reading something I, myself, might have written, if I had the knowledge of course.

On the third reading I knew this information had to be shared, regardless of the cost in precious time, labor and money. My approach to life seems to be somewhat cynical, at least verbally, and I do not really expect nor desire credit for the good that may flow through me to others. Here I had something that every sincere alchemical student ought to have. Was I going to sit on it, in the manner of those secretive, would be alchemists, who bought up every rare book on alchemy as collector's items, and refused to release the knowledge they contained, to the sincere seeker after truth? Of course not!

Most of those who are acquainted with me, through my writing, and the classes I have taught, consider me as a top ranking authority on Sidereal Astrology, with perhaps some lesser interest in Alchemy and the Quabalah. These people know that we go to extremes in attempting to make new discoveries and old truths available to all. With this in mind, the publication of "Eighteenth Century Chemistry", should come as no surprise to them.

The true alchemist must have more than a passing acquaintance with astrology and the Quabalah as well as in alchemy. Some schools of thought hold that the fourth pillar of alchemy is Ritual or Ceremonial Magic. The following pages will give us an interesting run down on the first part of alchemy, the breaking down of all matter into its four principles; fire, air, water and earth, and its three essentials; Mercury, Sulphur and Salt. This one division is more clearly listed below:

> Mercury   Spirit
> Sulphur   Soul
> Salt   Body

To phrase the matter as concisely as possible: "Everything contains within it the four elements and the three essentials".

January 18, 1978   Carl W. Stahl

INTRODUCTION

It is our hope, that the publication of this book on Eighteen Century will clarify some of the methods and practices used in the art of alchemy, the mother of chemistry. We want you to pay particular attention to the word 'clarify', which basically means 'to clear up'. We are using it in the sense of removing that which hinders understanding of the truth because it debases or clouds our perception ot it.

Perhaps an example will clarify what we mean. If you want pure water you must remove from it all impurities. This is usually done by distillation of the water which results in leaving most polutants behind while pure water comes over in the form of steam or condensation. Now let us suppose you wished to form a red colored liquid by adding a red dye. Surely common sense would indicate the use of the distilled, or purified, water as giving the clearest and most brilliant red color. Muddy or otherwise polluted water, on the other hand, would give us a duller, less brilliant red.

In order to do something correctly, or to begin something new, it is always a good idea to put aside all preconveived notions and conditioning. In some way we must remove the collection of falsehoods, predjudices and half-truths that we have adopted since we began to learn for ourselves the facts of life.

Since this book is on Eighteenth Century Chemistry we are going to have to get it clear in our minds what this means. In 1771 there was still very little difference between the processes and methods used in the early alchemistical steps and chemistry. The only real difference is that this article on chemistry makes no attempt to cloud the issue. It makes no effort to hide, to deceive, mislead or in any way to throw the seeker off the trail. A fault we find so frequently in so-called books on alchemy written by so-called alchemists whose only knowledge is that which they have copied from others who knew as little, or as much, depending on your point of view, as they did.

This book is being brought out for the practical alchemist. Those who attempt to practice what others only write about. Of course it will be of interest also to those whose interests run to ancient chemistry but this is not its main purpose.

We have given a combination of a table of contents and index. This will make it quite easy to find the material and process which you are seeking. This is an improvement you would find impossible to believe unless you had tried to find something without it in the article itself.

You will find misspelled words, what appear to be typographical errors and words that seem to mean absolutely nothing. We left all words, right or wrong, as we found them, with the exception of changing the (f's) for the (s's) they were intended to be. For some reason the printers of those days had either an excessive love of the German 'f' for 's', or an oversupply of the one type setting as opposed to the other. This makes for very difficult reading.

You will find the processes for breaking down the vegetable kingdom, the mininers (or semi-metal) kingdom, the metalline kingdome and the animal kingdom are all covered in this book.

Keep in mind that here chemistry is more or less the breaking down and cataloguing of all these steps which is very much to our advantage. Having mastered these steps we are now ready to go on to the more advanced processes of alchemy. The raising of the vibrations. The reuniting of the three essentials into a new and transmuted substance.

Study, analyze, and perform the experiments given; always in their relationship to their future use in alchemy. In this book you are being handed the equivilent of a seven year course of instruction in any school on alchemy of which I am at present aware. The study of alchemy, astrology and the Quabalah will round out your intellectual understanding of the cause and nature of life. And then, suddenly, by the Grace of God, illumination will come your way and with it the urge to serve the Lord by helping your fellow humans, whatever their problems.

January 19, 1978   Carl W. Stahl

C H E M I S T R Y

The object and chief end of chemistry is to separate the different substances that enter into the composition of bodies; to examine each of them apart; to discover their properties and relations; to decompose those very substances, if possible; to compare them together, and combine them with others; to reunite them again into one body, so as to reproduce the original compound with all its properties; or even to produce new compounds that never existed among the works of nature, from mixtures of other matters differently combined.

But this analysis, or decomposition of bodies is finite; for we are unable to carry it beyond a certain limit. In whatever way we attempt to go further, we are always stopped by substances in which we can produce no change, and which are incapable of being resolved into others. To these substances we may give the title of principles of elements. Of this kind the principal are earth, water, air, and fire. For though there be reason to think that these are not the first component parts, or the most simple elements of matter; yet, as we know by experience, that our senses cannot possibly discover, the principles of which they are themselves composed, it seems more reasonable to fix upon them, and consider them as simple homogeneous bodies, and the principles of the rest, than to tire our minds with vain conjectures about the parts of elements of which they may consist.

Before entering upon the examination of compound substances, it is necessary to consider the most simple ones, or the four first principles, with some attention.

PART I.   THEORY OF CHEMISTRY

OF THE PRINCIPLES OF BODIES. OF AIR.   Air is that fluid which we constantly breathe, and which encompasses the whole surface of the terrestrial globe. Being heavy, like other bodies, it penetrates into all places that are not either absolutely inaccessible, or filled with some other body heavier than itself. Its principal property is, to be susceptible of condensation and rarefaction; so that the very same quantity of air be heated, its bulk enlarges in proportion to the degree of heat applied to it; the consequence whereof is, that the same space now contains fewer particles of air than it did before. Cold again produces just the contrary effect.

On this property which air has of being condensed and dilated by heat its elasticity chiefly depends. For if air were forced by condensation into a less compass than it took up before, and then exposed to a very considerable degree of cold, it would remain quite inactive, without exerting such an effort as it usually makes against the depressing body. On the other hand, the elasticity of heated air arises only from hence, that being rarefied by the action of fire, it requires much more room than it occupied before.

Air enters into the composition of many substances, especially vegetable and animal bodies; For by analyzing most of them such a considerable quantity thereof is extricated, that some naturalists have suspected it to be altogether destitute of elasticity when thus combined with the other principles in the composition of bodies. According to them, the efficacy of the elastic power of the air is so prodigious, and its force when compressed so excessive, that it is not possible the other component parts of bodies should be able to confine so much of it in that state of compression which it must needs undergo, if retaining its elasticity when pent up among them.

However that be, this elastic property of the air produces the most singular and important phenomena observable in the resolution and composition of bodies.

OF WATER. Water is a thing so well known, that it is almost needless to attempt giving a general idea of it here. Every one knows that it is a transparent, insipid substance, and usually fluid. We say it is usually so; for being exposed to a certain degree of cold, it becomes solid: Solidity therefore seems to be its most natural state.

Water exposed to the fire grows hot; but only to a limited degree, beyond which its heat never rises, be the force of fire applied to it ever so violent; It is known to have acquired this degree of heat by its boiling up with great tumult. Water cannot be made hotter, because it is volatile, and incapable of enduring the heat without being evaporated and entirely dissipated.

If such a violent and sudden heat be applied to water as will not allow it time to exhale gently in vapours, as when for instance, a small quantiy thereof is thrown upon a metal in fusion, it is dissipated at once with vast impetuosity, producing a most terrible and dangerous explosion. This surprising effect may be deduced from the instantaneous dilatation of the parts of the water itself, or rather of the air contained in it. Moreover, water enters into the texture of many bodies, both compound and secondary principles; but, like air, it seems to be excluded from the composition of all metals, and most minerals. For although an immense quantity of water exists in the bowels of the earth, moistening all its contents, it does not therefore follow, that it is one of the principles of minerals. It is only interposed between their parts; for they may be entirely robbed of it, without any sort of decomposition: Indeed it is not capable of an intimate connection with them.

OF EARTH. We observed, that the two principles above treated of are volatile; that is, the action of fire separates them from the bodies they help to compose. But earth is fixed, and, when absolutely pure, refills the utmost force of fire. So that whatever remains of a body, after it hath been exposed to the power of the fiercest fire, must be considered as containing nearly all its earthy principles, and consisting chiefly there.

Earth therefore is a fixed principle which is permanent in the fire. There is reason to think it very difficult, if not impossible, to obtain the terrene principle wholly free from every other substance: For after our utmost endeavours to purify them, the earths we obtain from different compounds are found to have different properties, according to the different bodies from which they are procured; or else if those earths be pure, we must allow them to be essentially different, feeling they have different properties.

Earth, in general, with regard to its properties, may be distributed into fusible and unfusible; that is, into earth that is capable of melting or becoming fluid in the fire, and earth that constantly remains in a solid form, never melting in the strongest degree of heat to which we can expose it.

The former is also called vitrifiable, and the latter unvitrifiable earth; because, when earth is melted by the force of fire, it becomes what we call glass, which is nothing but the parts of earth brought into nearer contact, and more closely united by the means of fusion. Perhaps the earth, which we look upon as uncapable of vitrification, might be fused if we could apply to it a sufficient degree of heat. It is at least certain, that some earths, or stones, which separately resist the force of fire, so that they cannot be melted, become fusible when mixed together. Experience convinced Mr. du Hamel, that lime-stone and slate are of this kind. It is however undoubtedly true, that one earth differs from another in its degree of fusibility: And this gives ground to believe, that there may be a species of earth absolutely unvitrifiable in its nature, which, being mixed in different proportions with fusible earths, renders them difficult to melt.

Whatever may be in this, as there are earths which we are absolutely unable to vitrify, that is a sufficient reason of our division of them. Unvitrifiable earths seem to be porous, for they imbibe water; when they have also got the name of absorbent earths.

OF FIRE. The matter of the sun, or of light, the phlogiston, fire, the sulphureous principle, the inflammable matter, are all of them names by which the element of fire is usually denoted. But it should seem, that an accurate distinction hath not yet been made between the different states in which it exists; that is between the phenomena of fire actually existing as a principle in the composition of bodies, and those which it exhibits when existing separately and in its natural state; nor have proper distinct appelations been designed to it in those different circumstances. In the latter state we may properly give it the names of fire, matter of the sun, of light, and of heat; and may consider it as a substance composed of infinitely small particles continually agitated by a most rapid motion, and of consequence essentially fluid.

This substance, of which the sun may be called the general reservoir, seems to flow incessantly from that source, diffusing itself over the world, and through all the bodies we know; but not as a principle, or essential part of them, since they may be deprived thereof, at least in a great measure, without suffering any decomposition. The greatest change produced on them, by its presence or its absence, is the rendering them fluid or solid; so that all other bodies may be deemed naturally solid; fire alone essentially fluid, and the principle of fluidity in others. This being presupposed, air itself might become solid, if it could be entirely deprived of the fire it contains; as bodies of most difficult fusion become fluid, when penetrated by a sufficient quantity of the particles of fire.

One of the chief properties of this pure fire is to penetrate easily into all bodies, and to diffuse itself among them with a sort of uniformity and equality; for if a heated body be contiguous to a cold one, the former communicates the latter all its excess of heat, cooling to exact proportion as the other warms, till both come to have the very same degree of heat. Heat, however, is naturally communicable soonest to the upper parts of a body; and consequently, when a body cools, the under parts become soonest cold. It hath been observed, for instance, that the lower extremity of a heated body, freely suspended in the air, frows cold sooner than the upper; and that when a bar of iron is red-hot at one end, and cold at the other, the cold end is much sooner heated by placing the bar so that the hot end may be undermost, than when that end is turned uppermost. the levity of the matter of fire, and the vicinity of the earth, may possibly be the causes of this phenomenon.

Another property of fire is to dilate all bodies into which it penetrates. This hath already been shewn with regard to air and water; and it produces the same effect on earth.

Fire is the most powerful agent we can employ to decompose bodies; and the greatest degree of heat producible by man, is that excited by the rays of the sun collected in the focus of a large burning-glass.

OF THE PHLOGISTON. From what hath been said concerning the nature of fire, it is evidently impossible for us to fix and confine it in any body. Yet the phenomena attending the combustion of inflammable bodies shew that they really contain the matter of fire as a constituent principle. By what mechanism then is this fluid, so subtile, so active, so difficult to confine, so capable of penetrating into every other substance in nature, so fixed as to make a component part of the most solid bodies? It is no easy matter to give a satisfactory answer to this question. But, without pretending to guess the cause of the phenomenon, let us rest contented with the certainty of the fact, the knowledge of which will undoubtedly procure us considerable advantages. Let us therefore examine the properties of fire thus fixed and become a principle of bodies. To this substance in order to distinguish it from pure and unfixed fire, the chemists have assigned the peculiar title of the Phlogiston, which is indeed no other than a Greek word for the inflammable matter; by which latter name, as well as by that of the sulphureous principle, it is also sometimes called. It differs from elementary fire in the following particulars. 1. When united to a body, it communicates to it neither heat nor light. 2. It produces no change in its state, whether of solidity or fluidity; so that a solid body does not become fluid by the accession of the phlogiston and vice versa; the solid bodies to which it is joined being only rendered thereby more apt to be fused by the force of the culinary fire. 3. We can convey it from the body with which it is joined into another body, so that it shall enter into the composition thereof, and remain fixed in it.

On this occasion both these bodies, that which is deprived of the phlogiston and that which receives it, undergo very considerable alterations; and it is this last circumstance in particular that obliges us to distinguish the phlogiston from pure fire, and to consider it as the element of fire combined with some other substance, which serves it as a basis for constituting a kind of secondary principle. For if there were no difference between them, we should be able to introduce and fix pure fire itself where-ever we can introduce and fix the phlogiston: yet this is what we can by no means do, as will appear from experiments to be afterwards produced.

Hitherto chemists have never been able to obtain the phlogiston quite pure, and free from every other substance: for there are but two ways of separating it from a body of which it makes a part: to wit, either by applying some other body with which it may unite the moment it quits the former; or else by calcining and burning the compounds from which you desire to sever it. In the former case, it is evident that we do not get the phlogiston by itself, because it only passes from one combination into another; and in the latter, it is entirely dissipated in the decomposition, so that no part of it can possibly be secured.

The inflammability of a body is an infallible sign that it contains a phlogiston; but from a body's not being inflammable, it cannot be inferred that it contains none; for experiments have demonstrated that certain metals abound with it, which yet are by no means inflammable.

We have now delivered what is most necessary to be known concerning the principles of bodies in general. They have many other properties besides those abovementioned; but we cannot properly take notice of them here, because they presuppose an acquaintance with some other things relating to bodies, of which we have hitherto said nothing, intending to treat of them in the sequel as occasion shall offer. We shall only observe in this place that when animal and vegetable matters are burnt in such a manner as to hinder them from flaming, some part of the phlogiston contained in them unites intimately with their most fixed earthy parts, and with them forms a compound that can be consumed only by making it red-hot in the open air, where it sparkles and wafts away, without emitting any flame. This compound is called a coal. We shall inquire into the properties of this coal under the head of oils: at present it suffices that we know in general what it is, and that it readily communicates to other bodies the phlogiston it contains.

A GENERAL VIEW OF THE AFFINITIES OR ELECTIVE ATTRACTIONS THAT SUBSIST BETWEEN BODIES. Before we can reduce compound bodies to the first principles above pointed out, we obtain, by analyzing them, certain substances which are indeed more simple than the bodies they helped to compose, yet are themselves composed of our primary principles. Saline and oily matters chiefly constitute this class. But before we enter upon an examination of their properties, it is fit we lay before the reader a general view of what chemists understand by the relations or affinities of bodies; because it is necessary to know these, in order to get a distinct conception of the different combinations we are to treat of.

All the experiments hitherto made concur in proving, that different bodies, whether principles or compounds, have such a mutual conformity, relation, affinity, or attraction, as disposes some of them to join and unite together, while they are incapable of contracting any union with others. This effect, whatever be its cause, will enable us to account for, and connect together, all the phenomena that chemistry produces. The nature of this univeral affection of matter is laid down in the following propositions.

First, If one substance has any affinity or conformity with another, the two will unite together, and form one compound.

Secondly, All similar substances have an affinity with each other, and are consequently disposed to unite; as water with water, earth with earth, etc.

Thirdly, Substances that unite together lose some of their separate properties; and the compounds resulting from their union partake of the properties of those substances which serve as their principles.

Fourthly, The simpler any substances are, the more perceptible and considerable are their affinities: whence it follows, that the less bodies are compounded, the more difficult it is to analyse them; that is to separate from each other the principles of which they consist.

Fifthly, If a body consist of two substances, and to this compound be presented a third substance that has no affinity at all with one of the two primary substances aforesaid, but has a greater affinity with the other than those two substances have with each other, there will ensue a decomposition, and a new union: that is the third substance will separate the two compounding substances from each other, coalesce with that which has an affinity with it, form therewith a new combination, and disengage the other, which will then be left at liberty, and such as it was before it had contracted any union.

Sixthly, It happens sometimes that when a third substance is presented to a body consisting of two substances no decomposition follows; but the two compounding substances, without quitting each other, unite with the substance presented to them, and form a combination of three principles: and this happens when that third substance has an equal, or nearly equal, affinity with each of the compounding substances. The same thing may also happen even when the third substance hath no affinity but with one of the compounding substances only. To produce such an effect, it is sufficient that one of the two compounding substances have to the third body a relation equal to or nearly equal to that which it has to the other compounding substance with which it is already combined. Hence it follows, that two substances, which, when apart from all others, are incapable of contracting any union, may be rendered capable of incorporating together in some measure, and becoming parts of the same compound, by combining with a third substance with which each of them has an equal affinity.

Seventhly, A body, which of itself cannot decompose a compound consisting of two substances, because they have a greater affinity with each other than it has with either of them, becomes nevertheless capable of separating the two by uniting with one of them, when it is itself combined with another body having a degree of affinity with that one sufficient to compensate its own want thereof. In that case there are two affinities, and thence ensues a double decomposition, and a double combination.

These fundamental truths, from which we shall deduce an explanation of all the phenomena in chemistry, will be confirmed and illustrated by applying them to the several cases, of which our design in this treatise obliges uf to give a circumstantial account.

OF SALINE SUBSTANCES IN GENERAL. if a particle of water be intimately united with a particle of earth, the result will be a new compound, which, according to our third proposition of affinities, will partake of the properties of earth and of water; and this combination principally forms what is called a saline substance. Consequently every saline substance must have an affinity with earth and with water, and be capable of uniting with both or either of them, whether they be separate or mixed together: and accordingly this property characterises all salts or saline substances in general.

Water being volatile and earth fixed, salts in general are less volatile than the former, and less fixed than the latter; that is, fire, which cannot volatilize and carry off pure earth, is capable of rarefying and volatilizing a saline substance; but then this requires a greater degree of heat than is necessary for producing the same effects on pure water.

There are several sorts of salts, differing from one another in respect either of the quantity or the quality of the earth in their composition; or, lastly, they differ on account of some additional principles, which not being combined with them in sufficient quantity to hinder their saline properties from appearing, permit them to retain the name of salts, though they render them very different from the simplest saline substances.

Before we proceed further, it is proper just to mention the principal reasons which induce us to think that every saline substance is actually a combination of earth and water, as we supposed at our entering on this subject. The first is, the conformity salts have with earth and water, or the properties they possess in common with both. Of these properties we shall treat fully, as occasion offers to consider them, in examining the several sorts of salts. The second is, that all salts may be actually resolved into earth and water by sundry processes; particularly by repeated dissolution in water, evaporation, desiccation, and calcination. Indeed the chemists have not yet been able to produce a saline substance by combining earth and water together. This favours a suspicion, that besides these two there is some other principle in the composition of salts which escapes our researches, because we cannot preserve it when we decompose them: but it is sufficient to our purpose, that water and earth are demonstrably amongst the real principles of saline substances, and that no experiment hath ever shewn us any other.

OF ACIDS. The simplest saline substance is that called an acid, on account of its taste, which is like that of verjuice, sorrel, vinegar, and other sour things, which for the same reason are also called acids. By this peculiar taste are acids chiefly known. They have moreover the property of turning all the blue and violet colours of vegetable red, which distinguishes them from all other salts.

The form under which acids most commonly appear is that of a transparent liquour; though solidity is rather their natural state. This is owing to their affinity with water; which is so great, that when they contain but just as much of it as is necessary to constitute them salts, and consequently have a solid form, they rapidly unite therewith the moment they come into contact with it: and as the air is always loaded with moisture and aqueous vapours, its contact alone is sufficient to liquify them; because they unite with its humidity, imbibe it greedily and by that means become fluid. We therefor say, they attract the moisture of the air. This change of a salt from a solid to a fluid state, by the sole contact of the air, is called deliquium: so that when a salt changes in this manner from a solid into a fluid form, it is said to run per deliquium. Acids being the simplest species of saline bodies, their affinities with different substances are stronger than those of any other sort of salt with the same substances: which is agreeable to our fourth proposition concerning affinities.

Acids in general have a great affinity with earths: that with which they most readily unite is the unvitrifiable earth to which we gave the name of absorbent earth. They seem not to act at all upon vitrifiable earths, such as land; nor yet upon some other kinds of earths, at least while they are in their natural state. Yet the nature of these earths may be in some measure changed, by making them red hot in the fire, and then quenching them suddenly in cold water: for by repeating this often they are brought nearer to the nature of absorbent earths, and rendered capable of uniting with acids.

When an acid liquor is mixed with an absorbent earth, for instance with chalk, these two substances instantly rush into union with so much impetuosity, that a great ebullition is immediately produced, attended with considerable hissing, heat and vapours, which rise the very instant of their conjunction.

From the combination of an acid with an absorbent earth there arises a new compound, which some chemists have called sal salsum because the acid by uniting with the earth loses its sour taste, and acquires another not unlike that of the common sea-salt used in our kitchens; yet varying according to the different sorts of acids and earths combined together. The acid at the same time loses its property of turning blue or violet vegetable red.

If we inquire what is become of its propensity to unite with water, we shall find that the earth, which of itself is not soluble in water, hath by its union with the acid acquired a facility of dissolving there: so that our sal salsum is soluble in water, But on the other hand, the acid bath, by its union with the earth, lost part of the affinity it had with water; so that is a sal salsum be dried, and freed of all superfluous humidity, it will remain in that dry solid form, instead of attracting the moisture of the air and running per deliquium, as the acid would do if it were pure and unmixed with earth.

Acids have likewise a great affinity with the phlogiston. When we come to treat of each acid in particular, we shall examine the combinations of each with the phlogiston: they differ so widely from one another, and many of them are so little known, that we cannot at present give any general idea of them.

OF ALKALIS. Alkalis are saline combinations in which there is a greater proportion of earth than in acids. The principal arguments that may be adduced to prove this fact are these: First, if they be treated in the manner proposed above for analysing saline substances, we obtain from them a much greater quantity of earth than we do from acids. Secondly: by combining certain acids with certain earths we can produce alkalis; or at least such saline compounds as greatly resemble them. Our third and last argument is drawn from the properties of those alkalis which, when pure and unadulterated with any other principle, have less affinity with water than acids have, and are also more fixed, resisting the utmost force of fire. On this account it is that they have obtained the title of fixed, as well as to distinguish them from another species of alkali, to be considered hereafter, which is impure and volatile.

Though fixed alkalis, when dry sustain the utmost violence of fire without flying off in vapours, it is remarkable that, being boiled with water in an open vessel, considerable quantities of them rise with the steam; an effect which must be attributed to the great affinity between these two substances, by means whereof water communicates some part of its volatility to the fixed salt.

Alkalis freed of their superfluous humidity by calcination attract the moisture of the air, but not so strongly as acids: so that it is easier to procure and preserve them in a solid form.

They flow in the fire, and are then capable of uniting with vitrifiable earths, and of forming therewith true glass; which, however, will partake of their properties if they be used in sufficient quantity.

As they melt more readily than vitrifiable earth, they facilitate its fusion; so that a weaker fire will reduce it to glass, when a fixed alkali is joined with it, than will melt it without that addition.

Alkalis are known by their taste, which is acrid and firey; and by the properties they possess of turning blue or violet vegetables green; particularly syrup of violets.

Their affinity with acids is greater than that of absorbent earths; hence, if an alkali be presented to a combination of an acid with an absorbent earth, the earth will be separated from the acid by the alkali, and a new union between the acid and the alkali will take place. This is both an instance and a proof of our fifth proposition concerning affinities.

If a pure alkali be presented to a pure acid, they rush together with violence, and produce the same phenomena as were observed in the union of an absorbent earth with an acid, but in a greater and more remarkable degree.

Fixed alkalis may in general be divided into two sorts; one of these hath all the above recited properties; but the other possesses some that are peculiar to itself. We shall consider this latter sort more particularly under the head of seasalt.

OF NEUTRAL SALTS. The acid and the alkali thus uniting, mutually rob each other of their characteristic properties; so that the compound resulting from their union produces no change in the blue colours of vegetables, and has a taste which is neither sour nor acrid, but saltish. A saline combination of this kind is for that reason named sal salsum, sal medium, or neutral salt.

It must be observed, that in order to make these salts perfectly neutral, it is necessary that neither of the two saline principles of which they are compounded be predominant over the other; for in that case they will have the properties of the prevailing principle. The reason is this: neither of these saline substances can unite with the other but in a limited proportion beyond which there can be no further coalition between them. The action by which this perfect union is accomplished is termed saturation: and the instant when such proportions of the two saline substances are mixed together, that the one is incorporated with as much of the other as it can possibly take up, is called the point of saturation.

The point of saturation is known to be obtained, when, after repeated affusions of an acid in small quantities to an alkali, or an absorbent earth, we find those phenomena cease, which in such cases constantly attend the conflict of union, namely, ebullition, hissing, etc. and we may be assured the saturation is complete when the new compound hath neither an acid nor an acrid taste, nor in the least changes the blue colours of vegetables.

Natural salts have not so great an affinity with water as either acids or alkalis have, because they are more compounded; for we observed before, that the affinities of the most compounded bodies are generally weaker than those of the most simple. In consequence hereof few natural salts, when dried, attract the moisture of the air; and those that do attract it more slowly and in less quantity than either acids or alkalis do.

All neutral salts are soluble in water; but more or less readily, and in a greater or smaller quantity, according to the nature of their component principles.

Water made boiling hot dissolves a greater quantity of those salts which do not attract the moisture of the air, than when it is cold; and indeed it must be boiling hot to take up as much of them as it is capable of dissolving: but as for those which run in the air, the difference is imperceptible.

Some neutral salts have the property of shooting into crystals, and others have it not.

The nature of crystallization is this: Water cannot dissolve, nor keep in solution, more than a determinate quantity of any particular salt; when therefore such a quantity of water is evaporated from the solution of a salt capable of crystallization, that the remainder contains just as much salt as it can dissolve, then by continuing the evaporation the salt gradually recovers its solid form, and concretes into several little transparent masses called crystals. These crystals have regular figures, all differing from one another according to the species of salt of which they are formed. Different methods of evaporating saline solutions have different effects on the figure and regularity of the crystals; and each particular sort of salt requires a peculiar method of evaporation to make its crystals perfectly regular.

A solution of salt designed for crystallization is usually evaporated by means of fire to a pellicle: that is, till the salt begin to concrete; which is perceived by a kind of thin dark skin that gathers on the surface of the liquor, and is formed of the crystallized particles of salt. When this pellicle appears, the solution is suffered to cool and the crystals form therein falter or flower according to the sort of salt in hand. If the evaporation be carried on briskly to perfect dryness, no crystals will be formed, and only an irregular mass of salt will be obtained.

The reasons why no crystals appear when the evaporation is hastily performed, and carried on to dryness are first, that the particles of salt, being always in motion while the solution is hot, have not time to exert their mutual affinities, and to unite together as crystallization requires: secondly, that a certain quantity of water enters into the very composition of crystals; which is therefore absolutely necessary to their formation, and in a greater or smaller proportion according to the nature of the salt.

If these crystalized salts be exposed to the fire, they first part with that moisture which is not necessary to a saline generation, and which they retained only by means of their crystallization: afterwards they begin to flow, but with different degrees of fusibility.

It must be observed, that certain salts melt as soon as they are exposed to the fire; namely, those which retain a great deal of water in crystallizing. But this fluor which they so readily acquire must be carefully distinguished from actual fusion; for it is owing only to their superfluous humidity, which heat renders capable of dissolving and liquifying them; so that when it is evaporated, the salt ceases to be fluid, and requires a much greater degree of fire to bring it into real fusion.

The neutral salts that do not crystallize may indeed be dried by evaporating the water which keeps them fluid; but by becoming solid they acquire no regular form; they again attract the moisture of the air, and are thereby melted into a liquor. These may be called liquescent salts.

Most of the neutral salts, that consist of an acid joined with a fixed alkali, or with an absorbent earth, are themselves fixed and resist the force of fire; yet several of them, if they be dissolved in water, and the solutions boiled and evaporated, flie off along with the steams.

OF THE SEVERAL SORTS OF SALINE SUBSTANCES

1. OF THE UNIVERSAL OR VITRIOLIC ACID. The universal acid is so called, because it is in fact the acid which is most universally diffused through all nature, in waters, in the atmosphere, and in the bowels of the earth. But it is seldom pure; being almost always combined with some other substance. That from which we obtain it, with most ease, and in the greatest quantity, is vitriol; and this is the reason why it is called the vitriolic acid; the name by which it is best known.

When the vitriolic acid contains but little phlegm, yet enough to give it a fluid form, it is called oil of vitriol: on account of a certain unctuosity belonging to it.

If the vitriolic acid contains much water, it is then called spirit of vitriol. When it does not contain enough to render it fluid, and so is in a solid form, it is named the icy oil of vitriol.

When oil of vitriol, highly concentrated, is mixed with water, they rush into union with such an impetuosity that, the moment they touch each other, there arises a hissing noise, like that of red-hot iron plunged in cold water, together with a very considerable degree of heat proportioned to the degree in which the acid was concentrated,

If instead of mixing this concentrated acid with water, you only leave it exposed to the air for some time, it attracts the moisture thereof, and imbibes it most greedily. Both its bulk and its weight are increased by this accession; and if it be under an icy form, that is, if it be concreted, the phlegm thus acquired will soon resolve it into fluid.

The addition of water renders the vitriolic acid, and indeed all other acids, weaker in one sense; which is, that when they are very aqueous, they leave on the tongue a much fainter taste of acidity, and are less active in the solution of some particular bodies: But that occasions not change in the strength of their affinities, but in some cases rather enables them to dissolve several substances which, when well dephlegmated, they are not capable of attacking.

The vitriolic acid combined to the point of saturation with a particular absorbent earth, well known, forms a neutral salt that crystallizes. This salt is called alum, and the figure of its crystals is that of an octahedron or solid of eight sides. These octahedra are triangular pyramids, the angles of which are so cut off that four of the surfaces are hexagons, and the other four triangles.

There are several sorts of alum, which differ according to the earths combined with the vitriolic acid. Alum dissolves easily in water, and in crystallization retains a considerable quantity of it; which is the reason that being exposed to the fire it readily melts, swelling and puffing up as its superfluous moisture exhales. When that is quite evaporated, the remainder is called burnt alum and is very difficult to fuse. The acid of the alum is partly dissipated by this calcination. Its taste is saltish, with a degree of roughness and astringency.

The vitriolic acid combined with certain earths forms a kind of neutral salt called selenites, which crystallizes in different forms according to the nature of its earth. There are numberless springs of water infected with dissolved selenutes; but when this salt is once crystallized, it is exceeding difficult to dissolve it in water a second time. For that purpose a very great quantity of water is necessary and moreover it must boil; for, as it cools, most of the dissolved selenites takes a solid form, and falls in a powder to the bottom of the vessel.

If an alkali be presented to the selenites, or to alum, these salts will be thereby decomposed; that is, the acid will quit the earths, and join the alkali, with which it hath a greater affinity. And from this conjunction of the vitriolic acid with a fixed alkali there results another sort of neutral salt, which is called arcanum duplicatum, sal de duobus; and vitriolated tartar, because one of the fixed alkalis most in use is called salt of tartar.

Vitriolated tartar is almost as hard to dissolve in water as the selenites. It shoots into eight-sided crystals, leaving the apices of the pyramids pretty obtuse. Its taste is saltish, inclining to bitter; and it decrepitates on burning coals. It requires a very great degree of fire to make it flow.

The vitriolic acid is capable of uniting with the phlogiston, or rather it has a greater affinity with it than with any other body: whence it follows, that all compounds of which it makes a part may be decomposed by means of the phlogiston.

From the conjunction of the vitriolic acid with the phlogiston arises a compound called mineral sulphur, because it is found perfectly formed in the bowels of the earth. It is also called sulphur vivum, or simply sulphur.

Sulphur is absolutely insoluble in water, and incapable of contracting any sort of union with it. It melts with a very moderate degree of heat, and sublimes in fine light downy tufts called flowers of sulphur. By being thus sublimed it suffers no decomposition, let the operation be repeated ever so often; so that sublimed sulphur, or flower of sulphur, hath exactly the same properties as sulphur that has never been sublimed.

If sulphur be exposed to a brisk heat in the open air, it takes fire, burns, and is wholly consumed. This deflagration of sulphur is the only means we have of decomposing it, in order to obtain its acid in purity. The phlogiston is destroyed by the flame, and the acid exhales in vapours; these vapours collected have all the properties of the vitriolic acid, and differs from it only as they still retain some portion of the phlogiston; which, however, soon quits them of its own accord, if the free access of the common air be not precluded.

The portion of phlogiston retained by the acid of sulphur is much more considerable when that mineral is burnt gradually and slowly: in that case the vapours which rise from it have such a penetrating odour, that they instantaneously suffocate any person who draws in a certain quantity of them with his breath. These vapours constitute what is called the volatile spirit of sulphur. There is reason to think this portion of phlogiston which the acid retains is combined therewith in a manner different from that in which these two are united in the sulphur itself: for nothing but actual burning is capable of separating the vitriolic acid and the phlogiston, which by their union form sulphur; whereas in the volatile spirit of sulphur they separate spontaneously when exposed to the open air; that is, the phlogiston flies off and leaves the acid, which then becomes in every respect similar to the vitriolic acid.

That the volatile spirit of sulphur is a compound, appears evidently from hence, that whenever the vitriolic acid touches any substance containing the phlogiston, provided that phlogiston be disengaged or opened to a certain degree, a volatile spirit of sulphur is infallibly and immediately generated. This spirit hath all the properties of acids, but considerably weakened, and of course less perceptible. It unites with absorbed earths or fixed alkalis; and with them forms neutral salts: but when combined therewith it may be separated from them by the vitriolic acid, and indeed by any of the mineral acids, because its affinities are weaker. Sulphur hath the property of uniting with absorbent earth but not near so intimately as with fixed alkalis.

If equal parts of sulphur and an alkali be melted together, they incorporate with each other; and from their conjunction proceeds a compound of a most unpleasant smell, much like that of rotten eggs, and of a red colour nearly resembling that of an animal liver, which has occasioned it to bear the name of hepar sulphuris, or liver of sulphur.

In this composition the fixed alkali communicates to the sulphur the property of dissolving in water: and hence it comes that liver of sulphur may be made as well when the alkali is dissolved by water into a fluid, as when it is fused by the action of fire.

Sulphur has less affinity than any acid with the fixed alkalis: and therefor liver of sulphur may be decompounded by any acid whatever; which will unite with the fixed alkali, form therewith a neutral salt, and separate the sulphur.

If liver of sulphur be dissolved in water, and an acid poured thereon, the liquor, which was transparent before, instantly turns to an opaque white; because the sulphur, being forced to quit its union with the alkali, loses at the same time the property of dissolving in water, and appears again in its own opaque form. The liquor thus made white by the sulphur is called milk of sulphur.

If this liquor be suffered to stand still for some time, the particles of sulphur, now most minutely divided, gradually approach each other, unite and fall insensibly to the bottom of the vessel; and then the liquor recovers its transparency. The sulphur thus deposited on the bottom of the vessel is called the magistery or precipitate sulphur. The names of magistery and precipitate are also given to all substances whatever that are separated from another by this method; which is the reason that we use the expression of precipitating one substance by another, to signify the separating one of them by means of the other.

2. OF THE NITROUS ACID. The nitrous acid combined with certain absorbent earths, such as chalk, marble, boles, forms neutral salts which do not crystallize; and which, after being dried, run in the air per deliquium.

All those neutral salts which consist of the nitrous acid joined to an earth, may be decomposed by a fixed alkali, with which the acid unites, and deserts the earth; and from this union of the nitrous acid with a fixed alkali results a new neutral salt, which is called nitre, or salt petre. This latter name signifies the salt of stones, and in fact, nitre is extracted from the stones and plaister, in which it forms by boiling them in water saturated with a fixed alkali.

Nitre shoots in long crystals adhering sideways to each other; it has a saltish taste, which produces a sensation of cold on the tongue.

This salt easily dissolves in water; which when it boils, takes up still a greater quantity thereof.

It flows with a pretty moderate degree of heat, and continues fixed therein; but being urged by a brisk fire, and in the open air, it lets go some part of its acid, and indeed flies off itself in part.

The most remarkable property of nitre, and that which characterizes it, is its fulmination of explosion; the nature of which is as follows:

When nitre touches any substance containing a phlogiston, and actually ignited, that is red hot, it bursts out into a flame, burns, and is decompounded with much noise.

In this deflagration the acid is dissipated, and totally separated from the alkali, which now remains by itself.

Indeed the acid, at least the greatest part of it, is by this means quite destroyed. The alkali which is left when nitre is decompounded by deflagration, is called in general fixed nitre, and, more particularly, nitre fixed by such and such a substance as was used in the operation. But if nitre be deflagrated with an inflammable substance containing the vitriolic acid, as sulphur, for instance, the fixed salt produced by the deflagration is not a pure alkali but retains a good deal of the vitriolic acid, and, by combining there with, hath now formed a neutral salt.

The reason why nitre flames, and is decompounded in the manner above mentioned, when it comes in contact with phlogiston properly circumstanced, is, that the nitrous acid, having a greater affinity with the phlogiston than with the fixed alkali, naturally quits the latter to join with the former, and so produces a kind of sulphur, differing probably from the common sulphur, formed by the vitriolic acid, in that it is combustible to such a degree, as to take fire and be consumed in the very moment of its production; so that it is impossible to prevent its being thus destroyed, and consequently impossible to save it. In support of this opinion let it be considered, that the concurrence of the phlogiston is absolutely necessary to produce this deflagration, and that the matter of pure fire is altogether incapable of effecting it; for though nitre be exposed to the most violent degree of fire, even that in the focus of the most powerful burning-glass, it will not flame; nor will that effect ever happen till the nitre be brought into contact with a phlogiston properly so called, that is, the matter of fire existing as a principle of some body; and it is moreover necessary that this phlogiston be actually on fire, and agitated with the igneous motion, or else, that the nitre itself be red-hot, and so penetrated with fire as to kindle any inflammable matter that touches it.

This experiment, among others, helps to shew the distinction that ought to be made between pure elementary fire, and fire become a principle of bodies to which we have given the name of phlogiston.

Before we leave this subject, we shall observe, that nitre deflagrates only with such substances as contain the phlogiston in its simplest and purest form; such as charcoal, sulphur, and the metalline substances; and that, though it will not deflagrate without the addition of some combustible matter, it is nevertheless the only known body that will burn, and make other combustibles burn with it, in close vessels, without the admission of fresh air.

The nitrous acid hath not so great an affinity with earths and alkalis as the vitriolic acid hath; whence it follows, that the vitriolic acid decomposes all neutral salts arising from a combination of the nitrous acid with an earth or an alkali. The vitriolic acid expells the nitrous acid, unites with the substance which served it for a basis, and therewith forms a neutral salt, which is an alum, a selenites, or a vitriolated tartar, according to the nature of that basis.

The nitrous acid, when thus separated from its basis by the vitriolic acid, is named spirit of nitre, or aqua fortis. If it be dephlegmated, or contain but little superfluous water, it exhales in reddish vapours; these vapours being condensed and collected, form a liquor of a brownish yellow that incessantly emits vapours of the same colour, and of a pungent disagreeable smell. These characters have procured it the names of smoking spirit of nitre, and yellow aqua fortis. This property in the nitrous acid of exhaling in vapours, shews it to be less fixed than the vitriolic acid; for the latter, though ever so thoroughly dephlegmated, never yields any vapours, nor has it any smell.

3. OF THE ACID OF SEA-SALT. The acid of sea-salt is so called, because it is in fact obtained from such sea-salt as is used in our kitchens. It is not certainly known in what this acid differs from the vitriolic and the nitrous, with regard to its constituent parts.

When it is combined with absorbent earths, such as lime and chalk, it forms a neutral salt that does not crystallize; and, when dried, attracts the moisture of the air. If the absorbent earth be not fully saturated with the marine acid the salt thereby formed has the properties of a fixed alkali: And this is what made us say, when we were on the subject of those salts, that they might be imitated by combining an earth with an acid. The marine acid, like the rest, hath not so great an affinity with earths as with fixed alkalis.

When it is combined with the latter, it forms a neutral salt which shoots into cubical crystals. This salt is inclined to grow moist in the air, and is consequently one of those which water dissolves in equal quantities, at least as to sense, whether it be boiling hot or quite cold.

The affinity of this acid with alkalis and absorbent earths is not so great as that of the vitriolic and nitrous acids: Whence it follows, that, when combined therewith, it may be separated from them by either of those acids.

The acid of sea-salt, thus disengaged from the substance which served it for a basis, is called spirit of salt. When it contains but little phlegm, it is of a lemon colour, and continually emits many white, very dense, and very elastic vapours; on which account it is named the smoking or volatile spirit of salt. Its smell is not disagreeable, nor much unlike that of saffron; but extremely quick and suffocating when it smokes.

The acid of sea-salt, like the other two, seems to have a greater affinity with the phlogiston, than with fixed alkalis. We are led to this opinion by the very curious operation, which gives ground to think, that sea-salt may be decomposed by the proper application of a substance containing the phlogiston.

From the marine acid, combined with a phlogiston, results a kind of sulphur, differing from the common sort in many respects; but particularly in this property, that it takes fire of itself upon being exposed to the open air. This combination is called English phosphorus, phosphorus of urine, because it is generally prepared from urine, or only phosphorus.

This combination of the marine acid with a phlogiston is not easily affected; because it requires a difficult operation in appropriated vessels. For these reasons it does not always succeed; and phosphorus is so scarce and dear, that hitherto chemists have not been able to make on it the experiments necessary to discover all its properties. If phosphorus be suffered to burn away in the air, a small quantity of an acid liquor may be obtained from it, which seems to be spirit of salt, but either altered, or combined with some adventitious matter; for it has several properties that are not to be found in the pure marine acid; such as, leaving a fixed fusible substancebehind it when exposed to a strong fire, and being easily combined with the phlogiston so as to reproduce phosphorus.

Phosphorus resembles sulphur in several of its properties: It is soluble in oils; it melts with a gentle heat; it is very combustible; it burns without producing soot; and its flame is vivid and bluish.

From what has been said of the union of the acid of sea-salt with a fixed alkali, and of the neutral salt resulting therefrom, it may be concluded, that this neutral salt is no other than the common kitchen salt. But it must be observed, that the fixed alkali, which is the natural basis of the common salt obtained from sea-water, is of a sort somewhat differing from fixed alkalis in general, and hath certain properties peculiar to itself. For,

1. The basis of sea-salt differs from other fixed alkalis in this, that it crystallizes like a neutral salt.

2. It does not grow moist in the air: On the contrary, when exposed to the air, it loses part of the water that united with it in crystallization, by which means its crystals los their transparency, become as it were mealy, and fall into a fine flour.

3. When combined with the vitriolic acid to the point of saturation, it forms a neutral salt differing from vitriolated tartar, first in the figure of its crystals which are oblong six-sided solids; secondly, in its quantity of water, which in crystallization unites therewith in a much greater proportion than with vitriolated tartar; whence it follows, that this salt dissolves in water more readily than vitriolated tartar; thirdly, in that it flows with a very moderate degree of heat, whereas vitriolated tartar requires a very fierce one.

If the acid of sea-salt be separated from its basis by means of the vitriolic acid, it is easy to see, that, when the operation is finished, the salt we have been speaking of must be the result. A famous chemist, named Glauber, was the first who extracted the spirit of salt in this manner, examined the neutral salt resulting from his process, and finding it to have some singular properties, called it his sal mirabile, or wonderful salt: On this account it is still called Glauber's sal mirabile, or Glauber's salt.

4. When the basis of the sea-salt is combined with the nitrous acid to the point of saturation, there results a neutral salt, or a sort of nitre, differing from the common nitre, first, in that it attracts the moisture of the air pretty strongly; and this makes it difficult to crystallize; secondly, in the figure of its crystals, which are parallelopipeds; and this has procured it the name of quadrangular nitre.

Common salt, or the neutral salt formed by combining the marine with this particular sort of fixed alkali, has a taste well known to every body. The figure of its crystals is exactly cubical. It grows moist in the air, and, when exposed to the fire, it bursts, before it melts, into many little fragments with a crackling noise; which is called the decrepitation of sea-salt.

That neutral salt mentioned above, which is formed by combining the marine acid with a common fixed alkali, and called sol sebrisugum sylvii, hath also this property.

India furnishes us with a saline substance, known by the name of borax, which flows very easily, and then takes the form of glass. It is of great use in facilitating the fusion of metallic substances. It possesses some of the properties of fixed alkalis, which has induced certain chemists to represent it, through mistake as a pure fixed alkali.

By mixing borax with the vitriolic acid, Mr. Homberg obtained from it a salt, which sublimes in a certain degree of heat, whenever such a mixture is made. This salt has very singular properties; but its nature is not yet thoroughly understood. It dissolves in water with great difficulty; it is not volatile, though it rises by sublimation from the borax. According to Mr. Rouelle's observation it rises then only by means of the water which carries it up; for when once made, it abides the fiercest fire, flows and vitrifies just as borax does, provided care be taken to free it previously from moisture by drying it properly. Mr. Homberg called it sedative salt, on account of it medical effects. The sedative salt hath the appearance and some of the properties, of a neutral salt; for it shoots into crystals and does not change the colour of violets; but it acts the part of an acid with regard to alkali, uniting with them to the point of saturation, and thereby forming a true neutral salt. It also acts like the acid of vitriol, on all neutral salts; that is, it discharges the acid of such as have not the vitriolic acid in their composition.

Since Mr. Homberg's time it hath been discovered, that a sedative salt may be made either with the nitrous or with the marine acid; and that sublimation is not necessary to extract it from the borax, but that it may be obtained by crystallization only. For this latter discovery we are indebted to Mr. Geoffroy, as we are to Mr. Lemery for the former.

Since that time M. Baron d'Henouville, an able chemist, hath shewn that a sedative salt may be obtained by means of vegetable acids; and hath lately demonstrated, that the sedative salt exists actually and perfectly in the borax, and that it is not produced by mixing acids with that saline substance, as it seems all the chemists before him imagined. This he proves convincingly from his analysis of borax, (which thereby appears to be nothing else but the sedative salt united with that fixed alkali which is the basis of sea-salt) and from his regenerating the same borax by uniting together that alkali and the sedative salt: a proof the most complete that can possibly be produced in natural philosophy, and equivalent to demonstration itself.

In order to finish what remains to be said upon the several sorts of saline substances, we should now speak of the acids obtained from vegetables and animals, and also of the volatile alkalis; but, seeing these saline substances differ from those of which we have already treated, only as they are variously altered by the unions they have contracted with certain principles of vegetables and animals, of which nothing has been yet said, it is proper to defer being particular concerning them, till we have explained those principles.

OF LIME. Any substance whatever, that has been roasted a considerable time in a strong fire without melting, is commonly called a calx. Stones and metals are the principle subjects that have the property of being converted into calces. We shall treat of metalline calces in a subsequent chapter, and in this confine ourselves to the calx of stone, known by the name of lime.

In treating of earths in general, we observed that they may be divided into two principal kinds; one of which actually and properly flows when exposed to the action of fire, and turns to glass; whence it is called a fusible or vitrifiable earth; the other resists the utmost force of fire, and is therefore said to be an unfusible or unvitrifiable earth. The latter is also not uncommonly called calcinable earth; though sundry sorts of unfusible earths are incapable of acquiring by the action of fire all the qualities of calcined earth, or lime properly so called; such earths are particularly distinguished by the denomination of refractory earths.

As the different sorts of stones are nothing more than compounds of different earths, they have the same properties with the earths of which they are composed and may, like them, be divided into fusible or bitrifiable and unfusible or calcinable. The fusible stones are generally denoted by the name of flints; the calcinable stones, again, are the several sorts of marbles, cretaceous stones, those commonly called free-stones, etc. some of which as they make the best lime, are, by way of eminence, called lime-stones. Sea-shells also, and stones that abound with fossile shells, are capable of being burnt to lime.

All these substances being exposed for a longer or shorter time to the action of fire, are said to be calcined. By calcination they lose a considerable part of their weight, acquire a white colour, and become friable, though ever so solid before; as, for instance, the very hardest marbles. These substances, when thus calcined, take the name of quick-lime.

Water penetrates quick-lime, and rushes into it with vast activity. If a lump of newly calcined lime be thrown into water, it instantly excites almost as great a noise, ebullition, and smoke, as would be produced by a piece of red hot iron; with such a degree of heat too, that, if the lime be in due proportion to the water, it will set fire to combustible bodies; as hath unfortunately happened to vessels laden with quick lime, on their springing a small leak.

As soon as quick-lime is put into water, it swells, and falls asunder into a infinite number of minute particles; in a word, it is in a manner dissolved by the water, which forms therewith a sort of white paste called slacked lime.

If the quantity of water be considerable enough for the lime to form with it a white liquor, this liquor is called lac calcis; which, being left some time to settle, grows clear and transparent, the lime which was suspended therein and occasioned its opacity subsiding to the bottom of the vessel. Then there forms on the surface of the liquor a crystalline pellicle, somewhat opaque and dark coloured, which being skimmed off is reproduced from time to time. This matter is called cremor calcis.

Slacked lime gradually grows dry, and takes the form of a solid body, but full of cracks and destitute of firmness. The event is different when you mix it up, while yet a paste, with a certain quantity of uncalcined stony matter, such as sand for example; then it takes the name of mortar, and gradually acquires, as it grows drier and older, a hardness equal to that of the best stones. This is a very singular property of lime, nor is it easy to account for it; but it is a beneficial one, for every body knows the use of mortar in building.

Quick-lime attracts the moisture of the air in the same manner as concentrated acids and dry fixed alkalis, but not in such quantities as to render it fluid; it only falls into extremely small particles, takes the form of a find powder, and the title of lime slacked in the air.

Lime once slacked, however dry it may afterwards appear, always retains a large portion of the water it had imbibed; which cannot be separated from it again but by means of a violent calcination. Being so recalcined it returns to be quicklime, recovering all its properties.

Besides this great affinity of quick-lime with water, which discovers a saline character, it has several other saline properties, to be afterwards examined, much resembling those of fixed alkalis. In chemistry it acts very nearly as these salts do, and may be considered as holding the middle rank between a pure absorbent earth and a fixed alkali; and this hath induced many chemists to think that lime contains a true salt, to which all the properties it possesses in common with salt may be attributed.

But as the chemical examination of this subject hath long been neglected, the existence of a saline substance in lime hath been long doubtful. Mr. du Fay was one of the first who obtained a salt from lime, by lixiviating it with a great deal of water, which he afterwards evaporated. But the quantity of salt he obtained by that means was very small; nor was it of an alkaline nature, as one would think it should have been, considering the properties of lime. Mr. du Fay did not carry his experiments on this subject any further, probably for want of time; nor did he determine of what nature the salt was.

Mr. Malouin had the curiosity to examine this salt of lime and soon found that it was nothing else but what was above called cremor calcis. He found moreover, that by mixing a fixed alkali with lime-water, a vitriolated tartar was formed; that, by mixing therewith an alkali with the basis of sea-salt, a Glauber's salt was produced; and, lastly, by combining lime with a substance abounding in phlogiston, he obtained a true sulphur. These very ingenious experiments prove to a demonstration, that the vitriolic acid constitutes the salt of lime; for, as hath been shewn, no other acid is capable of forming such combinations. On the other hand, Mr. Malouin, having forced the vitriolic acid of this salt to combine with phlogiston, found its basis to be earthy, and analogous to that of the selenites; whence he concluded, that the salt of lime is a true neutral salt, of the same kind as the selenites. Mr. Malouin tells us he found several other salts in lime. But as none of them was a fixed alkali, and as all the saline properties of lime have an affinity with those of that kind of salt, there is great reason to think that all those salts are foreign to lime, and that their union with it is merely accidental.

Lime unites with all acids, and in conjunction with them exhibits various phenomena.

The vitriolic acid poured upon lime dissolves it with effervescence and heat. From this mixture there exhales a great quantity of vapours, in smell and colour perfectly like those of sea-salt; from which however they are found to be very different when collected into a liquor. From this combination of the vitriolic acid with lime arises a neutral salt, which shoots into crystals, and is the same kind with the selenite salt obtained from lime by Mr. Malouin.

The nitrous acid poured upon lime dissolves it in like manner with effervesence and heat; but the solution is transparent, and therein differs from the former, which is opaque. From this mixture there arises a neutral salt, which does not crystallize, and has withal the very singular property of being volatile, and rising wholly by distillation in a liquid form. This phenomenon is so much the more remarkable, as lime, the basis of this salt, is one of the most fixed bodies known in chemistry.

With the acid of sea salt lime forms also a singular sort of salt, which greedily imbibes the moisture of the air. We shall have occasion to take further notice of it in another place.

Lime applied to fixed alkalis adds considerably to their caustic quality and makes them more penetrating and active. An alkaline lixivium in which lime hath been boiled, being evaporated to driness, forms a very caustic substance, which flows in the fire much more easily; attracts and retains moisture much more strongly, than fixed alkalis that have not been so treated. An alkali thus actuated by lime is called the caustic stone, or potential cautery, because it is employed by surgeons to produce eschers on the skin and cauterize it.

OF METALLIC SUBSTANCES IN GENERAL. Metallic substances are heavy, glittering, opaque, fusible bodies. They consist chiefly of a vitrifiable earth united with the phlogiston.

Several chemists insist on a third principle in these bodies, and have given it the name of mercurial earth; which according to Becher and Stahl, is the very same that being combined with the vitriolic acid forms and characterises the acid of the sea-salt. The existence of this principle hath not yet been demonstrated by any decisive experiment; but we shall shew that there are pretty strong reasons for admitting it.

We shall begin with mentioning the experiments which prove metallic substances to consist of a vitrifiable earth united with the phlogiston. The first is this: if they be calcined in such a manner as to have no communication with any inflammable matter, they will be spoiled of all their properties, and reduced to an earth or calx, that has neither the splendour nor the ductility of a metal, and in a strong fire turns to an actual glass, instead of flowing like a metal.

The second is, that the calx or the glass resulting from a metal thus decomposed, recovers all its metalline properties by being fused in immediate contact with an inflammable substance, capable of restoring the phlogiston of which calcination had deprived it.

On this occasion we must observe, that chemists have not yet been able, by adding the phlogiston, to give the properties of metals to all sorts of vitrifiable earths indiscriminately, but to such only as originally made a part of some metallic body. For example, a compound cannot be made with the phlogiston and sand that shall have the least resemblance of a metal; and this is what seems to point out the reality of a third principle as necessary to form the metalline combination. This principle may probably remain united with the vitrifiable earth of a metallic substance, when reduced to a glass; whence it follows that such vitrified metals require only the addition of a phlogiston to enable them to appear again in their pristine form.

It may be inferred from another experiment, that the calx and the glass of a metal are not its pure vitrifiable earth properly so called: for by repeated or long continued calcinations, such a calx or glass may be rendered incapable of ever resuming the metalline form, in what ever manner the phlogiston be afterwards applied to it; so that by this means it is brought into the condition of a pure vitrifiable earth, absolutely free from any mixture.

When by adding the phlogiston to a metallic glass; we restore it to the form of a metal, we are said to reduce, resuscitate, or revivify that metal.

Metallic substances are of different kinds, and are divided into metals and semi-metals.

Those are called metals, which besides their metalline splendor and appearance, are also malleable; that is, have the property of stretching under the hammer.

Those which have only the metalline splendor and appearance, without malleability, are called semi-metals.

Metals also are further subdivided into two sorts; vis. perfect and imperfect metals.

The perfect metals are those which suffer no damage or change whatever by the most violent and most lasting action of fire.

The imperfect metals are those which by the force of fire may be deprived of their phlogiston, and consequently of their metalline form.

When a moderate degree of fire only is employed to deprive a metal of its phlogiston, the metal is said to be calcined; and then it appears in the form of a powdered earth, which is called a calx; and this metalline calx being exposed to a more violent degree of fire, melts and turns to glass.

Metallic substances have an affinity with acids, but not equally with all; that is, every metallic substance is not capable of uniting and joining with every acid.

When an acid unites with a metallic substance, there commonly arises an ebullition, attended with a kind of hissing noise and fuming exhalations. By degrees, as the union becomes more perfect, the particles of the metal combining with the acid becomes invisible and this is termed dissolution; and when a metalline mass thus disappears in an acid, the metal is said to be dissolved by that acid. It is proper to observe, that acids act upon metalline substances, in one respect, just as they do upon alkalis and absorbent earths: for an acid cannot take up above such a certain proportion thereof as is sufficient to saturate it, to destroy several of its properties, and weaken others. For example, when an acid is combined with a metal to the point of saturation, it loses its taste, does not turn the blue colour of a vegetable red, and its affinity with water is considerably impaired. On the other hand, metalline substances, which when pure, are incapable of uniting with water, by being joined with an acid, acquire the property of dissolving in water. These combinations of metalline substances with acids form different sorts of neutral salts; some of which have the property of shooting into crystals, while others have it not: most of them, when thoroughly dried, attract the moisture of the air.

The affinity which metalline substances have with acids is less than that which absorbent earths and fixed alkalis have with the same acid; so that all metalline salts may be decompounded by one of these substances, which will unite with the acid, and precipitate the metal.

Metalline substances thus separated from an acid solvent are called magisteries, and precipitates of metals. None of these precipitates, except those of the perfect metals, retain the metalline form: most of their phlogiston hath been destroyed by the solution and precipitation, and must be restored before they can recover their properties. In short, they are nearly in the same state with metalline substances deprived of their phlogiston by calcination; and accordingly such a precipitate is called a calx.

A metalline calx prepared in this manner loses a greater or a less portion of its phlogiston, the more or less effectually and thoroughly the metalline substance of which it made a part was dissolved by the acid.

Metallic substances have affinities with each other which differ according to their different kinds; but this is not universal, for some of them are incapable of any sort of union with some others.

It must be observed, that metallic substances will not unite, except they be both in a similar state; that is, both in a metalline form, or both in the form of a glass; for a metalline substance, retaining its phlogiston, cannot contract a union with any metallic glass, even its own.

OF METALS. There are six metals, of which two are perfect, and four imperfect. The perfect metals are gold and silver; the others are copper, tin, lead, and iron. Some chemists admit a seventh metal, viz. quick-silver; but, as it is not malleable, it has been generally considered as a metallic body of a particular kind.

The ancient chemists, or rather the alchemists, who fancied a certain relation or analogy between metals and the heavenly bodies, bestowed on the seven metals, reckoning quick-silver one of them, the names of the seven planets of the ancients, according to the affinity which they imagined they observed between those several bodies.

Thus gold was called Sol, silver Luna, copper Venus, tin Jupiter, lead Saturn, iron Mars, and quick-silver Mercury. Though these names were assigned for reasons merely chimerical, yet they still keep their ground; so that it is not uncommon to find the metals called by the names, and denoted by the characters, of the planets, in the writings even of the best chemists. Metals are the heaviest bodies known in nature.

OF GOLD. Gold is the heaviest of all metals. The arts of wire-drawing and gold-beating shew its wonderful ductility. The greatest violence of fire is not able to produce any alteration in it.

Gold cannot be dissolved by any pure acid: but if the acid of nitre be mixed with the acid of sea-salt, there results a compound acid liquor, with which it has so great an affinity, that it is capable of being perfectly dissolved thereby. The chemists have called this solvent aqua regis, on account of its being the only acid that can dissolve gold, which they consider as the king of metals. The solution of gold is of a beautiful orange colour.

If gold dissolved in aqua regis be precipitated by an alkali or an absorbent earth, the precipitate gently dried, and then exposed to a certain degree of heat, is instantly dispersed into the air, with a most violent explosion and noise: gold thus precipitated is therefore called aurum fulminous. But if the precipitated gold be carefully washed in plenty of water, so as to clear it of all the adhering saline particles, it will not fulminate; but may be melted in a crucible without additament, and will then appear in its usual form. The acid of vitriol being poured on aurum fulminous likewise deprives it of its fulminating quality.

Gold does not begin to flow till it be red-hot like a live coal. Though it be the most malleable and most ductile of all metals, it has the singular property of losing its ductility more easily than any of them: even the fumes of charcoal are sufficient to deprive it thereof, if they come to contact with it while it is in fusion.

The malleability of this metal, and indeed of all the rest, is also considerably diminished by exposing it suddenly to cold when it is red-hot; for example, by quenching it in water, or even barely exposing it to the cold air. The way to restore ductility to gold, when lost by its coming in contact with the vapour of coals, and in general to every other metal rendered less malleable by being suddenly cooled, is to heat it again, to keep them red hot a considerable time, and then to let them cool very slowly and gradually: this operation frequently repeated will by degrees much increase the malleability of a metal.

Pure sulphur hath no effect on gold; but being combined with an alkali into a hepar sulphuris, it unites therewith very readily. Nay, so intimate is their union, that the gold by means thereof becomes soluble in water; and this new compound of gold and liver of sulphur, being dissolved in water, will pass through the pores of brown paper without suffering any decomposition; which does not happen, at least in such a manifest degree, to other metallic substances dissolved by liver of sulphur.

Aurum fulminous mixed and melted with flour of sulphur loses its fulminating quality: which arises from hence, that on this occasion the sulphur burns, and its acid, which is the same with the vitriolic, being thereby set at liberty, becomes as capable of acting upon the gold as a vitriolic acid would: which, as was said above, deprives the gold of its fulminating quality.

OF SILVER. Next to gold, silver is the most perfect metal. Like gold, it resists the utmost violence of fire, even that in the focus of a burning-glass. However, it holds only the second place among metals: because it is lighter than gold by almost one half; is also somewhat less ductile; and lastly, because it is acted upon by a greater number of solvents.

Yet silver hath one advantage over gold, namely that of being a little harder. which makes it also more sonorous.

This metal, like gold, begins to flow when it is so thoroughly penetrated by the fire as to appear ignited like a live coal.

While this metal is in fusion, the immediate contact of the vapour of burning coals deprives it almost entirely of its malleability, in the same manner as we observed happens to gold: but both these metals easily recover that property by being melted with nitre.

The nitrous acid is the truu solvent of silver, and being somewhat dephlegmated will very readily and easily take up a quantity of silver equal in weight to itself.

Silver thus combined with the nitrous acid forms a metallic salt which shoots into crystals, called by the name of lunar crystals, or crystals of silver.

These crystals are most violently caustic: applied to the skin, they quickly affect it much as a live coal would; they produce a blackish escher, corroding and entirely destroying the parts they touch. Surgeons use them to eat away the proud fungous flesh of ulcers. As silver united with the nitrous acid hath the property of blackening all animal substances, a solution of this metallic salt is employed to die hair, or other animal matters, of a beautiful and durable black.

These crystals flow with a very moderate heat, and even before they grow red. Being thus melted, they form a blackish mass; and in this form they are used by surgeons, under the title of lapis infernalis, infernal stone, or silver caustic.

Silver is also dissolved by the vitriolic acid: but then the acid must be concentrated, and in quantity double the weight of the silver: nor will the solution succeed without a considerable degree of heat.

Spirit of salt and aqua regis, as well as the other acids, are incapable of dissolving this metal, at least in the ordinary way.

Though silver be not soluble in the acid of sea-salt, nor easily in the acid of vitriol, as hath just been observed, it doth not follow, that it hath but a weak affinity with the latter, and none at all with the former: on the contrary, it appears from experiment, that it hath with these two acids a much greater affinity than with the acid of nitre: which is singular enough, considering the facility with which this last acid dissolves it.

The experiment which proves the fact is this. To a solution of silver in the nitrous acid add the acid either of vitriol or of sea-salt, and the silver will instantly quit its nitrous solvent to join with the superadded acid.

Silver thus united with the vitriolic or the marine acid is less soluble in water than when combined with the nitrous acid: and for this reason it is, that when either of these two acids is added to a solution of silver, the liquor immediately becomes white, and a precipitate is formed, which is no other than the silver united with the precipitating acid. If the precipitation be effected by the vitriolic acid, the precipitate will disappear upon adding a sufficient quantity of water, because there will then be water enough to dissolve it. But the case is not the same when the precipitation is made by the marine acid: for silver combined therewith is scarce soluble in water.

This precipitate of silver procured by means of the marine acid is very easily fused, and when fused changes to a substance in some measure transparent and flexible; which hath occasioned it to be called by the name of luna cornea. If it be proposed to decompound this luna cornea, that is, to separate the marine acid from the silver with which it is united, the luna cornea must be melted along with fatty and absorbent matter, with which the acid will unite, and leave the metal exceeding pure.

It must be observed, that if, instead of the marine acid, sea-salt in substance be added to a solution of silver in the nitrous acid, a precipitate is also produced, which by fusion appears to be a true luna cornea. The reason is, that the sea-salt is decomposed by the nitrous acid, which seizes its basis, as having a greater affinity therewith than its own acid bath: and this acid being consequently disengaged, and set at liberty unites with the silver, which, as has been shewn, has greater affinity with it than with the nitrous acid. This is an instance of decomposition effected by means of one of those double affinities mentioned in the seventh proposition concerning affinities.

From what hath been already said it is clear, that all these combinations of silver with acids may be decompounded by absorbent earths and by fixed alkalis; it being a general law with regard to all metallic substances.

Silver, when separated by these means from the acids in which it was dissolved, requires nothing but simple fusion to restore it to its usual form: because it does not, any more than gold, lose its phlogiston by those solutions and precipitations.

Silver unites with sulphur in fusion. If this metal be only made red hot in a crucible, and sulphur be then added, it immediately flows; the sulphur acting as a flux to it. Silver thus united with sulphur forms a mass that may be cut, is half malleable, and hath nearly the colour and consistence of lead. It this sulphurated silver be kept a long time in fusion, and in a great degree of heat, the sulphur flies off and leaves the silver pure. But if the sulphur be evaporated by a violent heat, it carries off with it part of the silver.

Silver unites and mixes perfectly with gold in fusion. The two metals thus mixed form a compound with properties partaking of both.

Metallurgists have hitherto sought in vain for a perfectly good and easy method of separating these two metals by the dry way only: (This term is used to signify all operations performed by fusion:) but they are conveniently enough parted by the moist way, that is, by acid solvents. This method is founded on the above mentioned properties of gold and silver with respect to acids. It hath been shewn, that aqua regis only will dissolve gold; that silver, on the contrary, is not soluble by aqua regis, and that its proper solvent is the acid of nitre: Consequently, when gold and silver are mixed together, if the compound mass be put in aqua fortis, this acid will take up all the silver, without dissolving a particle of the gold, which will therefore remain pure; and by this means the desired separation is effected. This method, which is commonly made use of by goldsmiths and in mints, is called parting assay.

It is plain, that if aqua regis were employed instead of aqua fortis, the separation would be equally effected: and that the only difference between this process and the former would consist in this, that now the gold would be dissolved, and the silver remain pure. But the operation by aqua fortis is preferable; because aqua regis does take up a little silver, whereas aqua fortis hath not the least effect on gold.

It must be observed, that when gold and silver are mixed together in equal parts, they cannot be parted by the means of aqua fortis. To enable the aqua fortis to act duly on the silver, this metal must be, at least, in a triple proportion to the gold. If it be in a less proportion, you must either employ aqua regis to make the separation, or, if you prefer the use of aqua fortis, melt the metalline mass, and add as much silver as is necessary to make up the proportion above mentioned: And hence this process is called quartasion.

This effect, which is pretty singular, probably arises from hence, that when the gold exceeds, or even equals the silver in quantity, the parts of both being intimately united, the former are capable of coating over the latter, and covering them so as to defend them from the action of the aqua fortis; which is not the case when there is thrice as much silver as gold.

There is one thing more to be taken notice of with regard to this process; which is, that perfectly pure aqua fortis is rarely to be met with, for two reasons: First. it is difficult in making it wholly to prevent the rising of the medium employed to disengage the nitrous acid; that is, a little of the vitriolic acid will mix with the vapours of the aqua fortis: Secondly, unless the saltpetre be very well purified, it will always hold some small portion of sea-salt, the acid of which, we know, is very readily set loose by the vitriolic acid, and consequently rise together with the vapours of the aqua fortis. It is easy to see, that aqua fortis, mixed either with the one or the other, is not proper for the parting process; because, as has just been said, the vitriolic and the marine acid equally precipitate silver dissolved in the nitrous acid: by which means, when they are united with that acid, they weaken its action upon the silver, and hinder the dissolution. Add, that aqua fortis adulterated with a mixture of spirit of salt becomes aqua regis; and consequently is rendered capable of dissolving gold, in proportion as its action upon silver is diminished.

In order to remedy this inconvenience, and free aqua fortis from the vitriolic or marine acid with which it is tainted, silver must be dissolved therein: By degrees, as the metal dissolves, those heterogeneous acids lay hold of it, and precipitate with it in the form of a white powder, as we observed before. This precipitate being wholly fallen, the liquor grows clear; after which, if it be found capable of dissolving more silver, without turning milky, it may be depended on as perfectly pure aqua fortis. Then filtre it, dissolve more silver in it, as long as it will take up any, and you will have a solution of silver in a very pure aqua fortis. By means of this solution may other aqua fortis be purified: For, pour a few drops thereof into a very impure aqua fortis, and immediately the vitriolic or marine acid, with which the aqua fortis is contaminated, will join the silver and fall therewith to the bottom. When the solution of silver prepared as above does not in the least affect the transparency of the aqua fortis, it is then very pure, and fit for the purposes of quartation.

This operation of purifying aqua fortis by a solution of silver is called the precipitation of aqua fortis; and aqua fortis thus purified is called precipitated aqua fortis.

When silver is dissolved in aqua fortis it may be separated therefrom, as has been shewn, by absorbent earths and fixed alkalis.

OF COPPER. Of all the imperfect metals, copper comes the nearest to gold and silver. Its natural colour is a deep red yellow. It resists a very violent degree of fire for a considerable time; but losing its phlogiston at last, it changes its metalline form for that of a calx, or a pure reddish earth. This calx is hardly, if at all, reducible to glass, without the addition of something to promote its fusion: all that the fiercest heat can do being only to render it soft. Copper, even while it retains its metalline form, and is very pure, requires a considerable degree of fire to melt it, and does not begin to flow till long after it is red-hot. When in fusion, it communicates a greenish colour to the flame of the coals.

This metal is inferior to silver in point of gravity; nor is its ductility so great, though it be pretty considerable: But, on the other hand, it exceeds that metal in hardness. It unites readily with gold and silver; nor does it greatly lessen their beauty when added to them in a small quantity: Nay, it even procures them some advantages; such as making them harder, and less subject to lose their ductility. This may probably arise from hence, that the ductility of copper has the peculiarity of resisting most of those causes which rob the perfect metals of theirs.

The property which other metalline substances have in common with copper, of losing the phlogiston by calcining and then vitrifying, furnishes us with a method of separating them from gold and silver, when they are combined therewith. Nothing more is required than to expose the mass, compounded of the perfect metals and other metalline substances, to a degree of heat sufficient to calcine whatever is not either gold or silver. It is evident that by this means these two metals will be obtained as pure as possible; for, as hath already been said, no metalline calx or glass is capable of uniting with metals possessed of their phlogiston. On this principle is formed the whole business of refining gold and silver.

When the perfect metals have no other alloy but copper, as this metal is not to be calcined or vitrified without great difficulty, which is increased by its union with the unvitrifiable metals, it is easy to see that it is almost impossible to separate them without adding something to facilitate the vitrification of the copper. Such metals as have the property of turning easily to glass are very fit for this purpose; and it is necessary to add a certain quantity thereof, when gold or silver is to be purified from the alloy of copper. We shall have occasion to be more particular on this subject when we come to treat of lead.

Copper is soluble in all the acids, to which it communicates a green colour, and sometimes a blue. Even the neutral salts, and water itself, act upon this metal. With regard to water indeed, as the procuring it absolutely pure and free from any saline mixture is next to an impossibility, it remains a question, whether the effect it produces on copper be not owing to certain saline particles contained in it. It is this great facility of being dissolved that renders copper so subject to rust; which is nothing else but some parts of its surface corroded by saline particles contained in the surrounding air and water.

The rust of copper is always green or blue, or of a colour between these two. Internally used it is very noxious, being a real poison, as are all the solutions of this metal made by any acid whatever. The blue colour, which copper constantly assumes, when corroded by any saline substance, is a sure sign by which it may be discovered where-ever it exists, even in a very small quantity.

Copper dissolved in the vitriolic acid forms a kind of metalline salt, which shoots into rhomboidal crystals of a most beautiful blue colour. These crystals are called blue vitriol, or vitriol of copper. They are sometimes found ready formed in the bowels of the earth; and may be artificially made by dissolving copper in the vitriolic acid; but the solution will not succeed unless the acid be well dephlegmated. The taste of this vitriol is saltish and astringent. It retains a considerable quantity of water in crystallizing, on which account it is easily rendered fluid by fire.

It must be observed, that when it is exposed to a certain degree of heat in order to free it of its humidity, a great part of its acid flies off at the same time: And hence it is that, after calcination, there remains only a kind of earth, or metalline calx, of a red colour, which contains but very little acid. This earth cannot be brought to flow but with the greatest difficulty.

A solution of copper in the nitrous acid forms a salt which does not crystallize, but, when dried, powerfully attracts the moisture of the air. The same thing happens when it is dissolved in the spirit of salt, or in aqua regis.

If the copper, thus dissolved by any of these acids, be precipitated by an earth or an alkali, it retains nearly the colour it had in the solution: But these precipitates are scarce any thing more than the earth of copper, or copper deprived of most of its phlgiston; so that if they were exposed to a violent fire, without any additament, a great part of them would be converted into an earth that could never be reduced to a metalline form. Therefore, when we intend to reduce these precipitates to copper, it is necessary to add a certain quantity of a substance capable of restoring to them the phlogiston they have lost.

The substance which hath been found fittest for such reductions is charcoal dust; because charcoal is nothing but phlogiston closely combined with an earth, which renders it exceedingly fixed, and capable of resisting a violent force of fire. But as charcoal will not melt, and consequently is capable of preventing rather than forwarding the flux of a metalline calx or glass, which nevertheless is essentially necessary to complete the reduction, it hath been contrived to mix it, or any other substance containing the phlogiston, with such fixed alkalis as easily flow, and are fit to promote the flux of other bodies. These mixtures are called reducing fluxes; because the general name of fluxes is given to all salts, or mixtures of salts, which facilitate fusion.

If sulphur be applied to copper made perfectly red hot, the metal immediately runs; and these two substances uniting, form a new compound much more fusible than pure copper.

This compound is destroyed by the sole force of fire, for two reasons: The first is, that, sulphur being volatile, the fire is capable of subliming a great part of it, especially when it is in a great proportion to the copper with which it is joined; the second is, that the portion of sulphur which remains, being more intimately united with the copper, though it be rendered less combustible by that union, is nevertheless burnt and consumed in time. Copper being combined with sulphur, and together with it exposed to the force of fire, is found to be partly changed into a blue vitriol; because the vitriolic acid, being disengaged by burning the sulphur, is by that means qualified to dissolve the copper. The affinity of copper with sulphur is greater than that of silver.

This metal, as well as the other imperfect metals and the semi-metals, being mingled with nitre and exposed to the fire, is decomposed and calcined much sooner than by itself; because the phlogiston which it contains occasions the deflagration of the nitre, and consequently the two substances mutually decompose each other. There are certain metalline substances who phlogiston is so abundant, and so weakly connected with their earth, that, when they are thus treated with nitre, there arises immediately a detonation, accompanied with flame, and as violent as if sulphur or charcoal dust had been employed; so that in a moment the metalline substance loses its phlogiston, and is calcined. The nitre, after these detonations, always assumes an alkaline character.

OF IRON. Iron is lighter and less ductile than copper; but it is much harder, and of more difficult fusion.

It is the only body that has the property of being attracted by the magnet, which therefore serves to discover it where-ever it it. But it must be observed, that it hath this property only when in its metalline state, and loses it when converted to an earth or calx. Hence very few iron-ores are attracted by the loadstone; because, for the most part, they are only sorts of earths, which require a phlogiston to be added before they can be brought to the form of true iron.

When iron hath undergone no other preparation but the fusion which is necessary to smelt it from its ore, it is usually quite brittle, and flies to pieces under the hammer: Which arises in some measure from its containing a certain portion of un-metallic earth interposed between its parts. This we call pig-iron.

By melting this a second time it is rendered purer, and more free from hetero-geneous matters: But still, as its proper parts are probably not brought sufficiently near, or closely enough united, till the iron hath undergone some further preparation besides that of fusion, it seldom hath any degree of malleability.

The way to give it this property is to make it just red-hot, and then hammer it for some time in all directions; to the end that its parts may be properly united, in-corporated, and welded together, and that the heterogeneous matter which keep them assunder may be separated. Iron made by this means as malleable as possible, we call bar-iron, or forged iron.

Bar-iron is still harder to fuse than pig-iron: To make it flow requires the utmost force of fire.

Iron has the property of imbibing a greater quantity of phlogiston than is necessary to give it the metalline form. It may be made to take in this superabundant phlogiston two ways: The first is by fusing it again with matters that contain the phlogiston; the second is, by encompassing it with a quantity of such matter, charcoal-dust, for instance, and then exposing it so encompassed, for a certain time, to a degree of fire barely sufficient to keep it red-hot. This second method, whereby one substance is incorporated with another by means of fire, but without fusing either of them, is in general called cementation.

Iron thus impregnated with an additional quantity of phlogiston is called steel. The hardness of steel may be considerably augmented by tempering it; that is, by making it red-hot, and suddenly quenching it in some cold liquor. The hotter the metal, and the colder the liquor in which it is quenched, the harder will the steel be. By this means tools are made, such as files and sheers, capable of cutting and dividing the hardest bodies, as glass, pebbled, and iron itself. The colour of steel is darker than that of iron, and the facets which appear on breaking it are smaller. It is also less ductile and more brittle, especially when tempered.

As iron may be impregnated with an additional quantity of phlogiston, and thereby converted into steel, so may steel be again deprived of that superabundant phlogiston, and brought back to the condition of iron. This is effected by cementing it with poor earths, such as calcined bones and chalk. By the same operation steel may be untempered; nay, it will lose the hardness it had acquired by tempering, if it be but made red-hot, and left to cool gradually. As iron and steel differ only in the respects we have here taken notice of, their properties being in all other respects the same, what follows is equally applicable to both.

Iron being exposed to the action of fire for some time, especially when divided into small particles, such as filings, is calcined, and loses its phlogiston. By this means it turns to a kind of reddish yellow earth, which on account of its colour is called crocus Martis, or saffron of Mars.

This calx of iron has the singular property of flowing in the fire with somewhat less difficulty than iron itself; whereas every other metalline calx flows with less ease than the metal that produced it. It has moreover the remarkable property of uniting with the phlogiston, and of being reduced to iron without fusion; requiring for that purpose only to be made red-hot.

Iron may be incorporated with silver, and even with gold, by means of certain operations. Under the article of lead, we shall see how it may be separated from these metals.

The acids produce on it much the same effects as on copper; every one of them acts upon it. Certain neutral salts, alkalis, and even water itself, are capable of dissolving it; and hence it is also very subject to rust.

The vitriolic acid dissolves it with the greatest ease; but the circumstances which attend the dissolution thereof are different from those with which the same acid dissolves copper. For, 1. Whereas the vitriolic acid must be concentrated to dissolve copper, it must on the contrary be diluted with water to dissolve iron, which it will not touch when well dephlegmated. 2. The vapours which rise in this dissolution are inflammable; so that if it be made in a small necked bottle, and the flame of a candle be applied to the mouth thereof, the vapours in the bottle take fire with such rapidity as to produce a considerable explosion.

This solution is of a beautiful green colour; and from this union of the vitriolic acid with iron, there results a neutral metalline salt, which has the property of shooting into crystals of a rhomboidal figure, and a green colour. These crystals are called green vitriol, and vitriol of Mars.

Green vitriol hath a saltish and astringent taste. As it retains a great deal of water in crystallizing it quickly flows by the action of fire; but this fluidity is owing to its water only, and is not a real fusion; for as soon as its moisture is evaporated it resumes a solid form. Its green transparent colour is now changed into an opaque white; and, if the calcination be continued, its acid also exhales, and is dissipated in vapours; and as it loses that, it turns gradually to a yellow colour, which comes so much the nearer to a red the longer the calcination is continued, or the higher the force of the fire is raised; which being driven to the utmost, what remains is of a very deep red. This remainder is nothing but the body of the iron, which, having lost its phlogiston, is now no more than an earth, nearly of the same nature with that which is left after calcining the metal itself.

Green vitriol dissolved in water spontaneously lets fall a yellowish earthy sediment. If this solution be desecated by filtration, it still continues to deposit some of the same substance, till the vitriol be wholly decomposed. This sediment is nothing but the earth of iron, which is then called ochre.

The nitrous acid dissolves iron with great ease. This solution is of a yellow colour, inclining more or less to a russet, or dark-brown, as it is more or less saturated with iron. Iron dissolved by this acid also falls spontaneously into a kind of calx, which is incapable of being dissolved a second time; for the nitrous acid will not act upon iron that has lost its phlogiston. This solution does not crystallize, and if evaporated to dryness attracts the moisture of the air.

Spirit of salt likewise dissolves iron, and this solution is green. The vapours which rise during the dissolution are inflammable, like those which ascend when this metal is attacked by the vitriolic acid. Aqua regis makes a solution of iron, which is of a yellow colour.

Iron hath a greater affinity than either silver or copper with the nitrous and vitriolic acids; so that if iron be presented to a solution of either, on one of these two acids, the dissolved metal will be precipitated; because the acid quits if for the iron, with which it has a greater affinity.

On this occasion it must be observed, that if a solution of copper in the vitriolic acid be precipitated by means of iron, the precipitate has the form and splendour of a metal, and does not require the addition of a phlogiston to reduce it to true copper; which is not the case, when the precipitation is effected by earths or alkaline salts.

The colour of this metalline precipitate hath deceived several persons, who being unacquainted with such phenomena, and with the nature of blue vitriol, imagined that iron was transmuted into copper, when they saw a bit of iron, laid in a solution of that vitriol, become, in form and external appearance, exactly like copper; whereas the surface only of the iron was crusted over with the particles of copper contained in the vitriol, which had gradually fallen upon, and adhered to the iron, as they were precipitated out of the solution.

Among the solvents of iron we mentioned fixed alkalis; and that they have such a power, is proved by the following phenomenon. If a large proportion of alkaline salts be suddenly mixed with a solution of iron in an acid, no precipitation ensues, and the liquor remains clear and pellucid; or if at first it look a little turbid, that appearance lasts but a moment, and the liquor presently recovers its transparency. The reason is, that quantity of alkali is more than sufficient to saturate all the acid of the solution; and the superabundant portion thereof, meeting with the iron already finely divided by the acid, dissolves it with ease as fast as it falls, and so prevents its mudding in liquor. To evince that this is so in fact, let the alkali be applied in a quantity that is not sufficient, or but barely sufficient, to saturate the acid, and the iron will then precipitate like any other metal.

Water also acts upon iron; and therefore iron exposed to moisture grows rusty.

If iron filings be exposed to the dew, they turn wholly to rust, which is called crocus Martis aperient.

Iron exposed to the fire, together with nitre, makes it detonate pretty briskly, sets it in a flame, and decomposes it with rapidity.

This metal hath a greater affinity than any other metalline substance with sulphur; on which account, it is successfully used to precipitate, and separate all metalline substances combined with sulpjur.

Sulphur uniting with iron communicates to it such a degree of fusibility, that if a mass of this metal, heated red-hot, be rubbed with a bit of sulphur, it incessantly runs into as perfect a fusion as a metal exposed to the focus of a large burning-glass.

OF TIN. Tin is the lightest of all metals. Though it yields easily to the impression of hard bodies, it has but little ductility. Being bent backwards and forwards it makes a small crackling noise. It flows with a very moderate degree of fire, and long before it comes to be red-hot. When it is in fusion, its surface soon grows dusky, and there forms upon it a thin dark-coloured dusty pellicle, which is no other than a part of the tin that has lost its phlogiston, or a calx of tin. The metal thus calcined easily recovers its metalline form, on the addition of a phlogiston. If the calx of tin be urged by a strong fire it grows white, but the greatest violence of heat will not fuse it; which makes some chemists consider it as a calcinable or absorbent earth, rather than a vitrifiable one. Yet it turns to glass in some sort, when mixed with any other substance that vitrifies easily. However, it always produces an imperfect glass only, which is not at all transparent, but of an opaque white. The calx of tin thus vitrified is called enamel. Enamels are made of several colours by the addition of this or that metalline calx.

Tin unites easily with all the metals; but it destroys the ductility and malleability of every one of them, lead excepted. Nay, it possesses this property of maing metals brittle, in such an eminent degree, that the very vapour of it, when in fusion, is capable of producing this effect. Moreover, which is very singular, the most ductile metals, even gold and silver, are those on which it works this change with the most ease, and in the greatest degree. It has also the property of making silver, mixed with it, flow over a very small fire.

It adheres to, and in some measure incorporates with the surface of copper and of iron; whence arose the practice of coating those metals with tin. Tin-plates are no other than thin plates of iron tinned over.

If to twenty parts of tin one part of copper be added, this this alloy renders it much more solid, and the mixed mass continues tolerably ductile.

If, on the contrary, to one part of tin ten parts of copper be added, together with a little zinc, a semi-metal to be considered hereafter, from this combination there results a metalline compound, which is hard, brittle, and very sonorous; so that it is used for casting bells: This composition is called bronze and bell-metal.

Tin hath an affinity with the vitriolic, nitrous, and marine acids. All of them attack and corrode it; yet none of them is able to dissolve it without great difficulty: So that if a clear solution thereof be desired, particular methods must be employed for that purpose; for the acids do but in a manner calcine it, and convert it to a kind of white calx or precipitate. The solvent which has the greatest power over it is aqua regis, which has even a greater affinity therewith than with gold itself; whence it follows, that gold dissolved in aqua regis may be precipitated by means of tin; but then the aqua regis must be weakened. Gold thus precipitated by tin is of a most beautiful colour, and is used for a red in enamelling and painting on porcelain, as also to give a red colour to artificial gems. If the aqua regis be not lowered, the precipitate will not have the purple colour.

Tin hath the property of giving a great lustre to all red colours in general; on which account it is used by the dyers for striking a beautiful scarlet, and tin-vessels are employed in making fine syrup of violets. Water does not act upon this metal, as it does upon iron and copper; for which reason it is not subject to rust; nevertheless, when it is exposed to the air, its surface soon loses its polish and splendor.

Tin mixed with nitre, and exposed to the fire, deflagrates with it, makes it detonate, and is immediately converted to a refractory calx; for so all substances are called which are incapable of fusion.

Tin readily unites with sulphur, and with it becomes a brittle and friable mass.

OF LEAD. Next to gold and mercury, lead is the heaviest of all metalline substances, but in hardness is exceeded by every one of them. Of all metals also it melts the easiest, except tin. While it is in fusion there gathers incessantly on its surface, as on that of tine, a blackish, dusty pellicle, which is nothing but calx of lead.

This calx further calcined by a moderate fire, the flame being reverberated on it, soon grows white. If the calcination be continued it becomes yellow, and at last of a beautiful red. In this state it is called minium, and is used as a pigment. Minium is not easily made, and the operation succeeds well in large manufactures only.

To convert lead into litharge, which is the metal in a manner half vitrified, you need only keep it melted by a pretty strong fire; for then, as its surface gradually calcines, it tends more and more to fusion and vitrification.

All these preparations of lead are greatly disposed to perfect fusion and vitrification, and for that purpose require but a moderate degree of fire; the calx or earth of lead being of metalline earths that which vitrifies the most easily.

Lead hath not only the property of turning into glass with the greatest facility, but it hath also that of promoting greatly the vitrification of all the other imperfect metals; and, when it is actually vitrified, procures the ready fusion of all earths and stones in general, even those which are refractory, that is, which could not be fused without its help.

Glass of lead, besides its great fusibility, hath also the singular property of being so subtile and active as to corrode and penetrate the crucible in which it is melted, unless they be of an earth that is exceeding hard, compact, and withal very refractory; for glass of lead being one of the most powerful fluxes that we know, if the earth of the crucible in which it is melted be in the smallest degree fusible, it will be immediately vitrified; especially there be any metallic matter in its composition.

The great activity of glass of lead may be weakened by joining it with other vitrifiable matters; but unless these be added in a very great proportion, it will still remain powerful enough to penetrate common earths, and carry off the matters combined with it.

On these properties of lead, and of the glass of lead, depends the whole business of refining gold and silver. It hath been shewn, that as these two metals are indestructible by fire, and the only ones which have that advantage, they may be separated from the imperfect metals, when mixed therewith, by exposing the compound to a degree of fire sufficiently strong to vitrify the latter; which when once converted into glass can no longer remain united with any metal that has its metalline form. But it is very difficult to procure this vitrification of the imperfect metals, when united with gold and silver; nay, it is in a manner impossible to vitrify them entirely, for two reasons; first, because most of them are naturally very difficult to vitrify; secondly, because the union they have contracted with the perfect metals defends them, in a manner, from the action of the fire, and that so much the more effectually as the proportion of the perfect metals is greater; which being indestructible, and in some sort coating over those with which they are alloyed, serve them as a preservative and impenetrable shield against the utmost violence of fire.

It is therefore clear, that a great deal of labour may be saved, and that gold and silver may be refined to a much greater degree of purity than can otherwise be obtained, if to a mixture of these metals with copper, for instance, or any other imperfect metal, be added a certain quantity of lead. For the lead, by its known property, will infallibly produce the desired vitrification; and as it likewise increases the proportion of the imperfect metals, and so lessens that of the perfect metals, in the mass, it evidently deprives the former of a part of their guard, and so effects a more complete vitrification. As the glass of lead hath the property of running through the crucible, and carrying with it the matters which it has vitrified, it follows, that when the vitrification of the imperfect metals is effected by its means, all those vitrified matters together penetrate the vessel containing the fused metalline mass, disappear, and leave only the gold and silver perfectly pure, and freed, as far as possible, from all admixture of heterogenious parts.

The better to promote the separation of such parts, it is usual to employ in this process a particular sort of small crucibles, made of the ashes of calcined bones, which are exceedingly porous and easily pervaded. They are called cupels, on account of their figure, which is that of a wide-mouthed cup; and from hence the operation takes its name; for when we refine gold and silver in this manner, we are said to cupel those metals. It is easy to perceive, that the more lead is added, the more accurately will the gold and silver be refined; and that so much the more lead ought to be added as the perfect metals are alloyed with a greater proportion of the imperfect. This is the most severe trial to which a perfect metal can be put, and consequently any metal that stands it may be fairly considered as such.

In order to denote the fineness of gold, it is supposed to be divided into twenty-four parts called carats; and gold, which is quite pure and free from all alloy, is said to be twenty-four carats fine; that which contains 1/24 part of alloy is called gold of twenty-three carats; that which contains 2/24 of allow is but twenty-two carats; and so on. Silver again is supposed to be divided into twelve parts only, which are called penny-weights; so that when absolutely pure it is said to be twelve penny-weights fine; when it contains 1/12 of alloy, it is then called eleven penny-weights fine; when it contains 2/12 of alloy, it is called ten penny-weights fine; and so on.

In treating of copper, we promised to shew under the article of lead how to separate it from iron. The process is founded on that property of lead which renders it incapable of mixing and uniting with iron, though it readily dissolves all other metalline substances. Therefore if you have a mass compounded of copper and iron, it must be fused with a certain quantity of lead, and then the copper, having a greater affinity with lead than with iron, will desert the latter and join the former, which being incapable of any union with iron, as was said, will wholly exclude it from the new compound. The next point is to separate the lead from the copper; which is done by exposing the mass compounded of these two metals to a degree of fire strong enough to deprive the lead of its metalline form, but too weak to have the same effect on the copper; and this may be done, since of all the imperfect metals lead is, next to tin, the easiest to be calcined, and copper, on the contrary, resists the greatest force of fire longest, without losing its metalline form. Now what we gain by this exchange, viz. by separating copper from iron, and uniting it with lead, consists in this, that as lead is calcined with less fire than iron, the copper is less exposed to be destroyed; for it must be observed, that, however moderate the fire be, it is hardly possible to prevent a certain quantity thereof from being calcine in the operation.

Lead melted with a third part of tine forms a compound, which being exposed to a fire capable of making it thoroughly red hot, swells, puffs up, seems in some sort to take fire, and is presently calcined. These two metals mixed together are much sooner calcined than either of them separately.

Both lead and tin are in some measure affected by water, and by a moist air; but they are both much less subject than iron or copper to be corroded by these solvents, and of course are much less liable to rust.

The vitriolic acid acts upon and dissolves lead much in the same manner as it doth silver.

The nitrous acid dissolves this metal with much ease, and in great quantities; and from this solution a small portion of mercury may be obtained.

When this solution of lead is diluted with a good deal of water, the lead precipitates in the form of a white powder; which happens because the acid is rendered too weak to keep the lead dissolved.

If this solution of lead be evaporated to a certain degree, it shoots into crystals formed like regular pyramids with square bases. These crystals are of a yellowish colour, and of a saccharine taste; they do not easily dissolve in water. This nitrous metalline salt has the singular property of detonating in a crucible, without any additament, or the contact of any other inflammable substance. This property it derives from the great quantity of phlogiston contained in, and but loosely connected with the lead, which is one of its principles.

If spirit of salt, or even sea-salt in substance, be added to a solution of lead in the nitrous acid, a white precipitate immediately falls; which is no other than the lead united with the marine acid. This precipitate is extremely like the precipitate of silver made in the same manner; and that being called luna cornea, hat occasioned this to be named plumbum corneum. Like the luna cornea, it is very fusible, and, being melted, hardens like it into a kind of horny substance; it is volatile, and may be reduced by means of inflammable matters combined with alkalis. But it differs from the luna cornea in this chiefly, that id dissolves easily in water; whereas the luna cornea, on the contrary, dissolves therein with great difficulty, and in a very small quantity.

As this precipitation of lead from its solution is spirit of nitre is procured by the marine acid, lead is thereby proved to have a greater affinity with the latter acid than with the former. Yet, if you attempt to dissolve lead directly by the acid of sea-salt, the solution is not so easily effected as by the spirit of nitre, and it is always imperfect; for it wants one of the conditions essential to every solution in a liquor; namely transparenct.

If lead be boiled for a long time in a lixivium of fixed alkali, part of it will be dissolved.

Sulphur renders this metal refractory and scarce fusible; and the mass they form when united together is friable. Hence it appears that sulphur acts upon lead much in the same manner as upon tin; that is, it renders both these metals less fusible, which are naturally the most fusible of any, while it exceedingly facilitates the fusion of silver, copper, and iron, metals which of themselves flow with the greatest difficulty.

OF QUICKSILVER. We treat of quick-silver in a chapter apart, because this metallic substance cannot be classed with the metals properly so called, and yet has some properties which will not allow us to confound it with the semi-metals. The reason why quick-silver, by the chemists commonly called Mercury, is not reputed a metal, is, that it wants one of the essential properties thereof, viz. malleability. When it is pure and unadulterated with any mixture, it is always fluid, and of course unmalleable. But as, on the other hand, it eminently possesses the opacity, the splendor, and above all the gravity of a metal, being next to gold, the heaviest of all bodies, it may be considered as a true metal, differing from the rest no otherwise than by being constantly in fusion; which we may suppose arises from its aptness to flow with such a small degree of heat, that be there ever so little warmth on earth, there is still more than enough to keep mercury in fusion; which would become solid and malleable if it were possible to apply to it a degree of cold considerable enough for that purpose. These properties will not allow us to confound it with the semi-metals. Add, that we are not yet assured by any undoubted experiment that it can be wholly deprived of its phlogiston, as the imperfect metals may. Indeed we cannot apply the force of fire to it as could be wished; for it is so volatile, that it flies off and exhales in vapours with a much less degree of fire than is necessary to make it red-hot. The vapours of mercury thus raised by the action of fire, being collected and united in a certain quantity, appear to be no other than true mercury retaining every on of its properties; and no experiment hath ever been able to shew the least change thus produced in its nature.

If mercury be exposed to the greatest heat that it can bear without sublimation, and continued in it for several months, or even a whole year together, it turns to a red powder, which the chemists mercurius pracipitatus per se. But to succeed in this operation, it is absolutely necessary that the heat be such as is above specified; for this metallic substance may remain exposed to a weaker heat for a considerable number of years, without undergoing any sensible alteration.

Some chemists fancied that by this operation they had fixed mercury, and changed its nature; but without any reason; for if the mercury thus seemingly transmuted be exposed to a somewhat stronger degree of fire, it sublimes and exhales in vapours as usual; and those vapours collected are nothing else but running mercury, which has recovered all its properties without the help of any additament.

Mercury has the property of dissolving all the metals, iron only excepted. But it is a condition absolutely necessary to the success of such dissolution, that the metalline substances be possessed of their phlogiston; for if they be calcined, mercury cannot touch them; and hence it follows, that mercury doth not unite with substances that are purely earthy. Such a combination of a metal with mercury is called an amalgam. Trituration alone is sufficient to effect it; however, a proper degree of heat also is of use.

Mercury amalgamated with a metal gives it a consistence more or less soft, and even fluid, according to the greater or smaller proportion of mercury employed. All amalgams are softened by heat, and hardened by cold.

Mercury is very volatile; vastly more so than the most unfixed metals; moreover, the union it contracts with any metal is not sufficiently intimate to entitle the new compound resulting from that union to all the properties of the two substances united; at least with regard to their degree of fixity and volatility. From all which it follows, that the best and surest method of separating it from metals dissolved by it, is to expose the amalgam in a degree of heat sufficient to make all the quick-silver rise and evaporate; after which the metal remains in the form of a powder, and being fused recovers its malleability. If it be thought proper to save the quick-silver, the operation must be performed in close vessels, which will confine and collect the mercurial vapours. This operation is most frequently employed to separate gold and silver from the several sorts of earths and sands with which they are mixed in the ore; because these two metals, gold especially, are of sufficient value to compensate the loss of mercury, which is inevitable in this process; besides, as they very readily amalgamate with it, this way of separating them from every thing unmetallic is very commodius.

Mercury is dissolved by acids; but with circumstances peculiar to each particular acid.

The vitriolic acid concentrated and made boiling hot seizes on it, and presently reduces it to a kind of white powder, which turns yellow by the affusion of water, but does not dissolve in it; it is called turbith mineral. However, the vitriolic acid on this occasion unites with a great part of the mercury in such a manner that the compound is soluble in water. For if to the water which was used to wash the turbith a fixed alkali be added, there falls instantly a russet-coloured precipitate, which is no other than mercury separated from the vitriolic acid by the intervention of the alkali.

This dissolution of mercury the the vitriolic acid is accompanied with a very remarkable phenomenon; which is, that the acid contracts a strong smell of volatile spirits of sulphur; a notable proof that part of the phlogiston of the mercury hath united therewith. And yet, if the mercury be separated by means of a fixed alkali, it does not appear to have suffered any alteration. Turbith mineral is not so volatile as pure mercury.

The nitrous acid dissolves mercury with ease. The solution is limpid and transparent, and as it grows cold shoots into crystals, which are a nitrous mercurial salt.

If this solution be evaporated to driness, the mercury remains impregnated with a little of the acid, under the form of a red powder, which hath obtained the names of red precipitate, and arcanum corallinum. This precipitate, as well as turbith, is less volatile than pure mercury.

If this solution of mercury be mixed with a solution of copper made likewise in the nitrous acid, and the mixture evaporated to driness, there will remain a green powder called green precipitate. These precipitates are caustic and corrosive; and are used as such in surgery.

Though mercury be dissolved more easily and completely by the nitrous acid than by the vitriolic yet it has a greater affinity with the latter than with the former; for if a vitriolic acid be poured into a solution of mercury in spirit of nitre, the mercury will quit the latter acid in which it was dissolved, and join the other which was added. The same thing happens when the marine acid is employed instead of the vitriolic.

Mercury combined with spirit of salt forms a singular body; a metalline salt which shoots into long crystals pointed like daggers. This salt is volatile, and sublimes easily without decomposition. It is moreover the most violent of all the corrosives hitherto discovered by chemistry. It is called corrosive sublimate, because it must absolutely be sublimed to make the combination perfect. There several ways of doing this; but the operation will never fail, if the mercury be rarefied into vapours and meet with the marine acid in a similar state.

Corrosive sublimate is dissolved by water, but in very small quantities only. It is decompounded by fixed alkalis, which precipitate the mercury in a reddish yellow powder, called, on account of its colour, yellow precipitate.

If corrosive sublimate be mixed with tin, and the compound distilled, a liquor comes over, which continually emits abundance of dense fumes, and from the name of its inventor is called the smoking liquor of Libavius. This liquor is no other than the tin combined with the marine acid of the corrosive sublimate, which therefore it hath actually decompounded; whence it follows, that this acid hath a greater affinity with tin than with mercury.

The marine acid in corrosive sublimate is not quite saturated with mercury; but is capable of taking up a much greater quantity thereof. For if corrosive sublimate be mixed with fresh mercury, and sublimed a second time, another compound will be produced containing much more mercury, and less acrimonious; for which reason it is named sweet sublimate of mercury, mercurius dulcis, aquila alba. This compound may be taken internally, and is purgative or emetic according to the dose administered. It may be still more gentle by repeated sublimations, and then it takes the title of panacea mercurialis. No way hath hitherto been found to dissolve mercury in aqua regis without great difficultry, and even then it is but inperfectly dissolved.

Mercury unites easily and intimately with sulphur. If these two substances be only rubbed together in a gentle heat, or even without any heat, they will contract an union, though but an incomplete one. This combination takes the form of a black powder, which has procured it the name of AEthiops mineral.

If a more intimate and perfect union be desired, this compound must be exposed to a stronger heat; and then a red ponderous substance will be sublimed, appearing like a mass of shining needles; this is the combination desired, and is called cinabar. In this form chiefly is mercury found in the bowels of the earth. Cinabar finely levigated acquires a much brighter red colour, and is known to painters by the name vermilion.

Cinabar rises wholly by sublimation, without suffering any decomposition; because the two substances of which it consists, viz. mercury and sulphur, are both volatile.

Though mercury unites and combines very well with sulphur, as hath been said, yet it hath less affinity with that mineral than any other metal, gold only excepted; whence it follows, that any of the other metals will decompound cinabar, by uniting with its sulphur, and for settong the mercury at liberty to appear in its usual form. Mercury thus separated from sulphur, is esteemed the purest, and bears the name of mercury revivified from cinabar.

Iron is generally used in this operation preferably to the other metals, because among them all it has the greatest affinity with sulphur, and is the only one that has none with mercury.

Cinabar may also be decompounded by means of fixed alkalis; the affinity of these salts with sulphur being generally greater than that of any metalline substance whatever.

OF THE SEMI-METALS

OF REGULUS OF ANTIMONY. Regulus of antimony is a metallic substance of a pretty bright white colour. It has the splendor, opacity, and gravity of a metal; but it is quite unmalleable, and crumbles to dust, instead of yielding or stretching under the hammer; on which account it is classed with the semi-metals.

It begins to flow as soon as it is moderately red; but, like the other semi-metals, it cannot stand a violent degree of fire; being thereby dissipated into smoke and white vapours, which adhere to such cold bodies as they meet with, and so are collected into a kind of farina called flowers of antimony.

If regulus of antimony, instead of being exposed to a strong fire, be only heated so moderately that it shall not even melt, it will calcine, lose its phlogiston, and take the form of a greyish powder destitute of all splendor; this powder is called calx of antimony.

This calx is not volatile like the regulus, but will endure a very violent fire; and being exposed thereto will flow, and turn to a glass of the yellowish colour of a hyacinth.

It is to be observed, that the more the regulus is deprived of its phlogiston by continued calcination the more refractory is the calx obtained from kt. The glass thereof has also so much the less colour, and comes the nearer to common glass.

The calx and the glass of antimony will recover their metalline form, like every other calx and glass of a metal, if reduced by restoring to them their lost phlogiston. Yet if the calcination be carried too far, their reduction will become much more difficult, and a much smaller quantity of regulus will be resuscitated.

Regulus of antimony is capable of dissolving the metals; but its affinities with them are various, and differ according to the following order. It affects iron the most powerfully, next copper, then tin, lead, and silver. It promotes the fusion of metals, but makes them all brittle and unmalleable.

It will not amalgamate with mercury; and though, by certain processes, particularly the addition of water and continued trituration. a sort of union between these two substances may be produced, yet it is but apparent and momentary; for being left to themselves, and undisturbed, they quietly disunite and separate.

The vitriolic acid, assisted by heat, and even by distillation, dissolves regulus of antimony. The nitrous acid likewise attacks it; but the solution can by no art be made clear and limpid; so that the regulus is only calcined, in a manner, by this acid.

The marine acid dissolves it well enough; but then it must be exceedingly concentrated, and applied in a peculiar manner, and especially by distillation. One of the best methods of procuring a perfect union between the acid of sea-salt and regulus of antimony, is to pulverize the latter, mix it with corrosive sublimate, and distil the whole. There rises in the operation a white matter, thick, and scarce fluid, which is no other than the regulus of antimony united and combined with the acid of sea-salt. This compound is extremely corrosive, and is called butter of antimony.

It is plain, that the corrosive sublimate is here decompounded; that the mercury is revivified; and that the acid which was combined therewith hath quitted it to join the regulus of antimony with which its affinity is greater. This butter of antimony, by repeated distillations, acquires a considerable degree of fluidity and limpidness.

If the acid of nitre be mixed with butter of antimony, and the whole distilled, there rises an acid liquor, or a sort of aqua regis, which still retains some of the dissolved regulus, and is called bezoardic spirit of nitre. After the distillation there remains a white matter, from which fresh spirit of nitre is again abstracted, and which being then washed with water, is called bezoar mineral. This bezoar mineral is neither so volatile, nor so caustic, as butter of antimony; because the nitrous acid hath not the property of volatilizing metallic substances, as the marine acid does, and because it remains much more intimately combined with the reguline part.

Of butter of antimony be mixed with water, the liquor immediately becomes turbid and milky, and a precipitate falls, which is nothing but the metallic matter partly separated from its acid, which is too much weakened by the addition of water to keep it dissolved. Yet this precipitate still retains a good deal of acid; for which reason continues to be a violent emetic, and in some degree corrosive. It hath therefore been very improperly called mercurius vitae.

The proper solvent of regulus of antimony is aqua regis; by means whereof a clear and limpid solution of this semi-metal may be obtained.

Regulus of antimony mixed with nitre, and projected into a red-hot crucible, sets the nitre in a flame, and makes it detonate. As it produces this effect by means of its phlogiston, it must needs, as the same time, be calcined, and lose its metallic properties, which accordingly happens; and when the nitre is in a triple proportion to the regulus, the latter is so perfectly calcined as to leave only a white powder, which is fused with great difficulty, and then turns to a faintly coloured glass, not very different from common glass, and which is not reducible to a regulus by the addition of inflammable matter; at least it yields but a very small quantity thereof. If less nitre be used, the calx is not so white; the glass it produces is more like a metalline glass, and is more easily reduced. The calx of the regulus thus prepared by nitre is called, on account of the medicinal virtue ascribed to it, diaphoretic antimony, or diaphoretic mineral.

Nitre always becomes an alkali by deflagration, and in the present case retains part of the calx, which it even renders soluble in water. This calx may be separated from the alkali, if an acid be employed to precipitate it; and then it is called materia perlata. This pearly matter is a calx of antimony, so completely deprived of its phlogiston as to be altogether incapable of reduction to a regulus.

Regulus of antimony readily joins and unites with sulphur, forming therewith a compound which has a very faint metallic splendor. This compound appears like a mass of long needles adhering together laterally; and under this form it is usually found in the ore, or at least when only separated by fusion from the stones and earthy matters with which the ore is mixed. It is called crude antimony.

Antimony flows with a moderate heat, and becomes even more fluid than other metallic substances. The action of fire dissipates or consumes the sulphur it contains, and its phlogiston also, so as to convert it into a calx and a glass, as it does the regulus.

Aqua regis, which we observed to be the proper solvent of the regulus, being poured on antimony, attacks and dissolves the reguline part, but touches not the sulphur; in consequence whereof it decomposes the antimony, and separates its sulphur from its regulus.

There are several other ways of effecting this decomposition, and obtaining the reguline part of antimony by itself: They consist either in destroying the sulphureous part of the antimony by combustion, or in melting the antimony with some substance which has a greater affinity than its reguline part with sulphur. Most metals are very fit for this latter purpose: For though the regulus has a considerable affinity with sulphur, yet all the metals, except gold and mercury, have a greater.

If therefore iron, copper, lead, silver, or tin, be melted with antimony, the metal employed will unite with the sulphur, and separate it from the regulus.

It must be observed, that, as these metals have some affinity with the regulus of antimony, the regulus will be joined in the operation by some of the metal employed as a precipitant, (so those substances are called which serve as the means of separating two bodies from each other); and therefore the regulus procured in this manner will not be absolutely pure: On this account care is taken to distinguish each by adding the name of the metal employed in its precipitation; and thence come these titles, martial regulus of antimony, or only martial regulus, regulus veneris; and so of the rest.

Antimony is employed with advantage to separate gold from all other metals with which it may be alloyed. It has been shewn, that all the metals have a greater affinity, than the reguline part of antimony, with sulphur, gold only excepted; which is incapable of contracting any union therewith: And therefore, if a mass compounde of gold and several other metals be melted with antimony, every thing in that mass which is not gold will unite with the sulphur of the antimony. This union occasions two separations, to wit, that of the sulphur of the antimony from its reguline part, and that of the gold from the metals with which it was adulterated: and from the whole two new compounds arise; namely, a combination of the metals with the sulphur, which bekng lightest rise to the surface in fusion; and a metalline mass formed of the gold and the reguline part of the antimony united together, which being much the heaviest sinks to the bottom. There is no difficulty in parting the gold from the regulus of antimony with which it is alloyed: For the metalline mass need only be exposed to a degree of fire capable of dissipating into vapours all the semi-metal it contains; which being very volatile, the operation is much easier, and more expeditiously finished, than if the metals with which the gold was debased were to be vitrified on the cupel; without taking into the account that if silver were one of them, recourse must needs be had to the process of quartation after that of the cupel.

If equal parts of nitre and antimony be mixed together, and the mixture exposed to the action of fire, a violent detonation ensues; the nitre deflagrating consumes the sulphur of the antimony, and even a part of its phlogiston. After the detonation there remains a greyish matter which contains fixed nitre, vitriolated tartar, and the reguline part of the antimony in some measure deprived of its phlogiston, and half vitrified by the action of the fire, which is considerably increased by the deflagration. This matter is called liver of antimony.

If instead of equal parts of nitre and antimony, two parts of the former be used to one of the latter, then the reguline part loses much more of its phlogiston, and remains in the form of a yellowish powder.

Again, if three parts of nitre be taken to one of antimony, the regulus is thereby entirely robbed of its phlogiston, and converted to a white calx which bears the name of diaphoretic antimony, or diaphoretic mineral. The pearly matter may be precipitated by pouring an acid on the saline substances which remain after the detonation, in the same manner as we shewed above was to be done with regard to the regulus.

In the last two operations, where the nitre is in a double or triple proportion to the antimony, the reguline part is found after the detonation to be converted into a calx, and not into a half vitrified matter, which we have seen is the effect when equal parts only of nitre and antimony are used. The reason of this difference is, that in these two cases the reguline part, being wholly, or almost wholly, deprived of its phlogiston, becomes, as was observed, more difficult to fuse, and consequently cannot begin to vitrify in the same degree of heat as that which hath not lost so much of its phlogiston. If, instead of performing the operation with equal parts of nitre and antimony alone, a portion of some substance which abounds with phlogiston be added, in that case the sulphur only of the antimony will be consumed, and the regulus will remain united with its phlogiston, and separated from its sulphur.

The regulus prepared in this manner is absolutely pure, because no metalline substance being employed, none can mix with it and adulterate it. It is called regulus of antimony per se, or only regulus of antimony.

It is true indeed, that in this operation, much of the reguline part unavoidably loses its phlogiston and is calcined, and consequently a much smaller quantity of regulus is obtained than when metalline precipitants are employed: But this loss is easily repaired, if it be thought proper, by restoring to the calcined part its lost phlogiston.

Antimony melted with two parts of fixed alkali yields no regulus, but is entirely dissolved by the salt, and forms with it a mass of a reddish yellow colour.

The reason why no precipitate is produced on this occasion is, that the alkali uniting with the sulphur of the antimony forms therewith the combination called liver of sulphur, which by its nature is qualified to keep the reguline part dissolved. This mass, formed by the union of the antimony with the alkali, is soluble in water. If any acid whatever be dropt into this solution, there falls a precipitate of a reddish yellow colour; because the acid unites with the alkali, and forces it to quit the matters with which it is combined. This precipitate is called golden sulphur of antimony.

As in the operation for preparing regulus of antimony per se, some of the nitre is by the inflammable matters added thereto, turned to an alkali; this alkali seizes on part of the antimony, and therewith forms a compound like that just described. Hence it comes, that if the scoria formed in this process be dissolved in water, and an acid dropped into the solution, a true golden sulphur of antimony is thereby separated.

This union of antimony with an alkali may also be brought about by the humid way; that is, by making use of an alkali resolved into a liquor, and boiling the minera in it. The alkaline liquor, in proportion as it acts upon the antimony, gradually becomes reddish and turbid. If left to settle and cool, when well saturated therewith, it gradually deposites the antimony it had taken up, which precipitates in the form of a red powder: And this precipitate is the celebrated remedy known by the name of kermes mineral. It is plain, that the kermes is nearly the same thing with the golden sulphur: Yet it differs from it in some respects; and especially in this, that being taken inwardly it operates much more gently than the golden sulphur, which is a violent emetic. Nitre, fixed by charcoal, and resolved into a liquor, is the only alkali employed in preparing the kermes.

It was shewn above, that regulus of antimony, mixed and distilled with corrosive sublimate, decompounds it, disengages the mercury, and joining itself to the marine acid forms therewith a new combination, called butter of antimony. If the same operation be performed with crude antimony instead of its regulus, the same effects are produced; but then the antimony itself is also decomposed; that is, the reguline part is separated from the sulphur, which being set free unites with the mercury, now also at liberty, and these two together form a true cinabar, called cinabar of antimony.

OF BISMUTH. Bismuth, known also by the name tin-glass, is a semi-metal, having almost the same appearance as regulus of antimony; yet it has a more dusky cast, inclining somewhat to red, and even presents some changeable streaks, especially after lying long in the air.

When exposed to the fire it melts long before it is red, and consequently with less heat than regulus of antimony, which does not flow, as was shewn above, till it begin to be red hot. It becomes volatile, like all the other semi-metals, when acted on by a violent fire: Being kept in fusion by a proper degree of heat it loses its phlogiston with its metallic form, and turns to powder or a calx; and that again is converted into glass by the continued action of fire. The calx and glass of bismuth may be reduced, like any other metallic calx, by restoring their phlogiston.

Bismuth mixes with all the metals in fusion, and even facilitates the fusion of such as do not otherwise flow readily. It whitens them by its union, and destroys their malleability.

It amalgamates with mercury, if they be rubbed together with the addition of water: Yet after some time these two metalline substances desert each other, and the bismuth appears again in the form of a powder. Hence it is plain that the union it contracts with mercury is not perfect; and yet it has the singular property of attenuating lead, and altering it in such a manner that it afterwards amalgamates with mercury much more perfectly, so as even to pass with it through shamoy leather without any separation. The bismuth employed in making this amalgama afterwards separates from it spontaneously, as usual; but the lead still continues united with the mercury, and always retains the property thus acquired.

The vitriolic acid does not dissolve bismuth: Its proper solvent is the nitrous acid, which dissolves it with violence, and abundance of fumes.

Bismuth dissolved in the nitrous acid is precipitated not only by alkalis, but even by the bare addition of water. This precipitate is extremely white, and known by the name of magistery of bismuth.

The acid of sea-salt and aqua regis likewise act upon bismuth, but with less violence.

This semi-metal does not sensibly deflagrate with nitre; yet it is quickly deprived of its phlogiston, and turned into a vitrifiable calx, when exposed with it to the action of fire.

It readily unites with sulphur in fusion, and forms therewith a compound which appears to consist of needles adhering laterally to each other.

It may be separated from the sulphur with which it is combined, by only exposing it to the fire, without any additament; for the sulphur is either consumed or sublimed, and leaves the bismuth behind.

OF ZINC. Zinc to appearance differ but little from bismuth, and has even been confounded with it by several authors. Nevertheless, besides that it has somethinf of a bluish cast, and is harder than bismuth, it differs from it essentially in its properties, as will presently be shewn. These two metallic substances scarce resemble each other in any thing, but the qualities common to all semi-metals.

Zinc melts the moment it grows red in the fire, and then also begins to turn to a calx, which, like any other metallic calx, may be reduced by means of the phlogiston: But if the fire be considerably increased, it sublimes, flames, and burns like an oily matter; which is a proof of the great quantity of phlogiston in its composition. At the same time abundance of flowers rise from it in the form of white flakes, flying about in the air like very light bodies; and into this form may the whole substance of zinc be converted. Several names have been given to these flowers, such as pompholix, philosophic wool. They are supposed to be no other than the zinc itself deprived of its phlogiston; yet no body has hitherto been able to resuscitate them in the form of zinc. by restoring their phlogiston according to the methods used in the reduction of metals. Though they rise in the air with very great ease while the zinc is calcining, yet when once formed they are very fixed; for they withstand the utmost violence of fire, and are capable of being vitrified, especially if joined with a fixed alkali. They are soluble in acids.

Zinc unites with all metalline substances, except bismuth. It has this singular property, that being mixed with copper, even in a considerable quantity, such as a fourth part, it does not greatly lessen the ductility thereof, and at the same time communicates to it a very beautiful colour not unlike that of gold: On which account the composition is frequently made, and produces what is called brass. This metal melts much more easily than copper alone, because of the zinc with which it is alloyed. If it be exposed to a great degree of heat, the zinc which it contains takes fire and sublimes in white flowers, just as when it is pure.

It is to be observed, that brass is ductile only while it is cold, and not then unless the zinc used in making it was very pure; otherwise the composition will prove but tombac, or prince's metal, having very little malleability.

Zinc is very volatile, and carries off with it any metallic substance with which it is fused, making a kind of sublimate thereof. In the furnaces where they smelt ores containing zinc, the matter thus sublimed is called cadmia furnacum, to distinguish it from the native cadmia called also calamine, or lapis calaminaris; which, properly speaking, is an ore of zinc, containing a great deal of that semi-metal, together with some iron, and a stony substance. The name of cadmia furnacum is not appropriated solely to the metallic sublimates procured by means of zinc, but is given in general to all the metallic sublimates found in smelting houses.

If a violent and sudden heat be applied to zinc, it sublimes in its metalline form; there not being time for it to burn and be resolved into flowers.

This semi-metal is soluble in all the acids, but especially in spirit of nitre, which attacks and dissolves it with very great violence.

Zinc has a greater affinity than iron or copper with the vitriolic acid; and therefore it decompounds the green and blue vitriols, precipitating those two metals by uniting with the vitriolic acid, with which it forms a metallic salt or vitriol called white vitriol, or vitriol of zinc.

Nitre mixed with zinc, and projected into a red hot crucible, detonates with violence; and during the detonation there arises a great quantity of white flowers, like those which appear when it is calcined by itself.

Sulphur has no power over zinc. Even liver of sulphur, which dissolves all other metallic substances, contracts no union with this semi-metal.

OF REGULUS OF ARSENIC. Regulus of arsenic is the most volatile of all the semi-metals. A very moderate heat makes it wholly evaporate, and fly off in fumes; on which account it cannot be brought to fusion, nor can any considerable masses thereof be obtained. It has a metallic colour, somewhat resembling lead; but soon loses its splendor when exposed to the air.

It unites readily enough with metallic substances having the same affinities with them as regulus of antimony hath. It makes them brittle, and unmalleable. It hath also the property of rendering them volatile, and greatly facilitates their scorification.

It very easily parts with its phologiston and metallic form. When exposed to the fire it rises in a kind of shining crystalline calx, which on that account looks more like a saline matter than a metallic calx. To this calx or these flowers are given the names of white arsenic, crystalline arsenic, and most commonly plain arsenic.

Arsenic differs from every other metalline calx, first, in being volatile; whereas the calxes of all other metallic substances, not excepting those of the most volatile semi-metals, such as regulus of antimony and zinc, are exceedingly fixed; and secondly, in having a saline character, which is not found in any other metalline calx.

The saline character of arsenic appears, first, from its being soluble in water; secondly, from its corrosive quality, which makes it one of the most violent poisons; a quality from which the other metallic substances are free, when they are not combined with some saline matter. Regulus of antimony must however be excepted; but then the best chemists agree, that this semi-metal is either nearly of the same nature with arsenic, or contains a portion thereof in its composition; besides, its noxious qualities never discover themselves so plainly as when it is combined with some acid. Lastly, arsenic acts just like the vitriolic acid upon nitre; that is, it decompounds that neutral salt, by expelling its acid from its alkaline basis, of which it takes posession, and therewith forms a new saline compound.

This combination is a species of salt that is perfectly neutral. When the operation is performed in a close vessel, the salt shoots into crystals in the form of right-angled quadrangular prisms, terminated at each extremity by pyramids that are also quadrangular and right-angled; some of which, however, instead of ending in a point, are obtuse as if truncated. The consequence is different when the operation is performed in an open vessel; for then nothing is obtained but an alkaline salt impregnated with arsenic, which cannot be crystallized.

The cause of this different effect is this: When the arsenic is once engaged in the alkaline basis of the nitre, it can never be separated from it by the utmost force of fire, so long as it is kept in a close vessel; whereas, if you expose it to the fire without that precaution, it readily separates from it.

This salt possesses many singular properties, the chief of which are these: First, it cannot be decompounded by the intervention of any acid, even the strongest acid of vitriol; and this, joined to its property of expelling the nitrous acid from its basis, shews that it has a very great affinity with fixed alkalis.

Secondly, this very salt, on which pure acids have no effect, is decompounded with the greatest ease by acids united with metallic substances. The reason of this phenomenon is curious, and furnishes us with an instance of what we advanced concerning double affinities.

If to a solution of any metallic substance whatever, made by any acid whatever, (except that of mercury by the marine acid, and that of gold by aqua regis,) a certain quantity of this salt dissolved in water be added, the metallic substance is instantaneously separated from the acid in which it was dissolved, and falls to the bottom of the liquor.

All metallic precipitates obtained in this manner are found to be a combination of the metal with arsenic; whence it necessarily follows that the neutral salt is by this means decompounded, its arsenical part uniting with the metallic substance, and its alkaline basis with the acid in which that substance was dissolved.

The affinities of these several bodies must be considered as operating on this occasion in the following manner: The acids which tend to decompound the neutral salt of arsenic, by virtue of their affinity with its alkaline basis, are not able to accomplish it, because this affinity is powerfully counteracted by that which the arsenic has with the same alkaline basis, and which is equal or even superior to theirs. But if these acids happen to be united with a substance which naturally has a very great affinity with the arsenical part of the neutral salt, then, the two parts of which this salt consists, being drawn different ways by two several affinities, tending to separate them from each other, the salt will undergo a decomposition, which could not have been effected without the help of this second affinity. Now, as metallic substances have a great affinity with arsenic, it is not surprising that the neutral salt of arsenic, which cannot be decompounded by a pure acid, should nevertheless yield to an acid combined with a metal. The decomposition of this salt, therefore, and the preciptation which of course it produces in metallic solutions, are brought about by the means of a double affinity; namely, that of the acid with the alkaline basis of the neutral salt, and that of the metal with the arsenical part of that salt.

Arsenic has not the same effect on sea-salt as on nitre, and cannot expel its acid; a very singular phenomenon, for which it is hard to assign a reason; for the nitrous acid is known to have a greater affinity than the marine acid with alkali, and even with the basis of sea-salt itself.

Yet arsenic may be combined with the basis of sea-salt, and a neutral salt thereby obtained, like that which results from the decomposition of nitre by arsenic; but for that purpose a quadrangular nitre must be first prepared, and arsenic applied thereto as to common nitre.

The salt produced by uniting arsenic with the basis of sea-salt very much resembles the neutral salt of arsenic above treated of, as well in the figure of its crystals as in its several properties.

Arsenic presents another singular phenomenon, both with alkali of nitre and with that of sea-salt; which is, that if it be combined with these salts in a fluid state, it forms with them a saline compound, quite different from the neutral salts of arsenic which results from the decomposition of nitrous salts.

This saline compound, called liver of arsenic, takes up a much greater quantity of arsenic than is necessary for the perfect saturation of the alkali. It has the appearance of a glue, which is so much the thicker the more arsenic it contains. Its smell is disagreeable; it attracts the moisture of the air, and does not crystallize; it is easily decompounded by any acid whatever, which precipitates the arsenic and unites with the alkali. Lastly, the effects it produces on metallic solutions are different from those of our neutral arsenical salts.

Arsenic is easily reduced to a regulus. It need only be mixed with any matter containing the phlogiston, and by the help of a moderate heat a true regulus will sublime. This regulus is very volatile, and calcines with the greatest ease; which is the reason why it cannot be obtained but in small quantities; and also why, in order to obtain masses of it, some have thought of adding thereto some metal with which it has a great affinity, such as copper or iron; because, by joining with the metal, it is partly fixed and restrained from flying off. But it is plain the regulus obtained by this means is not pure, as it must partake considerably of the metal employed.

Arsenic readily unites with sulphur, and rises with it in a yellow compound called orpiment.

Sulphur cannot be separated from arsenic but by the intervention of two bodies only; to wit, a fixed alkali and mercury.

The property which mercury possesses of separating sulphur from arsenic is founded on this, that these two metallic substances are incapable of contracting any union; whereas, though most of the other metals and semi-metals have a greater affinity with sulphur than mercury hath, nevertheless they are all unable to decompound orpiment; because some of them have as great an affinity with arsenic as with sulphur; others have no affinity with either; and lastly, sulphur hath as great an affinity with arsenic as with any of them.

It must be observed, that, if fixed alkalis be employed to purify arsenic in this manner, no more must be used than is necessary to absorb the sulphur or the phlogiston, of which also it is their nature to deprive arsenic; for otherwise as it has been shewn that arsenic readily unites with alkalis, they would absorb a considerable quantity thereof.

OF OIL IN GENERAL. Oil is an unctuous body, which burns and consumes with flame and smoke, and is not soluble in water. It consists of the phlogiston united with water by means of an acid. There is, moreover, in its composition a certain proportion of earth, more or less according to each several sort of oil.

The inflammability of oil evidently proves that it contains the phlogiston. That an acid is one of its constituent principles may experiments demonstrate, of which these are the chief; If certain oils be long triturated with an alkaline salt, and the alkali afterwards dissolved in water, crystals of a true neutral salt will be produced; some metals, and particularly copper, are corroded and rusted by oils, just as they are by acids; again, acid crystals are found in some oils that have been long kept. This acid in oil serves undoubtedly to unite its phlogiston with its water; because these two substances having no affinity with each other cannot be united without the intervention of such a medium as an acid which has an affinity with both. As to the existence of salts in oils, it appears plainly when they are decomposed by repeated distillations, especially after mixing them with absorbent earths. Lastly, when an oil is destroyed by buring, a certain quantity of earth is constantly left behind.

Oils exposed to the fire in close vessels pass over almost wholly from the containing vessel into any other applied to receive them. There remains, however, a small quantity of black matter, which is extremely fixed, and continues unalterable as long as it has no communication with the external air, be the force of fire ever so violent. This matter is no other than part of the phlogiston of the oil united with its most fixed and grossest earth; and this is what we called charcoal, or plainly a coal.

OF CHARCOAL. When oil happens to be united to much earth, as it is in vegetable and animal bodies, it leaves a considerable quantity of coal or charred matter.

This coal, exposed to the fire in the open air, burns and wastes, but without blazing like other combustible matters; there appears only a small bluish flame, but not the least smoke. Most commonly it only glows and sparkles, and so gradually falls into ashes, which are nothing but the earth of the body combined with an alkaline salt in burining. This alkaline salt may be separated from the earth, by lixiviating the ashes with water, which dissolves all the salt, and leaves the earth quite pure.

Charcoal is unalterable and indestructible by any other body but fire; whence it follows, that when it is not actually kindled and ignited, the most powerful agents, such as the acids, though ever so strong and concentrated, have not the least effect on it.

The case is otherwise when it is lighted, that is, when its phlogiston begins to separate from its earth; for then the pure acid of vitriol being joined therewith contracts an instantaneous union with its phlogiston, and evaporates in a volatile sulphurous spirit. If the vitriolic acid, instead of being applied quite pure, be first clogged with some basis, especially an alkaline one, it quits that basis, enters into a more intimate union with the phlogiston of the burning coal, and so forms an actual sulphur, with which the alkali now unites and forms a hepar.

The pure acid sea-salt hath not been observed to act in the least upon charcoal, especially when it is not on fire. But when this acid is incorporated with an alkaline or metallic basis, and combined according to a peculiar process with burning charcoal, it in like manner quits its basis, unites with the phlogiston, and therewith forms a phosphorus.

Nor has the pure nitrous acid any effect on a charred coal, even when ignited; and so far is it from being able to kindle a cold one, that when poured on a live one, it extinguishes it like water. But when this acid is united with a basis, it quits it rapidly as soon as it touches a burning coal, and rushes violently into an union with the phlogiston thereof. From this union there probably arises, as we said before, a kind of sulphur or phosphorus, which is so inflammable as to be destroyed by the fire the very moment it is generated.

The acid of nitre and vitriol act upon oils; but very differently, according to the quantity of phlegm they contain. If they be awakened with much water, they have no effect at all upon oils; if they contain little watter, or dephlegmated to a certain degree, they dissolve them with heat, and with them form compounds of a thick consistence. Acids thus combined in a considerable proportion with oils render them soluble in water.

OF SOAP. Alkalis also have the same property. When an oil is combined with an acid, or an alkali, in such a manner that the compound resulting from their union is soluble in water; such a compound may in general be called soap. Soap itself hath the property of rendering fat bodies in some measure soluble in water; on which account it is very useful for scouring or cleansing any thing greasy.

Oily and saline substances, combined together, observe the same general rules as all other combinations; that is, they mutually communicate the properties belonging to each; thus oils, which naturally are not soluble in water, acquire by their union with saline matters the property cf dissolving therein; and salts lose by their conjunction with oils part of their natural tendency to incorporate with water; so that while they serve to constitute soap, they do not, as before, attract moisture of the air, and in like manner, as they are not inflammable, they considerably lessen the inflammability of the oils combined with them.

Acid soaps are decompounded by alkalis, as alkaline soaps are by acids, according to the general rules of affinities.

The acids of nitre and vitriol, when highly concentrated, dissolve oils with such violence as to heat them, make them black, burn them, and even set them on fire. How sea-salt affects oils is not yet sufficiently ascertained.

All oils have the property of dissolving sulphur; which is not at all surprising, seeing each of its component principles hath an affinity with oil.

It is also a property common to all oils to become more fluid, subtile, light, and limpid, the oftener they are distilled. On the contrary, by being incorporated with saline substances they acquire a greater consistence, and sometimes form compounds that are almost solid.

OF THE SEVERAL SORTS OF OILS. Oils are distinguished by the substances from which they are drawn; and as oils are extracted from minerals, from vegetables, and from animals, there are of course mineral, vegetable, and animal oils.

OF MINERAL OILS. In the bowels of the earth we find but one sort of oil, called petroleum: Its smell is strong, and not disagreeable, and its colour sometimes more, sometimes less yellow. There are certain mineral substances which yield by distillation a great deal of oil very like petroleum. This sort of substance is called bitumen, and is, indeed nothing but an oil rendered consistent and solid by being combined with an acid; as appears from hence that, by uniting petroleum with the acid of vitriol we can produce an artificial bitumen very like the native.

OF VEGETABLE OILS. Vegetable substances yield a very great quantity and variety of oils; for there is not a plant, or part of a plant, that does not contain one or more sorts thereof, generally peculiar to itself, and different from all others.

By expression only, that is, by bruising and squeezing vegetable substances, particularly certain fruits and seeds, a sort of oil is obtained which has scarce any smell or taste. Oils of this sort are very mild and unctuous; and, because in this respect they resemble animal fat more than the rest do; they are called fat-oils.

These oils, being exposed to the air for some time, sooner or later grow thick, aquire an acrid taste, and a strong disagreeable smell. Some of them congeal with the smallest degree of cold. This sort of oil is well adapted to dissolve those preparations of lead called litharge and minium, with which they form a thick tenatious substance, that is used for the basis of almost all plaisters. They also dissolve lead in its metalline form, but not so easily as the sorts of calx above mentioned; probably because its body is not so much opened, nor its parts so divided.

By expression alone we also procure from certain vegetable substances another sort of oil, which is thin, limpid, volatile, of a pungent taste, and retains the smell of the vegetable that yielded it; on which account it is called an essential oil. Of this there are several sorts, differing from one another, like the fat oils, according to the subjects from which they are obtained.

We must observe, that it is very dificult, or rather in most cases impossible, to force from the greatest part of vegetables, by expression only, all the essential oil they contain. For this purpose, therefore, recourse must be had to fire; a gentle heat, not exceeding that of boiling water, will extract all the essential oils of a vegetable; and this is the most usual and most convenient way of procuring them.

The fat oils cannot be obtained by the same method; these being much less volatile than the essential oils, require a much greater degree of heat to raise them; which, nevertheless, they cannot bear without being much spoiled and entirely changed in their nature, as shall presently be shewn. All oils, therefore, which rise with the heat of boiling water, and such alone, should be called essential oils.

Essential oils, in a longer or shrter time, according to the nature of each, lose the fragrant smell they had when newly distilled, and acquire another which is strong, rancid, and much less agreeable: They also lose their tenuity, becoming thick and vicid; and in this state they greatly resemble those substances abounding in oil which flow from certain trees, and which are called balsams or resins, according as they are less or more consistent.

Balsams and resins are not soluble in water. But there are other oily compounds which likewise run from trees; and, though not unlike resins, are however soluble in water. These are called gums; and their property of dissolving in water arises from their containing more water and more salt than resins have; or at least their saline parts are less clogged and more disengaged.

Balsams and resins distilled with the heat of boiling water yield great quantities of a limpid, subtile, odoriferous, and, in one word essential oil. In the still there remains a substance thicker and more consistent than the balsam or resin was before distillation. The same thing happens to essential oils which by length of time have acquired consistence, and are grown resinous. If they be redistilled, they recover their former tenuity, leaving behind them a remainder thicker and more resinous than they themselves were. This second distillation is called the rectification of an oil.

It must be observed, that an essential oil, combined with an acid strong enough to dissolve it, immediately becomes as thick and resinous, in consequence of this union, as if it had been long exposed to the air; which proves the consistence an oil acquires by long keeping to be owing to his, that its lightest and less acid parts being evaporated, the proportion of its acid to the remainder is so increased that it produces therein the same change as an additional acid mixed with the oil would have wrought before the evaporation.

This also shews us, that balsams and resins are only essentials combined with a great proportion of acid, and thereby thickened.

If vegetable substances, from which no more essential oil can be drawn by the heat of boiling water, be exposed to a stronger heat, they yield an additional quantity of oil; but it is thicker and heavier than the essential oil. These oils are black, and have a very disagreeable burnt smell which hath made them be called fetid or empyreumatic oils. They are moreover very acrid.

It must be observed, that if a vegetable substance be exposed to a degree of heat greater than that of boiling water, before the fat or the essential oil is extracted from it, an empyreumatic oil only will then be obtained; because both the fat and essential oils, when exposed to the force of fire, are thereby burnt, rendered acrid, acquire a smell of the fire, and, in a word, become truly empyreumatic. There is ground to think, that an empyreumatic oil is nothing else but an essential or fat oil burnt and spoiled by the fire, and that no other oil besides these two exists naturally in vegetables.

Empyreumatic oils, distilled and rectified several times by a gentle heat, acquire by every distillation a greater degree of tenuity, lightness, and limpidity. By this means also they lose something of their disagreeable odour; so that they gradually come nearer and nearer to the nature of essential oils, and if the rectifications be often enough repeated, ten or twelve times for instance, they become perfectly like those oils; except that their smell will never be so agreeable, nor like that of the substances from which they were obtained.

Fat oils may also be brought by the same means to resemble essential oils; but neither essential nor empyreumatic oils are capable of acquiring the properties of fat oils.

OF ANIMAL OILS. Distillation procures us considerable quantities of oil from all the parts of animal bodies, and especially from their fat. This oil at first is not very fluid, and is extremely fetid; but by many rectifications it gradually acquires a great degree of clearness and tenuity, and at the same time loses much of its disagreeable odour.

OF FERMENTATION IN GENERAL. By fermentation is meant an intestine motion, which, arising spontaneously among the insensible parts of a body, produces a new disposition and a different combination of those parts.

To excite a fermentation in a mixt body, it is necessary, first, that there be in the composition of that mix a certain proportion of watery, saline, oily, and earthy parts; but this proportion is not yet sufficiently ascertained. Secondly, it is requisite that the body to be fermented be placed in a certain degree of temperate heat; for much cold obstructs fermentation, and too much heat decomposes bodies. Lastly, the concurrence of the air is also necessary to fermentation.

All vegetable and animal substances are susceptible of fermentation, because all of them contain in a due proportion the principles above specified. However, many of them want the proper quantity of water, and cannot ferment while they remain in such a state of driness. But it is easy to supply that defect.

With respect to minerals properly so called, they are not subject to any fermentation, at least that our senses can perceive.

There are three sorts of fermentation, distinguished from one another by their several productions. The first produces wines and spiritous liquors; for which reason it is called the vinous or spirituous fermentation: The result of the second is an acid liquor; and therefore it is called the acetous fermentation; and the third generates an alkaline salt; which, however, differs from the alkaline salts hitherto treated of, in this respect chiefly, that, instead of being fixed, it is extremely volatile: This last sort takes the name of the putrid or putrifactive fermentation. We shall now consider these three sorts of fermentation and their effects a little more particularly.

These three sorts of fermentation may take place successively in the same subject; which proves them to be only three different degrees of fermentation, all proceeding from one and the same cause. These degrees of fermentation always follow the order in which we have here placed them.

OF THE SPIRITUOUS, OR VINOUS FERMENTATION. The juices of almost all fruits, all saccharine vegetable matter, all fatinaceous seeds and grains of every kind, being diluted with a suffient quantity of water, are proper subjects of spirituous fermentation. If such liquors be exposed, in vessels slightly stopped, to a moderate degree of heat, they begin in some time to grow turbid; there arises insensibly a small commotion among their parts, attended with a hissing noise; this by little and little increases, till the grosser parts appear, like little seeds or grains, moving to and fro, agitated among themselves, and thrown up to the surface. At the same time some air bubbles rise, and the liquor acquires a pungent, penetrating smell, occasioned by the very subtile vapours which exhale from it.

These vapours have never yet been collected, in order to examine their nature; and they are known only by their noxious effects. They are so actively pernicious, that if a man comes rashly into a close place, where large quantities of liquors are fermenting, he suddenly drops down and expires, as if he were knocked on the head.

When these several phenomena begin to go off, it is proper to stop the fermentation, if a very spirituous liquor be required; for if it be suffered to continue longer, the liquor will become acid, and from thence proceed to its last stage, that is, to putrifaction. This is done by stopping the containing vessels very close, and removing them into a cooler place. Then the impurities precipitate, and settling at the bottom leave the liquor clear and transparent: And now the palate discovers that the sweet sacharine taste it had before fermentation is changed to an agreeable pungency which is not acid.

Liquors thus fermented are in general called wines: For though in common life that word properly signifies the fermented juice of grapes only, and particular names are given to the fermented juices of other vegetable substances, as that obtained apples, is called cyder; that made from malt is called beer; yet in chemistry it is of use to have one general term denoting every liquor that has undergone this first degree of fermentation.

By distillation we draw from wine an inflammable liquor, of a yellowish white colour, light, and of a penetrating pleasant smell. This liquor is the truly spirituous part of the wine, and the product of fermentation. That which comes off in the first distillation is commonly loaded with much phlegm and some oily parts, from which it may be afterwards freed. In this state it goes by the name of brandy; but when freed from these heterogeneous matters by repeated distillations, it becomes still clearer, lighter, more fragrant, and much more inflammable, and then is called spirit of wine, and rectified spirit of wine, or ardent spirits, if considerably purified. The properties which distinguish an ardent spirit from all other substances are, it being inflamable; its burning and consuming entirely, without the least appearance of smoke or fulginosity; its containing no particles reducible to a coal; and its being perfectly miscible with water. Ardent spirits are lighter and more volatile than any of the principles of the mixes from which they were produced, and consequently more so than the phlegm, the acid, and the oil of which they themselves consist. This arises from a particular disposition of these principles, which are in a singular manner attenuated by fermentation, and thereby rendered more susceptible of expansion and rarefaction.

Ardent spirits are suppose to be the natural solvents of oils and oily matters. But it is very remarkable, that they dissolve essential oils only, without touching the fat of animals, or the fat oils obtained from vegetables by expression; yet when these oils have once undergone the action of fire, they become soluble in spirit of wine, and even acquire a new degree of solubility every time they are distilled. It is not so with essential oils, which can never be rendered more soluble in ardent spirits than they are at first; and are so far from acquiring a new degree of solubility every time they are distilled, that on the contrary they even in some measure lose that property by repeated rectifications.

Spirit of wine doth not dissolve fixed alkalis; or at least it takes up but a very small quantity thereof; and hence ardent spirits may be freed from much of their phlegm by means of these salts thoroughly dried: For as they strongly imbibe moisture, and have even a greater affinity than ardent spirits with water, if a fixed alkali well exsiccated be mixed with spirit of wine that is not perfectly dephlegmated, the alkali immediately attracts its superfluous moisture, and is thereby resolved into a liquor, which on account of its gravity descends to the bottom of the vessel. The spirit of wine which swims a-top is by this means as much dephlegmated, and as dry, as if it had been rectified by several distillations. As it takes up some alkaline particles in this operation, it is thereby qualified to dissolve oily matters with the greater facility. When rectified in this manner, it is called tartarified spirit of wine.

Yet spirit of wine, even when rectified to an alcohol, is not capable of dissolving all oily matters. Those named gums will by no means enter into any sort of union therewith; but it readily dissolves most of those which are known by the appellation of resins. When it has dissolved a certain proportion of resinous particles, it acquires a greater consistence, and forms what is called a spirit varnish, or a drying varnish, because it soon dries. This varnish is subject to be damaged by water. Many sorts thereof are prepared, different from each other according to the different resins employed, or the proportions in which they are used. Most of these varnishes are transparent and colourless.

Such bitumens or resins as spirit of wine will not touch are dissolved in oils by means of fire, and then form another kind of varnish which water does not hurt. These varnishes are usually coloured, and require much longer time to dry than the spirit-varnishes: They are called oil-varnishes.

Spirit of wine hath a much greater affinity with water than with oily matters; and therefore if a solution of any oil or resin in spirit of wine be mixed with water, the liquor immediately grows turbid, and acquires a whitish milky colour, owing entirely to the oily parts being separated from the spirituous menstruum by the accession of water, and too finely divided to appear in their natural form. But if the liquor stands some time quiet, several of these particles unite together, and gradually acquire a bulk sufficient to render them very perceptible to the eye.

Acids have an affinity with spirit of wine, and may be combined with it. By this union they lose most of their acidity, and on that account are said to be dulcified.

One part of highly concentrated oil of vitriol being mixed with four parts of well dephlegmated spirit of wine, there arises immediately a considerable ebullition and effervescence, attended with great heat, and abundance of vapours, which smell pleasantly, but are hurtful to the lungs. At the same time is heard a hissing like that produced by a piece of red-hot iron plunged in water. Indeed it is proper to mix the liquors very gradually; for otherwise the vessels in which the operation is performed will be in great danger of breaking.

If two liquors thus mixed be distilled with a very gentle heat, there rises first a spirit of wine of a most penetrating and grateful odour: When about half thereof is come over, what follows has a quicker and more sulphureous smell, and is also more loaded with phlegm. When the liquor begins to boil a little, there comes off a phlegm which smells very strong of sulphur, and grows gradually more acid. On this phlegm floats a small quantity of a very light and very limpid oil. In the still there remains a thick, blackish substance, somewhat like a resin or bitumen. From this substance may be separated a good deal of a vitriolic but sulphureous acid. When that is extracted, there remains a black mass like a charred coal, which, being put into a crucible, and exposed to a violent heat, leaves a small portion of earth, very fixed, and even vitrifiable.

By rectifying the ardent spirit, which came over in distilling the above mentioned mixture, a very singular liquor is obtained, which differs essentially both from oils and from ardent spirits, though in certain respects it resembles them both. This liquor is known in chemistry by the name of aether, and its chief properties are as follows.

AEther is lighter, more volatile, and more inflammable, than the most highly rectified spirit of wine. It quickly flies off when exposed to the air, and suddenly catches fire when any flame approaches it. It burns like spirit of wine without the least smoke, and consumes entirely without leaving the smallest appearance of a coal or of ashes. It dissolves oils and oily matters with great ease and rapidity. These properties it has in common with an ardent spirit. But it resembles an oil, in that it ks not miscible with water; and this makes it essentially different from spirit of wine, the nature of which is to be miscible with all aqueous liquors.

Another very singular property of aether is its great affinity with gold, exceeding even that of aqua regis. It does not indeed dissolve gold when in a mass, and in its metalline form: But if a small quantity of aether be added to a solution of gold in aqua regis, and the whole shaken together, the gold separates from the aqua regis, joins the aether, and remains dissolved therein,

The reason of all the phenomena above-mentioned, resulting from the mixture of spirit of wine with oil of vitriol, is founded on the great affinity between this acid and water. For if the vitriolic acid be weak, and as it were over-dosed with watery parts, neither oil nor aether can be obtained by means thereof: But when highly concentrated, it attracts the aqueous parts very powerfully; and therefore being mixed with spirit of wine, lays hold of most of the water contained in it, and even robs it of some portion of that which is essential to its nature, and necessary to constitute it spirit of wine: Whence it comes to pass, that a certain quantity of the oily particles in its composition being separated from the watery particles, and so brought nearer to each other, they unite and assume their natural form; and thus the oil that swims at top of the sulphureous phlegm is produced.

The vitriolic acid moreover thickens and even burns some of this oil; and hence comes the bituminous residuum left at the bottom of the still, which looks like the result of a vitriolic acid combined with common oil. Lastly, the vitriolic acid becomes sulphureous, as it always doth when united with oily matters, and also very aqueous, on account of the quantity of phlegm which it attracts from the spirit of wine.

AEther may be considered as a spirit of wine exceedingly dephlegmated, even to such a degree that its nature is thereby changed; so that the few aqueous particles left in it are not sufficient to dissolve the oily particles and keep them asunder; which therefore being now much nearer to one another than in common spirit of wine, the liquor hath lost its property of being miscible with water.

Spirit of nitre, well dephlegmated, and combined with spirit of wine, presents likewise some very singular appearances.

First, in the very instant of its mixture with spirit of wine, it produces a greater and more violent effervescence than the vitriolic acid occasions.

Secondly, this mixture, without the help of distillation, and only by stopping the bottle in which the liquors are contained, afford a sort of aether, produced probably by the vapours which ascend from, and swim atop of the mixture.

Thirdly, some authors pretend, that by distilling the mixture under consideration an oil is obtained greatly resembling that which rises from spirit of wine combined with vitriolic acid.

Fourthly, the two liquors we are speaking of, being intimately mixed by distillation, form a liquor slightly acid, used in medicine, and known by the name of sweet or culcified spirit of nitre; a very proper name, seeing the nitrous acid, by uniting with the spirit of wine, actually loses almost all its acidity and corrosive quality.

Fifthly, when the distillation is finished, there remains in the bottom of the vessel a thick, blackish substance, nearly resembling that which is found after distilling oil of vitriol and spirit of wine.

Spirit of salt hath likewise been combined with spirit of wine; but it does not unite therewith so easily or so intimately as the two acids above mentioned. To mix them thoroughly, the spirit of salt must be highly concentrated, and smoking; and moreover the assistance of the still must be called in. Some authors pretend, that from this mixture also a small quantity of oil may be obtained; which probably happens when the liquors have the qualities above specified. The marine acid likewise, by uniting with spirit of wine, loses most of its acidity; on which account it is in like manner called sweet or dulcified spirit of salt. A thick residuum is also found here after distillation.

OF THE ACETOUS FERMENTATION. Besides an ardent spirit, wine affords a great deal of water, oil, earth, and a sort of acid which shall be considered presently. When the spirituous part is separated from these other matters, they undergo no further change. But if all the constituent parts of wine remain combined together, then, after some time, shorter or longer as the degree of heat in which the wine stands is greater or less, the fermentation begins afresh, or rather arrives at its second stage. The liquor once more grows turbid, a new intestate motion arises, and after some days it is found changed into an acid; which, however, is very different from those hitherto treated of. The liquor then takes the name of vinegar. The acetous fermentation differs from the spirituous, not only in its effect, but also in several of its concomitant circumstances. Moderate motion is of service to this, whereas it obstructs the spirituous; and it is attended with much more warmth than the spirituous. The vapours it produces are not noxious, like those of fermenting wine. Lastly, vinegar deposites no tartar, even when the wine employed in this operation is quite new, and hath not had time to discharge its tartar; instead of tartar, vinegar deposites a viscid matter which is very apt to putrify.

OF VINEGAR. If wine, which has gone through this second stage of fermentation, be distilled, instead of an ardent spirit, only an acid liquor is obtained, which is called distilled vinegar.

This acid has the same properties as the mineral acids; that is, it unites with alkaline salts, absorbent earths, and metallic substances, and therewith forms neutral saline combinations.

Its affinity with these substances observes the same order as that observed by the mineral acids with regard to the same substances; but in general it is weaker; that is, any mineral acid is capable of expelling the acid of vinegar out of all matters with which it is united.

Vinegar hath likewise a greater affinity than sulphur with alkalis; whence it follows, that it is capable of decompounding that combination of sulphur with an alkali called liver of sulphur, and of precipitating the sulphur it contains.

The acid of vinegar is always clogged with a certain proportion of oily parts, which greatly weaken it, and deprive it of much of its activity; and for this reason it is not near so strong as the mineral acids, which are not entangled with any oil. By distillation, indeed, it may be freed from this oil, and at the same time from the great quantity of water which in a manner suffocates it, and by that means may be brought much nearer to the nature of the mineral acids; but this attempt has not yet been prosecuted with the assiduity it deserves. Besides distillation, there is another way of freeing vinegar from a good deal of its phlegm; and that is, by exposing it to a hard frost, which readily congeals the watery part into ice, while the acid retains its fluidity.

Vinegar, saturated with a fixed alkali, forms a neutral oily salt, of a dark colour, which is semi-volatile, melts with a very gentle heat, flames when thrown upon burning coals, and dissolves in spirit of wine, of which, however, it requires six parts to complete the solution. This solution being evaporated to dryness leaves a matter in the form of leaves lying on each other; on which account it hath obtained the name of terra foliata. The same foliated matter will be obtained, though the salt be not previously dissolved in spirit of wine; but not so readily. This salt is also called regenerated tartar. Under the head of tartar we shall see the reason of these different appellations. Regenerated tartar is also in some degree capable of crystallizing; for this purpose a resolution thereof in water must be slowly evaporated to the consistence of a syrup, and then suffered to stand quiet in a cool place; by which means it will shoot into clusters of crystals, lying one upon another, not unlike the feathers on a quill.

With vinegar and several absorbent earths, such as calcined pearls, coral, shells of fish, etc., are also formed neutral saline compounds, each of which take the name of the particular earth employed in its composition.

Vinegar perfectly dissolves lead, and converts it to a neutral metallic salt, which shoots into crystals, and has a sweet saccharine taste. This compound is called sugar of lead, or sal Saturni.

If lead be exposed to the bare vapour of vinegar, it will be thereby corroded, calcined, and converted into a white matter much used in painting, and known by the name of ceruse, or, when it is finer than ordinary, white-lead.

Vinegar corrodes copper likewise, and converts it into a beautiful green rust, which also is used in painting, and distinguished by the name of verdegris. However, vinegar is not commonly employed to make verdegris; for this purpose the use of wine, or the rape of wine, from which fire extricates an acid analogous to that of vinegar.

OF TARTAR. This substance is a saline compound, consisting of earthy, oily, and especially acid parts. It is found in the form of rusts, adhering to the inner sides of vessels in which wines have stood for sometime, particularly acid wines, such as those of Germany.

Tartar derives its origin from the superabundant quantiy of the acid contained in the juice of the grape. This superfluous acid, being more than is requisite to constitue the ardent spirit, unites with some of the oil and earth contained in the fermented liquor, and forms a kind of salt; which for sometime continued suspended in that liquor, but, when the wine stands undisturbed in a cool place, is deposited, and hath been said, on the sides of the cask.

When it is purified, there appears on the surface of the liquor a sort of white crystalline pellicle, which is skimmed off as it forms. This matter is called cream of tartar. The same liquor which produces this cream and in which the purified tartar is dissolved, being set to cool, yields a great number of white semi-transparent crystals, which are called crystals of tartar. The cream and crystals of tartar are therefore no other than purified tartar, and differ from each other in their form only.

Though the crystals of tartar have every appearance of a neutral salt, yet they are far from being such; for they have all the properties of a true acid, which scarce differs from that of vinegar, except that it contains less water, and more earth and oil; to which it owes its solid form, as well as its property of not being soluble in water without much difficulty; for a very great quantity of water is requisite to keep the crystals of tartar in solution; and it must moreover be boiling hot; otherwise as soon as it cools most of the tartar dissolved in it separates from the liquor, and falls to the bottom in the form of a white powder.

Tartar is decomposed by calcination in the open fire. All its oily parts are consumed or dissipated in smoke, together with most of its acid. The other part of its acid, uniting intimately with its earth, forms a very strong and very pure fixed alkali, called salt of tartar.

It will be shewn in its proper place, that almost every vegetable matter, as well as tartar, leaves a fixed alkali in its ashes; yet tartar has these peculiar properties; first, it assumes an alkaline character even when burnt or calcined in close vessels, whereas other substances acquire it only by being burnt in the open air; secondly, the alkali of tartar is stronger and more saline than almost any that is obtained from other matters.

This alkali, when thoroughly calcined, powerfully attracts the moisture of the air, and melts into an unctuous alkaline liquor, improperly called oil of tartar per deliquium. This is the alkali generally used in making the terra foliata, mentioned under the head of vinegar; for which reason this combination is called terra foliata tartari.

Crystals of tartar combined with alkali of tartar produce a great effervescence while they are mixing, as all acids usually do; and if the combination be brought exactly up to the point of saturation, a perfectly neutral salt is formed, which shoots into crystals, and easily dissolves in water; and this hath procured it the name of soluble tartar. It is also called the vegetable salt, as being obtained from vegetables only; and again tartarifed tartar, because it consists of the acid and the alkali of tartar combined together.

Crystals of tartar combined with alkalis procured from the ashes of sea-weeds, such as soda, which alkalis resemble the basis of sea-salt, form likewise a neutral salt, which crystallizes well, and dissolves easily in water. This salt is another sort of soluble tartar. It is called Saignette's salt, from the inventor's name.

Tartar likewise dissolves the absorbent earths, as lime, chalk, etc. and with them forms neutral salts which are soluble in water. It even attacks metallic bodies, and when combined with them becomes soluble. A soluble tartar for medical use is prepared with crystals of tartar and iron; the metallic salt thereby produced hath the name of chalybeated soluble tartar. This salt attracts the moisture of the air, and is one of those which do not crystallize.

Crystallized tartar acts also upon several other metallic substances; for instance, it dissolves the regulus, liver and glass of antimony, and thence acquires an emetic quality: It is then called stibiated, or emetic tartar. It likewise dissolves lead, and therewith forms a salt which, in the figure of its crystals, resembles tartarised tartar.

It is very extraordinary, that tartar, which of itself is not soluble in water, should be soluble therein when become a neutral salt by uniting either with alkalis or with absorbent earths, or even with metals. All the soluble tartars are easily decompounded by exposing them to a certain degree of heat. In distillation they yield the same principles which are obtained from tartar; and what remains fixed in the fire, after they are thoroughly burnt, is a compound of the alkali which tartar naturally produces, and of the alkaline or metallic substance with which it was converted into a neutral salt.

As crystal of tartar is the weakest of all acids, on account of the oily and earthy matters with which it is combined, soluble tartars are decompounded by all the acids; by any of which crystal of tartar may be separated from the substance that serves it for a basis and renders it a neutral salt.

OF THE PUTRID FERMENTATION, OR PUTREFACTION. Every body which hath gone through the two stages of fermentation above described, that is, the spirituous and the acetous fermentation, being left to itself in a due degree of warmth, which varies according to the subject, advances to the last stage of fermentation; that is, to putrefaction.

When a body is in a putrefying state, it is easy to discover, by the vapours which rise from it, by the opacity which invades it, if a pellucid liquor, and frequently even by a greater degree of heat than is found in the two other sorts of fermentation, that an intestine motion is begun among its constituent parts, which lasts till the whole be entirely putrefied.

The effect of this intestine motion is to break the union, and change the disposition, of the particles constituting the body in which it is excited, and to produce a new combination.

If we examine a substance that has undergone putrefaction, we shall soon perceive that it contains a principle which did not exist in it before. If this substance be distilled, there rises first, by means of a very gentle heat, a saline matter which is exceedingly volatile, and affects the organ of smelling briskly and disagreeably. Nor is the aid of distillation necessary to discover the presence of this product of putrefaction; it readily manifests itself in most substances where it exists, as any one may soon be convinced by observing the different smell of fresh and putrefied urine; for the latter not only affects the nose, but even makes the eyes smart, and irritates them so as to draw tears from them in abundance.

This saline principle, which is the product of putrefaction, when separated from the other principles of the body which affords it, and collected by itself, appears either in the form of a liquor, or in that of a concrete salt, according to the different methods used to obtain it. In the former state it is called a volatile urinous spirit; and in the latter a volatile urinous salt. The qualification of urinous is given it, because a great deal thereof is generated in putrefied urine, to which it communicates its small. It goes also by the general name of a volatile alkali, whether in a concrete or in a liquid form. The enumeration of its properties will shew why it is called an alkali.

Volatile alkalis, from whatever substance obtained, are all alike, and have the same properties; differing only according to their degrees of purity. The volatile alkali, as well as the fixed, consists of a certain quantity of acid combined with, and entangled by a portion of the earth of the mixt body from which it was obtained; and on that account it has many properties like those of a fixed alkali. But there is moreover in its composition a considerable quantity of a fat or oily matter, of which there is none in a fixed alkali; and on this account again there is a great difference between them. Thus the volatility of the alkali produced by putrefaction, which is the principal difference between it and the other kind of alkali, whose nature it is to be fixed, must be attributed to the portion of oil which it contains; for there is a certain method of volatilizing fixed alkalis by means of a fatty substance.

Volatile alkalis have a great affinity with acids, unite therewith rapidly, and with ebullition, and form with them neutral salts, which shoot into crystals, but differ from one another according to the kind of acid employed in the combination.

The neutral salts which have a volatile alkali for their basis are in general called ammoniacal salts. That whose acid is the acid of sea-salt is called sal ammoniac. As this was the first known, it gave name to all the rest. Great quantities of this salt are made in Egypt, and thence brought to us. They sublime it from the soot of cow's dung, which is the fuel of that country, and contains sea-salt, together with a volatile alkali, or at least the materials proper for forming it; and consequently all the ingredients that enter into the composition of sal ammoniac.

The neutral salts formed by combining the acids of nitre and of vitriol with a volatile alkali, are called; after their acids, nitrous sal ammoniac, and vitriolic sal ammoniac: The latter, from the name of its inventor, is also called Glauber's secret sal ammoniac.

A volatile alkali, then, has the same property as a fixed alkali with regard to a-cids' yet they differ in this, that the affinity of the former with acids is weaker than that of the latter; and hence it follows, that any sal ammoniac may be decompounded by a fixed alkali, which will lay hold of the acid, and discharge the volatile alkali.

A volatile alkali will decompound any neutral salt which has not a fixed alkali for its basis; that is, all such as consist of an acid combined with an absorbent earth or a metallic substance. By joining with the acids in which they are dissolved, it disengages the earths or metallic substances, takes their place, and, in conjunction with their acids, forms ammoniac salts.

Hence it might be concluded, that, of all substances, next to the phlogiston and the fixed alkalis, volatile alkalis have the greatest affinity with acids in general. Yet there is some difficulty in this matter; for absorbent earths and several metallic substances are also capable of decompounding ammoniacal salts, discharging their volatile alkali, and forming new compounds by uniting with their acids. This might induce us to think that these substances have nearly the same affinity with acids.

But it is proper to observe, that a volatile alkali decompounds such neutral salts as have for their basis either an absorbent earth or a metallic substance, without the aid of fire; whereas absorbent earths or metallic substances will not decompound an ammoniacal salt, unless they be assisted by a certain degree of heat.

Now, as all these matters are extremely fixed, at least in comparison with a volatile alkali, they have the advantage of being able to resist the force of fire, and so of acting in conjunction therewith; and fire greatly promotes the natural action of substances upon one another; whereas the volatile alkali in the ammoniacal salt, being unable to abide the force of fire, is compelled to desert its acid; and that so much the more quickly, as its affinity therewith is considerably weakened by the presence of an earthy or metallic substance, both of which have a great affinity with acids.

These considerations oblige us to conclude, that volatile alkalis have a somewhat greater affinity, than absorbent earths and metallic substances, with acids.

Ammoniacal salts projected upon nitre in fusion make it detonate; and the nitrous sal ammoniac detonates by itself, without the addition of any inflammable matter. This singular effect evidently demonstrates the existence of an oily matter in volatile alkalis; for it is certain that nitre will never deflagrate without the concurrence and even the immediate contact of some combustible matter.

This oily substance is often found combined with volatile alkalis in such a large proportion as to disguise it in some measure, and render it exceeding foul. The salt may be freed from its superfluous oil by repeated sublimations; and particularly by subliming it from absorbent earths, which readily drink up oils. This is called the rectification of a volatile alkali. The salt, which before was of a yellowish or dirty colour, by being thus rectified, becomes very white, and acquires an odour more pungent and less fetid than it had at first, that is, when obtained by one single distillation from a putrid substance.

It is proper to observe, that the rectification of a volatile alkali must not be carried too far, or repeated too often; for by that means it may be entirely decomposed at length; and particularly if an absorbent earth, and especially chalk, be employed for that purpose, the salt may be converted into an oil, an earth, and water.

Volatile alkalis act upon several metallic substances, and particularly on copper; of which they make a most beautiful blue solution. On this property depends a pretty singular effect, which happens sometimes when we attempt by means of a volatile alkali to separate copper from an acid with which it is combined. Instead of seeing the liquor grow turbid, and the metal fall, both which generally happen when any alkali whatever is mixed with a metallic solution, we are surprised to observe the solution of copper, upon adding a volatile alkali, retain its limpidity, and let fall no precipitate; or at least if the liquor does grow turbid, it remains so but for a moment, and instantly recovers its transparency. This is occasioned by adding such a quantity of volatile alkali as is more than sufficient fully to saturate the acid of the solution, and considerable enough to dissolve all the copper as fast as it is separated from the acid. On this occasion the liquor requires a deeper blue than it had before; which arises from the property which volatile alkalis have of giving this metal, when combined with them, a fuller blue than any other solvent can: Hence we have a touchstone to discover copper where-ever it is; for, let the quantity of this metal, combined with other metals, be ever so small, a volatile alkali never fails to discover it, by making it appear of a blue colour.

Though a volatile alkali be constantly the result of putrefaction, yet it must not therefore be imagined, that none can be produced by any other means; on the contrary, most of those which contain the ingredients necessary to form it, yield no inconsiderable quantity thereof in distillation. Tartar, for example, which by being burnt in an open fire is converted, as was shewn, into a fixed alkali, yields a volatile alkali when it is decomposed in close vessels; that is, when it is distilled: Because, in this latter case, the oily part is not dissipated or burnt, as it is by calcination in a naked fire, but has time to unite with some of the earth and acid of the mixt, in such a manner as to form a true volatile alkali.

To prove that on this occasion, as well as on all others, where unputrefied bodies yield a volatile alkali, this salt is the product of the fire, we need only observe, that in these distillations it never rises till after some part of the phlegm of the acid and even of the thick oil of the mixt, is come over; which never is the case when it is formed before hand in the body which is the subject of the operation, as it is in those which have undergone putrefaction: For this salt, being much lighter and more volatile than those other substances, rises of course before them in distillation.

A GENERAL VIEW OF CHEMICAL DECOMPOSITION. Though we have considered all the substances which enter into the composition of vegetables, animals, and minerals, whether as primary or as secondary principles, it will not be improper to shew in what order we obtain these principles from the several mixts; and especially from vegetables and animals, because they are much more complicated than minerals. This is called analysing a compound.

The method most commonly taken to decompose bodies is by applying to them successive degrees of heat, from the gentlest to the most violent, in appropriated vessels, so contrived as to collect what exhales from them. By this means the principles are gradually separated from each other; the most volatile rise first, and the rest follow in order, as they come to be acted on by the proper degree of heat; And this is called distillation.

But it being observed that fire, applied to the decomposition of bodies, most commonly alters their secondary principles very sensibly, by combining them in a different manner with each other, or even partly decomposing them, and reducing them to their primitive principles; other means have been used to separate those principles without the help of fire.

With this view the mixts to be decomposed are forcibly compressed, in order to squeeze out of them all such parts of their substance as they will by this means part with; or else those mixts are for a long time triturated, either along with water, which carries off all their saline and saponaceous contents; or with solvents, such as ardent spirits, capable of taking up every thing in them that is of an oily or resinous nature.

We shall here give a succinct account of the effects of these different methods, as applied to the principal substances among vegetables and animals, and likewise to some minerals.

THE ANALYSIS OF VEGETABLE SUBSTANCES. A vast many vegetable substances, such as kernels and seeds, yield by strong compression great quantities of mild, fat, unctuous oils, which are not soluble in ardent spirits: These are what we called expressed oils. They are also sometimes called fat oils, on account of their unctuousness, in which they exceed all other sorts of oil. As these oils are obtained without the aid of fire, it is certain that they existed in the mixt just as we see them, and that they are not in the least altered; which could not have been the case had they been obtained by distillation: For that never produces any oils but such as are acrid and soluble in spirit of wine.

Some vegetable matters, such as the rind of citrons, lemons, oranges, etc., also yield only be being squeesed between the fingers, a great deal of oil. This spits out in fine small jets, which being received upon any polished surface, such as a looking-glass, run together, and form a liquor that is a real oil.

But it must be carefully noted, that this sort of oil, though obtained by expression only, is nevertheless very different from the oils mentioned before to which the title of expressed oils peculiarly belongs: For this is far lighter and thinner; moreover, it retains the perfect odour of the fruit which yields it, and is soluble in spirit of wine; in a word, it is a true essential oil, but abounds so in the fruits which produce it, and is lodged therein in such a manner, occupying a vast number of little cells provided in the peel for its reception, that a very slight pressure discharges it; which is not the case with many vegetables that contain an essential oil.

Succulent and green plants yield by compression a great deal of liquor or juice, which consists of most of the phlegm of the salts, and a small portion of the oil and earth of the plant. These juices, being set in a cool place for some time, deposit saline crystals, which are a combination of the acid of the plant with part of it oil and earth, wherein the acid is always predominant. These salts, as is evident from the description here given, bear a great resemblance to the tartar of wine treated of above. They are called essential salts; so that tartar might likewise be called the essential salt of wine.

Dried plants, and such as are of a ligneous, or acid nature, require to be long triturated with water, before they will yield their essential salts. Trituration with water is an excellent way to get out of them all their saline and saponaceous contents.

A vegetable matter that is very oily yields its essential salt with much difficulty, if at all; because the excessive quantity of oil entangles the salt so that it cannot extricate itself or shoot into crystals. Mr. Gerike, in his PRINCIPLES OF CHEMISTRY, says, That if part of the oil of a plant be extracted by spirit of wine, its essential salt may be afterwards obtained with more ease and in greater quantity.

Essential salts are among those substances which cannot be extracted from mixts by distillation; for the first impression of fire decomposes them.

Though the acid which predominates in the essential salts of plants be most commonly analogous to the vegetable acid, properly so called, that is, to the acid of vinegar and tartar, which is probably no other than the vitriolic acid disguised; yet it sometimes differs therefrom, and somewhat resembles the nitrous or the marine acid. This depends on the places where the plants grow which produce these salts: If they be submarine plants, their acid is a kin to the acid of sea-salt; if, on the contrary, they grow upon walls, or in nitrous grounds, their acid is like that of nitre. Sometimes one and the same plant contains salts analogous to all the three mineral acids; which shews that the vegetable acids are no other than the mineral acids variously changed by circulating through plants.

Liquors containing the essential salts of plants being evaporated by a gentle heat to the consistence of honey, or even further, are called extracts. Hence it is plain, that an extract is nothing but the essential salt of a plant, combined with some particles of its oil and earth, that remained suspended in the liquor, and are now incorporated by evaporation.

Extracts of plants are also prepared by boiling them long in water, and then evaporating some part of it. But these extracts are of inferior virtue; because the fire dissipates many of the oily and saline parts.

EMULSIONS. Substances which abound much in oil, being bruised and triturated with water for some time, afford a liquor of an opaque dead-white colour like milk. This liquor consists of such juices as the water is capable of dissolving, together with a portion of the oil, which being naturally indissoluble in water, is only divided and dispersed in the liquor, the limpidity whereof is by that means destroyed. This sort of oily liquor, in which the oil is only divided, not dissolved, is called an emulsion. The oily particles in emulsions spontaneously separate from the water, when left at rest, and, uniting into greater masses, rise, on account of their lightness, to the surface of the liquor, which by that means recovers a degree of transparency.

If vegetables, abounding in essential oils and resins, be digested in spirit of wine, the menstruum takes up these oily matters, as being capable of dissolving them; and they may afterwards be easily separated from it by the affusion of water. The water, with which spirit of wine has a greater affinity than with oily matters, separates them by this means from their solvent, agreeable to the common laws of affinities.

Without the help of fire scarce any thing, besides the substances already mentioned, can be obtained from a plant: But by the means of distillation we are enabled to analyse them more completely. In prosecuting this method of extracting from a plant the several principles of which it consists, the following order is to be observed.

A plant being exposed to a very gentle heat, in a distilling vessel set in the balneum maria, yields a water which retains the perfect smell thereof. Some chemists, and particularly the illustrious Boerhaave, have called this liquor the spiritus rector. The nature of this odoriferous part of plants is not yet thoroughly known; because it is so very volatile, that it is difficult to subject it to the experiments necessary for discovering all its properties.

If instead of distilling the plant in the balneum maria, it be distilled over a naked fire, with the precaution of putting a certain quantity of water into the distilling vessel along with it, to prevent its suffering a greater heat than that of boiling water, all the essential oil contained in that plant will rise together with that water, and wotj tje same degree of heat.

On this occasion it must be observed, that no essential oil can be obtained from a plant after the spiritus rector hath been drawn off; which gives ground to think that the volatility of these oils is owing to that spirit.

The heat of boiling water is also sufficient to separate from vegetable matters the fat oils which they contain: That, however, is to be done by the way of decoction only, and not by distillation; because, though these oils will swim on water, yet they will not rise in vapours without a greater degree of heat.

When the essential oil is come over, if the plant be exposed to a naked fire, without the addition of water, and the heat be increased a little, a phlegm will rise that gradually grows acid; after which, if the heat be increased as occasion requires, there will come over a thicker and heavier oil; from some a volatile alkali; and last of all, a very thick, black, empyreumatic oil.

When nothing more rises with the strongest degree of heat, there remains of the plant a mere coal only, called the caput mortuum, or terra damnata. This coal when burnt falls into ashes, which being lixiviated with water give a fixed alkali.

It is observable, that in the distillation of plants which yield an acid and a volatile alkali, these two salts are often found quite distinct and separate in the same receiver; which seems very extraordinary, considering that they are naturally disposed to unite, and have a great affinity with one another. The reason of this phenomenon is, that they are both combined with much oil, which embarrasses them so that they cannot unite to form a neutral salt, as they would not fail to do were it not for that impediment.

All vegetables, except such as yield a great deal of volatile alkali, being burnt in an open fire, and so as to flame, leave in their ashes a large quantity of an acrid, caustic, fixed alkali. But if care be taken to smother them, so as to prevent their flaming hile they burn, by covering them with something that may continually beat down again what exhales, the salt obtained from their ashes will be much less acrid and caustic; the cause whereof is, that some part of the acid and oil of the plant being detained in the burning, and stopped from being dissipated by the fire, combines with its alkali. These salts crystallize, and being milder than the common fixed alkalis may be used in medicine, and taken internally. They are called Tachenius's salts, because invented by that chemist.

Marine plants yield a fixed alkali analogous to that of sea-salt. As for all other plants or vegetable substances, the fixed alkalis obtained from them, if rightly prepared and thoroughly calcined, are all perfectly alike, and of the same nature.

The last observation we have to make on the production of a fixed alkali is, that if the plant you intend to work upon be steeped or boiled in water before you burn it, a much smaller quantity of salt will be obtained from it; nay, it will yield none at all, if repeated boilings have robbed it entirely of those saline particles which must necessarily concur with its earth to form a fixed alkali.

THE ANALYSIS OF ANIMAL SUBSTANCES. Succulent animal substances, such as new-killed flesh yield by expression a juice or liquid, which is no other than the phlegm, replete with all the principles of the animal body except the earth, of which it contains but little. The hard or dry parts, such as the horns, bones etc., yield a similar juice, by boiling them in water. These juices become thick, like a glue or jelly, when their watery parts are evaporated; and in this state they are true extracts of animal matters. These juices afford no crystals of essential salt, like those obtained from vegetables, and shew no sign either of an acid or an alkali.

Great part of the oil which is in the flesh of animals may be easily separated without the help of fire; for it lies in a manner by itself: It is commonly in a concrete form, and is called fat. This oil somewhat resembles the fat oils of vegetables; for like them it is mild, unctuous, indissoluble in spirit of wine, and is subtilized and attenuated by the action of fire. But there is not in animals, as in vegetables, any light essential oil, which rises with the heat of boiling water; so that, properly speaking, animals contain but one sort of oil.

Few animal substances yield a perceptible acid. Ants and bees are almost the only ones from which any can be obtained; and indeed the quantity which they yield is very small, as the acid itself is extremely weak.

The reason thereof is that as animals do not draw their nourishment immediately from the earth, but feed wholly either on vegetables or on the flesh of other animals, the mineral acids, which have already undergone a great change by the union contracted between them and the oily matters of the vegetable kingdom, enter into a closer union and combination with these oily parts while they are passing through the organs and strainers of animals; whereby their properties are destroyed, or at least so impaired that they are no longer sensible.

Animal matters yield in distillation, first, a phlegm, and then, on increasing the fire, a pretty clear oil, which gradually becomes thicker, blacker, more fetid, and empyreumatic. It is accompanied with a great deal of volatile alkali; and if the fire be raised and kept up till nothing more comes over, there will remain in the distilling vessel a coal like that of vegetables; except that when it is reduced to ashes, no fixed alkali, or at least very little, can be obtained from them, as from the ashes of vegetables. This arises from hence that, as we said before, the saline principle in animals being more intimately united with the oil than it is in plants, and being consequently more attenuated and subtilized, is too volatile to enter into the combination of a fixed alkali; on the contrary, it is more disposed to join in forming a volatile alkali, which on this occasion does not rise till after the oil, and therefore must certainly be the production of the fire.

The chyle, and the milk of animals which feed on plants, still retain some likeness to begetables; because the principles of which these liquors are composed have not gone through all the changes which they must suffer before they enter into the animal combination.

Urine and sweat are excrementitious aqueous liquors, loaded chiefly with the saline particles which are of no service towards the nourishment of the animal, but pass through its strainers without receiving any alteration; such as the neutral salts which have a fixed alkali for their basis, and particularly the sea-salt which happens to be in the food of animals, whether it exist therein naturally, as it does in some plants, or whether the animals eat it to please their palates.

The saliva, the pancreatic juice, and especially the bile, are saponaceous liquors; that is, they consist of saline and oily particles combined together; so that being themselves dissolved in an aqueous liquor, they are capable of dissolving likewise the oily parts, and of rendering them miscible with water.

Lastly. The blood being the receptacle of all these liquors, partakes of the nature of each, more or less in proportion to the quantity thereof which it contains.

THE ANALYSIS OF MINERAL SUBSTANCES. Minerals differ greatly from vegetables, and from animals; they are not so complex as those organized bodies, and their principles are much more simple; whence it follows, that these principles are much more closely connected, and that they cannot be separated without the help of fire; which not having on their parts the same action and the same power as on organized bodies, hath not the same ill effect on them; we mean the effect of changing their principles, or even destroying them entirely.

We do not here speak of pure, vitrifiable, or refractory earths; of mere metals and semi-metals; of pure acids; or even of their simple conbinations, such as sulphur, vitriol, alum, sea-salt. Of all these we have said enough.

We are now to treat of bodies that are more complex, and therefore mor susceptible of decomposition. These bodies are compound masses or combinations of those above mentioned; that is, metallic substances as they are found in the bowels of the earth, united with several sorts of sand, stones, earths, semi-metals, sulphur, etc. When the metallic matter is combined with other matters in such a proportion to the rest that it may be separated from them with advantage and profit, these compounds are called ores; when the case is otherwise, they are called pyrites, and marcasites; especially if sulphur or arsenic be predominant therein, which often happens.

In order to analyse an ore, and get out of it the metal it contains, the first step is to free it from a great deal of earth and stones which commonly adhere to it very slightly and superficially. This is effected by pounding the ore, and then washing it in water; to the bottom of which the metalline parts presently sink, as being the heaviest, while the small particles of earth and stone remain suspended some time longer.

Thus the metallic part is left combined with such matters only as are most intimately complicated with it. These substances are most commonly sulphur and arsenic. Now, as they are much more volatile than other mineral matters, they may be dissipated in vapours, or the sulphur may be consumed, by exposing the ore which contains them to a proper degree of heat. If the sulphur and arsenic be desired by themselves, the fumes thereof may be catched and collected in proper vessels and places. This operation is called roasting in ore.

The metal thus depurated is now fit to be exposed to a greater force of fire, capable of melting it.

On this occasion the semi-metals and the imperfect metals require the addition of some matter abounding in phlogiston, particularly charcoal-dust; because these metallic substances lose their phlogiston by the action of the fire, or of the fluxes joined with them, and therefore without this precaution would never acquire either the splendor or the ductility of a metal. By this means the metallic substance is more accurately separated from the earthy and stony parts, of which some portion always remains combined therewith till it is brought to fusion. For, as we observed before, a metallic glass or calx only will contract an union with such matters; a metal possessed of it phlogiston and metalline form being utterly incapable thereof.

We took notice of the cause of this separation above, where we shewed that a metal possessed of its phlogiston and metalline form will not remain intimately united with any calcined or vitrified matter, not even with its own calx or glass.

The metal therefore on this occasion gathers into a mass, and lies at the bottom of the vessel, as being most ponderous; while the heterogeneous matters float upon it in the form of a glass, or a semi-vitrification. These floating matters take the name of scoria, and the metalline substance at bottom is called the regulus.

It frequently happens, that the metalline regulus thus precipitate, is itself a compound of several metals mixed together, which are afterwards to be separated.

It is proper to observe, before we quit this subject, that the rules here laid down for analysing ores are not absolutely general: For example, it is often adviseable to roast the ore before you wash it; for by that means some ores are opened, attenuated, and made very friable, which would cost much trouble and expence, on account of their excessive hardness, if you should attempt to pound them without a previous torrefaction.

It is also frequently necessary to separate the ore from part only of its stone; sometimes to leave the whole; and sometimes to add more to it, before you smelt it. This depends on the quality of the stone, which always helps to promote fusion when it is in its own nature fusible and vitrifiable: It is then called the fluor of the ore.

We shall now give a succinct account of the principal ores and mineral bodies, contenting ourselves with just pointing out the particulars of which they severally consist.

OF THE PYRITES. THE YELLOW PYRITES. The yellow pyrites is a mineral consisting of sulphur, iron, an unmetallic earth, and frequently a little copper: The sulphur, which is the only one of these principles that is volatile, may be separated from the rest by sublimation: It usually makes a fourth, and sometimes a third, of the whole weight of these pyrites. The other principles are separated from one another by fusion and reduction with the phlogiston, which, by metallizing the ferruginous and cupreous earths, parts them from the unmetallic earth; for this earth vitrifies, and cannot afterwards continue united with metallic matters possessed of their metalline form.

There is yet another way of decomposing the yellow pyrites, which is to let it lie till it effloresces, or begins to shoot into flowers; which is nothing but a sort of slow ascension of the sulphur it contains. The sulphur being by this means decomposed, its acid unites with the ferruginous and cupreous parts of the pyrites, and therewith forms green and blue vitriols; which may be extracted by steeping in water the pyrites which has effloresced or been burnt, and then evaporating the lixivium to a pellicle; for by this means the vitriol will shoot into crystals.

Sometimes the pyrites contains also an earth of the same nature with that of alum: A pyrites of this sort, after flowering, yields alum as well as vitriol.

THE WHITE PYRITES. The white pyrites contains much arsenic, a ferrugious earth, and an unmetallic earth. The arsenic being a volatile principle, may be separated by sublimation or distillation from the rest, which are fixed; and these again may be disjoined from each other by fusion and reduction, as was said in relation to the yellow pyrites.

THE COPPER PYRITES. The copper pyrites contains sulphur, copper, and an unmetallic earth. A great deal thereof likewise holds arsenic, and its colour approaches more or less to orange, yellow, or white, according to the quantity of arsenic in it. It may be decomposed by the same means as the yellow and white pyrites.

OF ORES. OF GOLD ORES. Gold being constantly found in its metalline form, and never combined with sulphur and arsenic, its ores are not, properly speaking, ores, because the metal contained in them is not mineralized. The gold is only lodged between particles of stone, earth, or sand, from which it is easily separated by lotion, and by

Amalgamation with quick-silver. The gold thus found is seldom pure, but is frequently alloyed with more or less silver, from which it is to be separated by quartatiion.

It is also very common to find gold in most ores of other metals or semi-metals, and even in the pyrites; but the quantity contained therein is generally so small, that it would not pay the cost of extracting it. However, if any should incline to attempt it, merely out of curiosity, it would be necessary to begin with treating these ores in the manner proper for separating their metalline part; then to cupel the metalline regulus so obtained; and lastly, to refine it by quartation.

OF SILVER ORES. It is no rare thing to find silver, as well as gold, in its metalline form, only lodged in sundry earths and stony matters, from which it may be separated in the same manner as gold. But the greatest quantities of this metal are usually dug out of the bowels of the earth in a truly mineral state; that is, combined with different substances, and particularly with sulphur and arsenic.

several silver ores are distinguished by peculiar characteristics, and are accordingly denoted by particular names. That which is called the vitreous silver ore, is scarce anything else but a combination of silver and sulphur. Another is known by the name of the horny silver ore, because when in thin plates it is semi-transparent: In this ore the silver is mineralized by sulphur and a little arsenic. The red silver ore is of the colour which its name imports, sometimes more, sometimes less vivid; and is chiefly composed of silver, arsenic, and sulphur: It also contains a little iron.

These three ores are very rich in silver; the first contains nearly three-fourths of its weight, and the others about two-thirds of theirs.

There is a fourth, called the white silver ore, which though it be heavier, is not so rich in silver, because it contains much copper. Many other ores contain silver, yet are not, properly speaking, silver ores; because a much greater quantity of other metals than of silver is found in them.

When a silver ore is to be decomposed, in order to have the silver pure, or when silver is to be extracted out of any ore that contains it, the first thing to be done is to roast the ore in order to clear it of the volatile minerals; and as silver cannot be had pure without the operation of the cupel, which requires more or less lead to be joined with it, it is usual to mix with the torrified silver ore a quantity of lead proportioned to that of the heterogeneous matters combined with the silver, and to melt the whole together. Part of the added lead vitrifies during the fusion, and at the same time converts some of the heterogeneous matter also into glass, with which it forms a scoria that rises to the surface of the matter. The other part of the lead, with which the silver is mixed, falls to the bottom in the form of a regulus, which must be cupelled in order to have the silver pure.

OF COPPER ORES. Copper is much seldomer found in a metalline form, than gold or silver; it is commonly in a mineral state; it is mineralized by sulphur and arsenic; almost all its ores contain also more or less iron; sometimes a little silver or even gold, together with unmetallic earths and stones, as all ores do.

Most copper ores are of a beautiful green or blue, or else in shades blended of these two colours. The minerals called mountain green, and mountain blue, are true copper ores; not in the form of hard stones, like other ores, but crumbly and friable like earth.

Nevertheless there are several copper ores of different colours, as ash-coloured, whitish, and shaded with yellow or orange; which colours arise from the different proportions of arsenic, sulphur, and iron, which these ores contain.

In order to decompose a copper ore, and to extract the copper it contains, it is first of all to be freed from as many of its earthy, stony, sulphureous, and arsenical parts, as is possible, by roasting and washing; then what remains is to be mixed with a flux compounded of a fixed alkali and some inflammable matter; a little sea-salt is to be put over all, and the whole melted by a strong fire. The salts facilitate the fusion and scorification of the unmetallic matters, and therewith form a slag, which being lighter rises to the surface. The metalline matters are collected below in the form of a thining regulus of copper; which however, is not usually fine copper, but requires to be purified.

In order to separate the copper from the unmetallic matters it is absolutely necessary to melt its ore along with the inflammable substances, abounding in phlogiston. For, as this metal is not possessed of its metalline form while it is in a mineral state, as it is destitute of the true quantity of phlogiston, and, though it were not, would lose it by the action of the fire, it would come to pass, that, if its ore were melted without the addition of any inflammable matter, the cupreous earth, or calx, would be scorified and confounded with the unmetallic matters; and as all metallic matters, except gold and silver, are subject to this inconvenience as well as copper, the addition of an inflammable substance, in fluxing all ores that contain them, is a general rule that ought constantly to be observed.

OF IRON ORES. Iron is seldom found pure and malleable in the earth; yet it is much seldomer found in the mineral state; properly so called, than any of the other metals; for most iron ores are scarce anything more than a ferruginous earth mixed in different proportions with unmetallic earths and stones. Some of them, however, contain also volatile minerals, such as sulphur and arsenic; and therefore it is necessary to roast the iron ores, like all others, before you attempt to extract the metal out of them. That being done, they are to be smelted with a flux consisting of fusible and inflammable matters, as the general rule directs.

Iron is the commonest of all metals; Nay, it is so universally diffused through the earth, that it is difficult to find any stone, earth, or sand, that does not contain some of it; and therefore none of these are usually considered and treated as iron ores, except such as contain a great deal of that metal, and melt easily. The hematites, emery, yellow pyrites, calamine, all contain a pretty considerably quantity of iron; but nobody attempts to extract it from them, because they are very hard to melt.

ferruginous earth being naturally of an orange colour, a stone or earth may be judged to contain iron, if either naturally or after roasting it appears to have any shade of yellow or red.

The singular property which iron has of being attracted by the magnet, and of being the only body, exclusive of all others, that is so, likewise affords us an easy method of discovering the presence of this metal among other matters, where it often exists in such a small quantity that it could not otherwise be found out. For this purpose the body in which iron is suspected to lurk, must be pulverised and torrefied with some inflammable matter; and then the powder thus roasted being touched with a magnet, or a magnetical bar, if it contains any particles of iron they will infallibly adhere to the magnet or bar.

OF TIN ORES. Tin is never found in the earth pure and malleable, but always in a mineral state, and always mineralised by arsenic. Tin ores are not sulphureous; whence it comes that though tin be the lightest of all metals, its ores are nevertheless heavier than those of other metals, as arsenic greatly exceeds sulphur in gravity. Some tin ores contain also a little iron. The ores of tin are to be washed, roasted, and smelted with a reducing flux, according to the general rules.

OF LEAD ORES. Lead, like tin, is never found but in a mineral state. It is most commonly mineralised by sulphur; yet there are some lead ores which also contain arsenic.

Lead ores, as well as all others, must be roasted and smelted with a reducing flux; however, as it is difficult to free them from all their sulphur by torrefaction only, the reducing flux employed in their fusion may be made up with a quantity of iron filings, which being incapable of any union with lead, and having a much greater affinity than that metal with sulphur, will on this occasion be of great service by interposing between them.

OF QUICK-SILVER ORES. Running mercury is sometimes found in certain earths, or grey friable stones; but most commonly in a mineral state. It is always mineralized by sulphur alone; so that cinabar is the only ore of quick-silver that we know of; and a very rich one it is, seeing it contains six or seven times as much mercury as sulphur.

Roasting can be of no use towards decomposing the ore of mercury, and separating its sulphur; because mercury being itself very volatile would be carried off by the fire together with the sulphur. In order therefore to part the two substances of which cinabar consists, recourse must necessarily be had to some third body, which will unite with one of them, and by that means separate it from the other. Now all the metals, except gold, having a greater affinity than mercury with sulphur, such a body is easily found; any metal but gold may be employed with success in this decomposition; but as iron hath a greater affinity with sulphur than any of the rest, and is, moreover, the only one that cannot unite with mercury, it must, on account of these two qualities, be preferred to all the rest.

Fixed alkalis are also well qualified to absorb the sulphur of cinabar. Cinabar must be decompounded in close vessels, and by the way of distillation; otherwise the mercury, as soon as it separates from the sulphur, will be dissipated in vapours and entirely lost.

In this operation it is needless to add either flux or phlogiston; because the cinabar is decomposed without melting, and the mercury, though in a mineral state, contains, like gold and silver, all the phlogiston requisite to secure its metalline properties.

OF THE ORES OF REGULUS OF ANTIMONY. Regulus of antimony is always found in a mineral state; it is mineralised by sulphur; but sometimes, tho rarely, it is also combined with a little arsenic.

When the ore of regulus of antimony is to be decomposed, the first thing to be done, is to expose it to a degree of heat too weak to melt its earthy and stony parts, but strong enough to fuse its reguline together with its sulphureous parts, which by this means are separated from the earth, and united into one mass, know by the name of Antimony.

It is plain, that this first operation, which is founded on the great fusibility of antimony, produces, with regard to the ore of regulus of antimony, the same effect that washing hath on other ores; so that after this first fusion nothing more is requisite to the obtaining of a pure regulus of antimony, but to separate it from its sulphur by roasting, and to melt it with some matter abounding in phlogiston, in the same manner as other metallic matters are treated. The term calcination is generally used to express this torrefaction of antimony, by means whereof the metallic earth of the regulus of antimony is separated from its sulphur.

As regulus of antimony hath, like mercury, much less affinity with sulphur than the other metals have, jt follows that the antimony may be decomposed by the same means as cinabar; but the regulus so obtained is adulterated with a portion of the additament made use of, which combines therewith.

OF THE ORES OF BISMUTH. The ore of bismuth consists of the semi-metal mineralised by the arsenic, and of an unmetallic earth. It is very easy to decompose this ore, and to extract the bismuth it contains; for this purpose it need only be exposed to a moderate heat, whereby the arsenic will be dissipated in vapours, and the bismuth melted, which will then separate from the unmetallic earth. This earth, at least in several ores of bismuth, possesses the property of tinging all vitrifiable matters with which it is melted of a beautiful blue colour.

To decompose the ore of bismuth no flux or inflammable matter is used; because this semi-metal is possessed, even in its mineral state, of all the phlogiston requisite to maintain its metalline properties; and its great fusibility makes it unnecessary to melt the metallic earth contained in its ore.

OF THE ORES OF ZINC. Zinc is not generally obtained from a particular ore of its own; but sublimes during the fusion of a mineral, or rather a confused mass of minerals, that contains this semi-metal together with iron, copper, lead, sulphur, arsenic, and like all other ores, an unmetallic earth.

Nevertheless there is a substance which may be considered as the proper ore of zinc because it contains a pretty large quantity of that semi-metal, a little iron, and an unmetallic earth. It is called calamine, or lapis calaminaris; but hitherto the art of procuring zinc directly from this mineral hath no where been practised. Calamine is commonly employed only to convert copper into brass, or a yellow metal, by cementing it therewith. Indeed till lately no easy or practicable method of obtaining pure zinc from calamine was publicly know; for that semi-metal being volatile and very inflammable, its ore cannot be fused like others. Mr. Margraaf was the first who, by mixing powdered charcoal with calamine in close vessels, obtained a perfect zinc from it, by the means of distillation or sublimation.

OF ARSENICAL MINERALS. Arsenic, as well as sulphur, is naturally combined with almost all ores, or minerals containing metallic substances. As it is very volatile, while the matters with which it is united are fixed, at least in comparison therewith, it is easily separated by sublimation.

The minerals that contain most arsenic are the white pyrites, orpiment, and cobalt. We have already considered the white pyrites; as to orpiment, it consists of sulphur and arsenic. Both these substances being very volatile, it is difficult to separate them by sublimation; yet, with proper management, and a due regulation of the fire, this separation may be effected; because sulphur sublimes a little more easily than arsenic. But it is more convenient, as well as more expeditious, to make use of some additament that hath a greater affinity with one of those substances than with the other. Fixed alkalis and mercury, both of which have more affinity with sulphur than with arsenic, may be very properly employed on this occasion. Cobalt is a mineral composed of arsenic, an unmetallic earth, and frequently bismuth; and as none of these are very volatile, except the arsenic, this may be easily separated from the rest by sublimation. The unmetallic earth which remains has, like that of the ore of bismuth, the property of giving a blue colour to any vitrifiable matters melted with it; whence it is conjectured, that cobalt and the ore of bismuth have a great resemblance, or are often blended with each other.

Besides the minerals already recited, there is found in the bowels of the earth another species of compound body, of which we have already taken notice; but which is supposed, with some degree of probability, to belong as much to the vegetable as to the mineral kingdom; we mean the bitumens; which the best observations oblige us to consider as vegetable oils, that by lying long in the earth have contracted an union with the mineral acids, and by that means acquired the thickness, consistence, and other properties observable in them.

By distillation they yield an oil, and an acid not unlike a mineral acid. Mr. Bourdelin has even demonstated, by a very artful and ingenious process, that amber contains a manifest acid of sea-salt.

EXPLANATION OF THE TABLE OF AFFINITIES OR ELECTIVE ATTRACTIONS. We have already explained what is meant by affinities, and have laid down the principal laws to which the relations of different bodies are subject. The late Mr. Geoffroy, being convinced of the advantages which all who cultivate chemistry would receive from having constantly before their eyes a state of the best ascertained relationsbetween the chief agents in chemistry, was the first who undertook to reduce them into order, and unite them all in one point of view, by means of a table. This table will be of considerable use to such as are beginning to study chemistry, in helping them to form a just idea of the relations which different substances have with one another; and the practical chemist will thereby be enabled to account for what passes in several of his operations, otherwise difficult to be understood, as well as to judge what may be expected to result from mixtures of different compounds. These reasons have induced us to insert it at the end of this elementary treatise, and to give a short explanation of it here; especially as it will serve at the same time for a recapitulation of the whole work, in which the several axioms of this table are dispersed. See Plate LXV.

The upper line of Mr. Geoffroy's table comprehends several substances used in chemistry. Under each of those substances are ranged in distinct columns several matters compared with them, in the order of their relation to that first substance; so as that which is the nearest to it is that which hath the greatest affinity with it, or that which none of the substances standing below it can separate therefrom; but which on the contrary, separates them all when they are combined with it, and expels them in order to join itself therewith. The same is to be understood of that which occupies the second place of affinity; that is, it has the same property with regard to all below it, yielding only to that which is above it; and so of all the rest.

At the top of the first column stands the character which denotes an acid in general. Immediately under this stands the mark of a fixed alkali, being placed there as the substance which has the greatest affinity with an acid. After the fixed alkali, appears the volatile alkali, whose affinity with acids yields only to the fixed alkali. Next come the absorbent earths; and, last of all, metallic substances. Hence it follows, that when a fixed alkali is united with an acid, it cannot be separated therefrom by any other substance; that a volatile alkali united with an acid cannot be separated from it by any thing but a fixed alkali; that an absorbent earth combined with an acid may be separated from it either by a fixed or by a volatile alkali; and lastly, that any metallic substance combined with an acid, may be separated from it by a fixed alkali, a volatile alkali, or an absorbent earth.

At the head of the second column stands the character of the marine acid, which signifies that the affinities of this acid are the subject of the column. Immediately below it is placed the mark of tin. As this is a metalline substance, and as the first column places metalline substances in the lowest degree of affinity with all acids, it is plain we must suppose fixed alkalis, volatile alkalis, and absorbent earths, to be placed here in order after the marine acids and before tin. Tin, then, is of all metalline substances that which has the greatest affinity with the marine acid; and then follow regulus of antimony, copper, silver, mercury. Gold comes last of all; and there are no less than two vacant places above it. By this means it is in some sort excluded from the rank of substances that have an affinity with the marine acid. The reason thereof is, that this acid alone is not capable of dissolving gold and combining therewith, necessarily requiring for that purpose the aid of the nitrous acid, or at least of the phlogiston.

The third column exhibits the affinities of the nitrous acid, the character whereof stands at its head. Immediately below it is the sign of iron, as the metal which has the greatest affinity with this acid; and then follow other metals, each according to the degree of its relation, viz. copper, lead, mercury, and silver. In this column, as in the preceding one, we must suppose the substances, which in the first column stand above metallic substances, to be placed in their proper order before iron.

The fourth column is intended to represent the affinities of the vitriolic acid. The phlogiston stands uppermost. Below it the fixed alkalis, volatile alkalis, and absorbent earths, to shew that this is an exception to the first column. As to metalline substances, Mr. Geoffroy has set down but three, being those with which the vitriolic acid has the most perceptible affinity; these metals, placed in the order of their affinities, are iron, copper, and silver.

The fifth column shews the affinities of absorbent earths. As these earths have no sensible affinity but with acids, this column contains only the characters of the acids ranked according to the degree of their strength, or affinity with the earths, viz. the vitriolic, the nitrous, and the marine acids. Underneath this last might be placed the acid of vinegar, or the vegetable acid.

The sixth column expresses the affinities of fixed alkalis with acids, which are the same with those of absorbent earths. Moreover, we find sulphur placed here below all the acids; because liver of sulphur, which is a combination of sulphur with a fixed alkali, is actually decompounded by any acid; for any acid precipitates the sulphur and unites with the alkali.

Immediately over the sulphur, or in the same square with it, might be set a mark denoting the volatile sulphureous spirit; because, like sulphur, it has less affinity than any other acid with fixed alkalis. Oils might also be ranked with sulphur, because they unite with fixed alkalis, and therewith form soaps which are decompounded by any acid whatever.

The seventh column points out the affinities of volatile alkalis, which are likewise the same as those of absorbent earths; and the vegetable acid might be placed here also under the marine acid.

The eighth column specifies the affinities of metallic substances with acids. The affinities of the acids, which with respect to fixed alkalis, volatile alkalis, and absorbent earths, succeed each other uniformly, do not appear in the same order here. The marine acid, instead of being placed below the vitriolic and nitrous acids, stands, on the contrary, at their head; because, in fact, this acid separates metalline substances from all the other acids with which they happen to be united, and, forcing these acids to quit possession, intrudes into their place. Nevertheless, this is not a general rule; for several metalline substances must be excepted, particularly iron and copper.

The ninth column declares the affinities of sulphur. Fixed alkalis, iron, copper, lead, silver, regulus of antimony, mercury, and gold, stand below it in the order of their affinities. With regard to gold, it must be observed, that it will not unite with pure sulphur; it suffers itself to be dissolved only by the liver of sulphur, which is known to be a composition of sulphur and fixed alkali.

At the head of the tenth column appears mercury, and beneath it several metalline substances, in the order of their affinities with it. Those metalline substances are gold, silver, lead, copper, zinc, and regulus of antimony.

The eleventh column shews that lead has a greater affinity with silver than with copper.

The twelfth, that copper has a greater affinity with mercury than with calamine.

The thirteenth, that silver has a greater affinity with lead than with copper.

The fourteenth contains the affinities of iron. Regulus of antimony stands immediately underneath it, as being the metallic substance which has the greatest affinity with it. Silver, copper, and lead, are placed together in the next square below, because the degrees of affinity which those metals have with iron are not exactly determined.

The same is to be said of the fifteenth column: Regulus of antimony stands at its head; iron is immediately below the iron the same three metals occupy one square as before.

Lastly, the sixteenth column indicates that water has a greater affinity with spirit of wine than with salts. By this general expression must not be understood any saline substance whatever; but only the neutral salts, which spirit of wine frees from the water that kept them is solution. Fixed alkalis, on the contrary, as well as the mineral acids, have a greater affinity than spirit of wine with water; so that these saline substances, being well dephlegmated and mixed with spirit of wine, imbibe the water it contains and rectify it.

THE THEORY OF CONSTRUCTING THE VESSELS MOST COMMONLY USED IN CHEMISTRY. Chemists cannot perform the operations of their art without the help of a considerable number of vessels, instruments, and furnaces, adapted to contain the bodies on which they intend to work, and to apply to them the several degrees of heat required by different processes.

Vessels intended for chemical operations should be able to bear, without breaking, the sudden application of great heat and great cold; be impenetrable to every thing, and unalterable by any solvent; unvitrifiable, and capable of enduring the most violent fire without melting: But hitherto no vessels have been found with all these qualities united.

They are made of sundry materials, namely, of metal, of glass, and of earth. Metalline vessels, especially those made of iron or copper, are apt to be corroded by almost

GEOFFROY'S TABLE of the COMPARATIVE AFFINITIES observed between different substances   Plate LXV

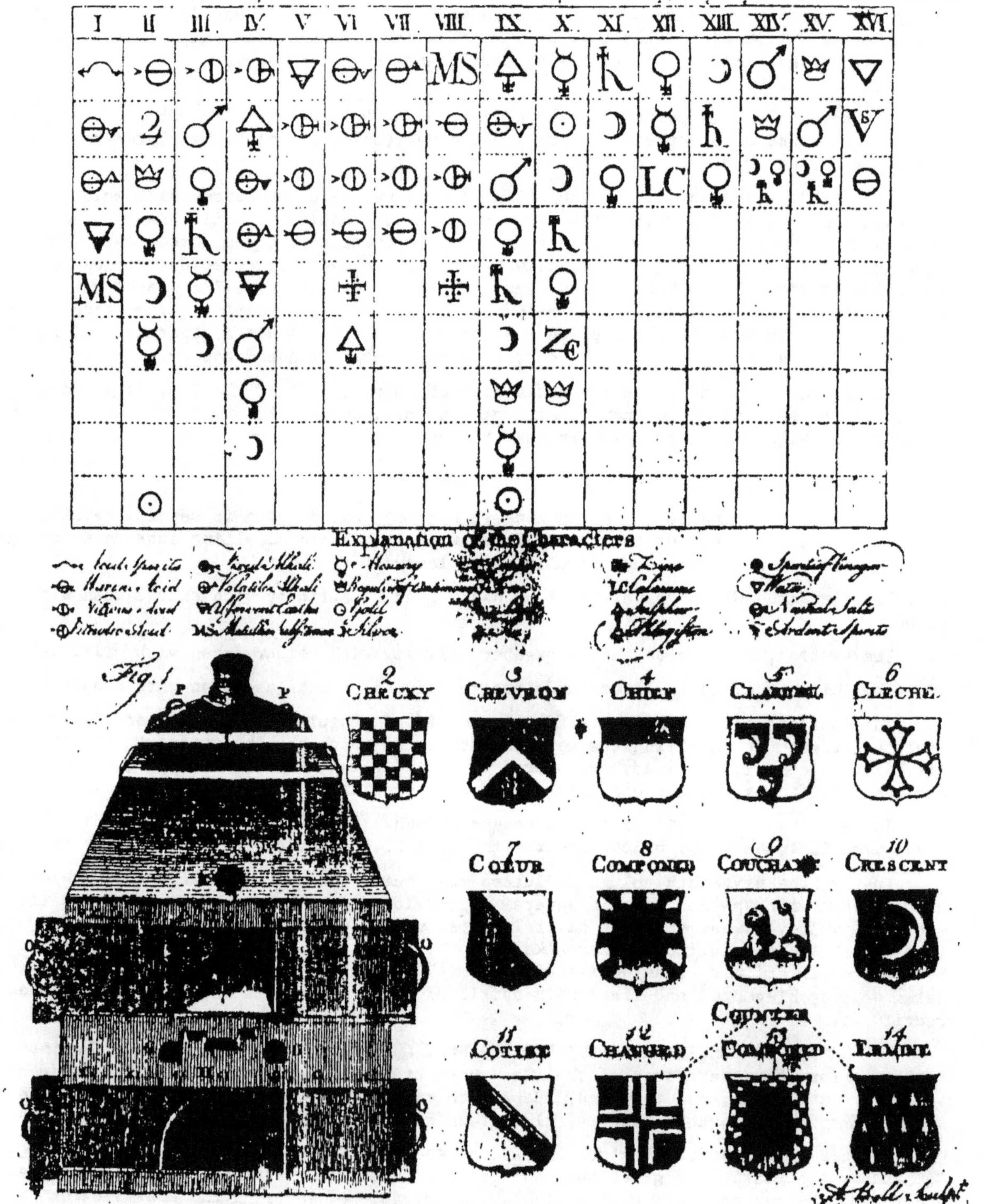

Explanation of the Characters

Fig. 1

| 2 CHECKY | 3 CHEVRON | 4 CHIEF | 5 CLARION | 6 CLECHE |

| 7 COEUR | 8 COMPONEE | 9 COUCHANT | 10 CRESCENT |

| 11 COTISE | 12 CHARGED | 13 COUNTER COMPONED | 14 ERMINE |

every saline, oily, or even aqueous substance. For this reason, in order to render the use of them a little more extensive, they are tinned on the inside. But, notwithstanding this precaution, they are on many occasions not to be trusted; and should never be employed in any nice operations which require great accuracy; they are, moreover, incapable of resisting the force of fire.

Earthen vessels are of several sorts. Some, that are made of a refractory earth, are capable of being suddenly exposed to a strong fire without breaking, and even of sustaining a great degree of heat for a considerable time: But they generally suffer the vapours of the matters which they contain, as well as vitrified metals, to pass through them; especially the glass of lead, which easily penetrates them, and runs through their pores, as through a sieve. There are others made of an earth, that, when well baked, looks as if it were half vitrified: These being much less porous are capable of retaining the vapours of the matters which they contain, and even glass of lead in fusion; which is one of the severest trials a vessel can be put to: But then they are more brittle than the other sort.

Good glass-vessels should constantly be employed in preference to all others, whenever they can possibly be used: And that not only because they are no way injured by the most active solvents, nor suffer any part of what they contain to pass through, but also because their transparency allows the chemist to observe what passes within them; which is always both curious and useful. But it is pity, that vessels of this sort should not be able to endure a fierce fire without melting.

Distillation, as hath been already said, is an operation by which we separate from a body, by the help of a gradual heat, the several principles of which it consists.

There are three methods of distilling. The first is performed by applying the heat over the body whose principles are to be extracted. In this case, as the liquors when heated and converted into vapours constantly endeavour to fly from the centre of heat, they are forced to reunite in the lower part of the vessel that contains the matter in distillation, and so passing through the pores or holes of that vessel, they fall into another cold vessel applied underneath to receive them. This way of distilling is, on this account, called distilling per descensum. It requires no other apparatus than two vessels figured like segments of hollow spheres, whereof that which is pierced with little holes, and intended to contain the matter to be distilled, ought to be much less than the other which is to contain the fire, and close its aperture exactly; the whole together being supported vertically upon a third vessel, which is to serve the purpose of a recipient, admitting into its mouth the convex bottom of the vessel containing the matter to be distilled, which must accurately fill it. This method of distilling is but little used.

The second method of distilling is performed by applying the heat underneath the matter to be decomposed. On this occasion the liquors being heated, rarefied, and converted into vapours, rise, and are condensed in a vessel contrived for that purpose, which we shall presently describe. This way of distilling is called distilling per ascensum, and is much used.

The vessel in which the distillation per ascensum is performed, we call an alembic. Plate LXIV, fig. I.

There are several sorts thereof differing from one another both in the matter of which, and the manner in which, they are made.

Those employed to draw the odoriferous waters and essential oils of plants are generally made of copper, and consist of several pieces. The first, which is designed to contain the plant, is formed nearly like a hollow cone, the vertex whereof is drawn out in the shape of a hollow cylinder or tube; This part is named the cucurbit, Plate LXIX, fig. I A; and its tube the neck of the alembic B. To the upper end of this tube another vessel is soldered: This is called the head C, and commonly has likewise the form of a cone, joined to the neck of the alembic by its base, round which on the inside is hollowed a small groove communicating with an orifice that opens at its most depending part. To this orifice is soldered a small pipe in a direction sloping downwards, which is called the nose, spout, or beak D of the alembic.

As soon as the matters contained in the alembic grow hot, vapours begin to arise from them, and ascending through the neck of the alembic into the head, are by the sides thereof stopped and condensed: From thence they trickle down in little streams to the groove, which conveys them to the spout; and by that they pass out of the alembic into a glass vessel or receiver G with a long neck, the end of the spout being introduced into that neck and luted thereto.

To facilitate the refrigeration and condensation of the vapours circulating in the head, all alembics of metal are moreover provided with another piece, which is a kind of large pan of the same metal, fitted and soldered round the head. This piece serves to keep cold water in, which incessantly cools the head, and therefore it is called the refrigeratory E. The water in the refrigeratory itself grows hot after some time, and must therefore be changed occasionally; the heated water being first drawn off by means of a cock fixed near the bottom of the refrigeratory. All copper alembics should be tinned on the inside for the reasons already given.

When saline spirits are to be distilled, alembics of metal must not be used; because the saline vapours would corrode them. In this case recourse must be had to alembics of glass. These consist of pieces only; namely, a cucurbit, whose superior orifice is admitted into, and exactly luted with its head, which is the second piece.

In general, as alembics require that the vapours of the matter to be distilled should rise to a considerable height, they ought to be used only when the most volatile principles are to be drawn from bodies: And the lighter and more volatile the substances to be separated by distillation are, the taller must the alembic be; because the most ponerous parts, being unable to rise above a certain heighth, fall back again into the cucurbit as soon as they arrive there, leaving the lighter to mount alone, whose volatility qualifies them to ascend into the head.

When a matter is to be distilled that requires a very tall alembic, and yet does not admit of a metalline vessel, the end will be best answered by a glass vessel of a round or oval shape, having a very long neck, with a small head fitted to its extremity. Such a vessel serves many purposes: It is sometimes employed as a receiver, and at other times as a digesting vessel; on which last occasion it goes under the name of a matrass, fig. 3. When one of these provided with a head, (fig. 3.C), is applied to the purpose of distilling, it forms a sort of alembic.

There are some alembics of glass, blown in such a manner by the workmen, that the body and head form but one continued piece. As these alembics do not stand in need of having their several pieces luted together, they are very useful on some occasions, when such exceeding subtile vapours rise as are capable of transpiring through lutes. The head must be open at the top, and provided with a short tube, through which by means of a funnel with a long pipe, the matter to be distilled may be introducded into the cucurbit. This is to be exactly closed with a glass stopple, the surface whereof must be made to fit the inside of the tube in every point, by rubbing those two pieces well together with emery.

Another sort of alembic hath also been invented, which may be used with advantage when cohobation is required; that is, when the liquor obtained by distillation is to be returned upon the matter in the cucurbit: and especially when it is intended that this cohobation shall be repeated a great number of times. The vessel we are speaking of is constructed exactly in the same manner as that last described; except that its beak, instead of being in a straight line as in the other alembics, forms a circular arch, and re-enters the cavity of the cucurbit, in order to convey back again the liquor collected in the head. This instrument hath commonly two beaks opposite to each other, both turned in this manner, and is called a pelican: It saves the artist the trouble of frequently unluting and reluting his vessels, as well as the loss of a great many vapours.

There are certain substances which in distillation afford matters in a concrete form, or rise wholly in the form of a very light powder, called flowers. When such substances are to be distilled, the cucurbit which contains them is covered with a head without a nose, which is named a blind-head.

When the flowers rise in great quantities and very high, a number of heads is employed to collect them; or rather a number of a kind of pots, consisting of a body only without any bottom, which fitting one into the other form a canal, that may be lengthened or shortened at pleasure, according as the flowers to be sublimed are more or less volatile. The last of the heads, which terminates the canal, is quite close at one end, and makes a true blind head. These vessels are called aludels; they are usually of earthen or stone ware.

All the vessels above mentioned are fit only for distilling such light volatile matters as can be easily raised and brought over; such as phlegm, essential oils, fragrant waters, acid oily spirits, volatile alkalis, etc. But when the point is to procure, by distillation, principles that are much less volatile, and incapable of rising high, such as the thick fetid oils, the vitriolic, the nitrous, and the marine acids, etc. we are under a necessity of having recourse to other vessels, and another manner of distilling.

It is easy to imagine, that such a vessel must be much lower than the alembic. It is indeed no more than a hollow globe, whose upper part degerates into a neck or tube, that is bent into a horizontal position; for which reason this instrument is called a retort: It is always of one single piece.

The matter to be distilled is introduced into the body of the retort by means of a ladle with a long tubular shank. Then it is set in a furnace built purposely for this use, and so that the neck of the retort coming out of the furnace may, like the nose of the alembic, stand in a sloping position, to facilitate the egress of the liquors, which by its means are conveyed to a receiver, into which it is introduced, and with which it is luted. This way of distilling, in which the vapours seem rather to be driven out of the vessel horizontally and laterally, than raised up and sublimed, is for that reason called distillation per latus.

Retorts are, of all the instruments of distillation, those that must sustain the greatest heat, and resist the strongest solvents; and therefore they must not be made of metal. Some, however, which are made of iron may do well enough on certain occasions. The rest are either of glass or earth. Those of glass, for the reasons above given, are preferable to the other sort, in all cases where they are not to be exposed to such a force of fire as may melt them. The best glass, that which stands both heat and solvents best, is that in which there are fewest alkaline salts: Of this sort is the green German glass: The beautiful white crystal glass is far from being equally serviceable.

Retorts, as well as alembics, may be of different forms. For example, some matters are apt to swell and rise over the neck of the retort in substance without suffering any decomposition; when such matters are to be distilled in a retort, it is proper that the body of the vessel, instead of being globular, be drawn out into the form of a pear, so as nearly to resemble that of a cucurbit, In a retort of this kind, the distance between the bottom and the neck being much greater than in those whose bodies are spherical, the matters contained have much more room for expansion; so that the inconvenience here mentioned is thereby prevented. Retorts of this form are called English retorts; as they hold the middle place between alembics and common retorts, they may be used to distill such matters as have a mean degree of volatility between the greatest and the least.

It is moreover proper to have in a laboratory sundry retorts with necks of different diameters. Wide necks will be found the fittest for conveying thick matters, and such as readily become fixed; for instance, some very thick fetid oils, butter of antimony, etc., for as these matters acquire a consistence as soon as they are out of the reach of a certain degree of heat, they would soon choke up a narrow neck, and by stopping the vapours, which rise at the same time from the retort, might occasion the bursting of the vessels.

Some retorts are also made with an opening on their upper side, like that of tubulated glass alembics, which is to be closed in the same manner with a glass stopple. These retorts are also called tubulated retorts, and ought always to be used whenever it is necessary to introduce fresh matter into the retort during the operation; seeing it may be done by means of this invention, without unluting and reluting the vessels; which ought always to be avoided as much as possible.

One of the things that most perplexes the chemists is, the prodigious elasticity of many different vapours, which are frequently discharged with impetuosity during the distillation, and are even capable of bursting the vessels with explosion, and with danger to the artist. On such occasions it is absolutely necessary to give these vapours vent, as we shall direct in its proper place: But as that can never be done without losing a great many of them; as some of them in particular are so elastic, that scarce any at all would remain in the vessel; for instance, those of the spirit of nitre, and especially those of the smoking spirit of salt; the practice is to make use of very large receivers, of about eighteen or twenty inches diameter, that the vapours may have sufficient room to circulate in, and, by applying to the wide surface presented them by the extensive inside of such a large vessel, may be condensed into drops. These huge receivers are commonly in the form of hollow globes, and are called ballons.

To give these vapours still more room, ballons have been contrived with two open gullets in each, diametrically opposite to one another; whereof one admits the neck of the retort, and the other is received by one of the gullets of a second ballon of the same form, which is joined in like manner to a third, and so on. By this artifice the space may be enlarged at pleasure. These ballons with two necks are called adopters.

Operations on bodies that are absolutely fixed, as metals, stones, sand, etc. require only such vessels as are capable of containing those bodies and resisting the force of fire. These vessels are little hollow pots, of different dimensions, which are called crucibles. Crucibles can hardly be made of any thing but earth; they ought to have a cover of the same material fitted to shut them close. The best earth we know is that whereof those pots are made in which butter is brought from Bretagne; These pots themselves are exceedingly good crucibles; and they are almost the only ones that are capable of holding glass of lead in fusion, without being penetrated by it.

For the roasting of ores, that is, freeing them by the help of fire from their sulphureous and arsenical parts, little cups made of the same material with crucibles are used; but they are made flat, shallow, and wider above than below, that these volatile matters may the more freely exhale. These vessels are called tests, or scorifiers: They are scarce used but in the docimastic art, that is, in making small assays of ores.

THE THEORY OF CONSTRUCTING THE FURNACES MOST COMMONLY USED IN CHEMISTRY. Skill in conducting and applying fire properly, and determining its different degrees, is of very great consequence to the success of chemical operations.

As it is exceeding difficult to govern and moderate the action of fire, when the vessels in which any operation is performed are immediately exposed to it, chemists have contrived to convey heat to their vessels, in nice operations, through different mediums, which they place occasionly between those vessels and the fire.

Those intermediate substances in which they plunge their vessels are called baths. They are either fluid or solid: The fluid baths are water, or its vapours. When the distilling vessel is set in water, the bath is called balneum maria, or the water bath; and the greatest degree of heat of which it is susceptible is that of boiling water. When the vessel is exposed only to the vapours which exhale from water, this forms the vapour bath; the heat of which is nearly the same with that of the balneum maria. These baths are useful for distilling essential oils, ardent spirits, sweet-scented waters; in a word, all such substances as cannot bear a greater heat without prejudice either to their odour, or to some of their other qualities.

Baths may also be made of any other fluids, such as oils, mercury, etc. which are capable of receiving and communicating much more heat; but they are very seldom used. When a more considerable degree of heat is required, a bath is prepared of any solid matter reduced to a fine powder, such as sand, ashes, filings of iron, etc. The heat of these baths may be pushed so far as to make the bottom of the vessel become faintly red. By plunging a thermometer into the bath, by the side of the vessel, it is easy to observe the precise degree of heat applied to the substance on which you are working. It is necessary that the thermometers employed on this occasion be constructed on good principles, and so contrived as to be easily compared with those of the most celebrated natural philosophers.

Those of the illustrious Reaumur are most used and best known, so that it would not be amiss to give them the preference. When a greater heat is required than any of those baths can give, the vessels must be set immediately on live coals, or in a flaming fire; this is called working with a naked fire; and in this case it is much more difficult than in the other to determine the degrees of heat.

There are several ways of applying a naked fire. When the heat or flame is reflected upon the upper part of the vessel which is exposed to the fire, this is called reverberated heat. A melting heat is that which is strong enough to fuse most bodies. A forging heat is that of a fire which is forcibly excited by the constant blast of a pair of bellows, or more.

There is also another sort of fire which serves very commodiously for many operations, because it does not require to be fed or frequently mended: This is afforded by a lamp with one or more wicks, and may be called a lamp-heat. It is scarce ever employed but to heat baths, in operations which require a gentle and long continued warmth; if it hath any fault, it is that of growing gradually hotter.

All these different ways of applying fire require furnaces of different constructions: We shall therefore describe such as are of principal and most necessary use.

Furnaces must be divided into different parts or stories, each of which has its particular use and name.

The lower part of the furnace designed for receiving the ashes, and giving passage to the air, is called the ash hole. The ash-hole is terminated above by a grate, the use of which is to support the coals and wood, which are to be burnt thereon: This part is called the fire-place. The fire-place is in like manner terminated above by several iron bars, which lie quite across it from right to left, in lines paralled to each other: The use of these bars is to sustain the vessels in which the operations are to be performed. The space above these bars to the top of the furnace is the upper story, and may be called the laboratory of the furnace. Lastly, some furnaces are quite covered above, by means of a kind of vaulted roof called the dome.

Furnaces have moreover several apertures; on of these is at the ash-hole, which gives passage to the air, and through which the ashes that fall through the grate are raked out; this aperture is called the ash-hole door; another is at the fire-place, through which the fire is supplied with fuel, as occasion requires; this is called the mouth or door of the fire-place, or the stoke-hole; there is a third in the upper story, through which the neck of the vessel passes; and a fourth in the dome, for carrying off the fuliginosities of combustible matters, which is called the chimney.

To conclude, there are several other openings in the several parts of the furnace, the use whereof is to admit the air into those places, and also, as they can be easily shut, to incite or slacken the activity of the fire, and so to regulate it; which has procured them the title of registers. All the other openings of the furnace should be made to shut very close, the better to assist in governing the fire; by which means they likewise do the office of registers.

In order to our forming a just and general idea of the construction of furnaces, and of the disposition of the several apertures in them, with a view to increase or diminish the activity of the fire, it will be proper to lay down, as our ground work, certain principles of natural philosophy, the truth of which is demonstrated by experience.

And first, every body knows that combustible matters will not burn or consume unless they have a free communication with the air; insomuch that if they be deprived thereof, even when burning most rapidly, they will be extinguished at once; that consequently combustion is greatly promoted by the frequent accession of fresh air; and that a stream of air, directed so as to pass with impetuosity through burning fuel, excites the fire to the greatest possible activity.

Secondly, It is certain that the air which touches or comes near ignited bodies is heated, rarefied, and rendered lighter than the air about it; that is, further distant from the centre of heat; and consequently that this air so heated and become lighter is necessarily determined thereby to ascend and mount aloft, in order to make room for that which is less heated and not so light, which by its weight and elasticity tends to occupy the place quitted by the other. Another consequence hereof is, that if fire be kindled in a place inclosed every where but above and below, a current of air will be formed in that place, running in a direction from the bottom to the top; so that if any light bodies be applied to the opening below, they will be carried up towards the fire; but, on the contrary, if they be held at the opening above, they will be impelled by a force which will drive them up and carry them away from the fire.

Thirdly, and lastly, it is a truth demonstrated in hydraulics, that the velocity of a given quantity of any fluid, determined to flow in any direction whatever, is so much the greater, the narrower the channel is to which that fluid is confined; and consequently that the velocity of a fluid will be increased by making it run from a wider through a narrower passage.

These principles being established, it is easy to apply them to the construction of furnaces. First, if a fire be kindled in the fire-place of a furnace, which is open on all sides, it burns nearly as if it were in the open air. It has with the surrounding air a free communication; so that fresh air is continually admitted to facilitate the entire combustion of the inflammable matters employed as fuel. But there being nothing to determine that air to pass with rapidity through the fire in this case, it does not at all augment the activity thereof, but suffers it to waste away quietly.

Secondly, If the ash-hole or dome of a furnace in which a fire is burning be shut quite close, then there is no longer any free communication between the air and the fire; if the ash-hole be shut, the air is debarred from having free access to the fire; if the dome be stopt, the egress of the air rarefied by the fire is prevented; and consequently the fire must in either case burn very faintly and slowly, gradually die away, and at last go quite out.

Thirdly, If all the openings of the furnaces be wholly closed, it is evident that the fire will be very quickly extinguished.

Fourthly, If only the lateral openings of the fire-place be shut, leaving the ash-hole and upper part of the furnace open; it is plain that the air entering by the ash-hole will necessarily be determined to go out at top, and that consequently a current of air will be formed, which will pass through the fire, and make it burn briskly and vigorously.

Fifthly, If both the ash-hole and the upper story of the furnace be of some length, and form canals either cylindric or prismatic, then the air being kept in the same direction through a longer space, the course of its stream will be both stronger and better determined, and consequently the fire will be more animated by it.

Sixthly, and lastly, if the ash-hole and the upper part of the furnace, instead of being cylindric or prismatic canals, have the form of truncated cones or pyramids, standing on their bases, and so ordered that the upper opening of the ash-hole adjoining to the fire-place may be wider than the base of the superior cone or pyramid; then the stream of air, being forced to pass incessantly from a larger channel through a smaller, must be considerably accelerated, and procure to the fire the greatest activity which it can receive from the make of a furnace.

The materials fittest for building furnaces are, 1. Bricks, joined together with potters clay mixed with sand, and moistened with water. 2. Potters clay mingled with potsherds, moistened with water, and baked in a violent fire. 3. Iron; of which all furnaces may be made; with this precaution, that the inside be provided with a great many prominent points, as fastenings for a coat of earth, with which the internal parts of the furnace must necessarily be covered to defend it from the action of the fire.

The reverberating furnace is one of those that are most employed in chemistry; it is proper for distillations by the retort, and should be constructed in the following manner.

First. The use of the ash-hole being, as was said, to give passage to the air, and to receive the ashes, no bad consequence can attend its being made pretty high: It may have from twelve to twenty or twenty-four inches in heighth. Its aperture should be wide enough to admit billets of wood when a great fire is to be made.

Secondly. The ash-hole must be terminated at its upper part by an iron grate, the bars of which should be very substantial, that they may resist the action of the fire: this grate is the bottom of the fire-place, and destined to support the coals. In the lateral part of the fire-place, and nearly about the same height with the grate, there should be a hole of such a size that it may easily admit charcoal, as well as little tongs and shovels for managing the fire. This aperture or mouth of the fire-place should be perpendicularly over the mouth of the ash-hole.

Thirdly, from six to eight or ten inches high above the grate, over the ash-hole, little apertures must be made in the walls of the furnace, of eight or ten lines in diameter, an inch from one another, and those in one side must be diametrically opposite to those in the other. The use of these holes is to receive bars of iron for the retort to rest on; which should be, as was said, at different heights, in order to accommodate retorts of different sizes. At the upper extremity of this part of the furnace, which reaches from the iron bars to the top, the heighth whereof should be somewhat less than the width of the furnace, must be cut a semi-circular aperture for the neck of the retort to come through. This hole must by no means be over the doors of the fire-place and ash-hole; for then, as it gives passage to the neck of the retort, it must of course be opposite to the receiver, and in that case the receiver itself would stand over against those two apertures; which would be attended with this double inconvenience, that the receiver would not only grow very hot, but greatly embarrass the operator, whose free access to the fire-place and ash-hole would be thereby obstructed. It is proper therefore, that the semi-circular cut we are speaking of be so placed, that, when the greatest ballons are luted to the retort, they may leave an open passage to the fire-place or ash-hole.

Fourthly, in order cover in the laboratory of the reverberating furnace, thre must be a roof made for it in the form of a cupola, or concave hemisphere, having the same diameter as the furnace. This dome should have a semi-circular cut in its rim answering to that above-directed to be made in the upper extremity of the furnace, so that, when adjusted to each other, the two together may form a circular hole for the neck of the retort to pass through. At the top of this dome there must also be a circular hole of three or four inches diameter, carrying a short tapering funnel of the same diameter, and three inches high, which will serve for a chimney to carry off all fuliginosities, and accerlerate the current of the air. This passage may be shut at pleasure with a flat cover. Moreover, as it is necessary that the dome should be taken off and put on with ease, it should have two ears or handles for that purpose; a portative or moveable furnace should also have a pair of handles fixed opposite to each other between the ash-hole and the fire-place.

Sixthly and lastly, a conical canal must be provided of about three foot long, and sufficiently wide at it lower end to admit the funnel of the aperture at the top of the dome. This conical tube is to be applied to the dome when the fire is required to be extremely active; it tapers gradually from its base upwards, and breaks off as if truncated at top, where it should be about two inches wide.

Besides the apertures already mentioned as necessary to a reverberating furnace, there must also be many other smaller holes made in its ash-hole, fire-place, laboratory, and dome, which must all be so contrived as to be easily opened and shut with stopples of earth; these holes are the registers of the furnace, and serve to regulate the activity of the fire according to the principles before laid down.

When the action of the fire is required to be exactly uniform and very brisk, it is necessary to stop carefully with moist earth all the little chinks in the juncture of the dome with the furnace, between the neck of the retort and the circular hole through which it passes, and which it never fills exactly, and lastly the holes which receive the iron bars that sustain the retort.

It is proper to have in a laboratory several reverberating furnaces of different magnitudes; because they must be proportioned to the size of the retorts employed. The retort ought to fill the furnace, so as to leave only the distance of an inch between it and the inside of the furnace.

Yet when the retort is to be exposed to a most violent fire, and especially when it is required that the heat shall act with equal force on all parts of the furnace, and as strongly on its vault as on its bottom, a greater distance must be left between the retort and the inside of the furnace; for then the furnace may be filled with coals, even to the upper part of the dome. If moreover some pieces of wood be put into the ash-hole, the conical canal fitted on to the funnel of the dome, and all the apertures of the furnace exactly closed, except the ash-hole and the chimney, the greatest heat will then be excited that this furnace can produce.

The furnace now described may also be employed in many other chemical operations. If the dome be laid aside, an alembic may very well be placed therein; but then the space, which will be left between the body of the alembic and the top of the upper part of the furnace, must be carefully filled up with Windsor-loam moistened; for without that precaution the heat would soon reach the very head, which ought to be kept as cool as possible, in order to promote the condensation of the vapours.

On this occasion therefore it will be proper to leave no holes open in the fire-place, but the lateral ones; of which also those over against the receiver must be stoppled.

A pot or broad-brimmed earthen pan may be placed over this furnace, and being so fitted to it as to close the upper part thereof accurately, and filled with sand, may serve for a sand-heat to distill with.

The bars designed to support distilling vessels being taken out, a crucible may stand therein, and many operations be performed that do not require the utmost violence of fire. In a word, this furnace is one of the most commodious that can be, and more extensively useful than any other.

The melting furnace is designed for applying the greatest force of heat to the most fixed bodies, such as metals and earths. It is never employed in distilling; it is of no use but for calcination and fusion; and consequently need not admit any vessels but crucibles.

The ash-hole of this furnace differs from that of the reverberating furnace only in this, that it must be higher, in order to raise the fire-place to a level with the artist's hand; because in that all the operations of this furnace are performed. The ash-hole therefore must be about three foot high; and this height procures it moreover the advantage of a good draught of air. For the same reason, and in consequence of the principles we laid down, it should be so built that its width lessening insensibly from the bottom to the top, it may be narrower where it opens into the fire-place than anywhere below.

The ash-hole is terminated at its upper end, like that of the reverberating furnace, by a grate which serves for the bottom of the fire-place, and ought to be very substantial that it may resist the violence of the fire. The inside of this furnace is commonly an elliptic curve; because it is demonstrated by mathematicians, that surfaces having that curvature reflect the rays of the sun, or of fire, in such a manner, that, meeting in a point or a line, they produce there a violent heat. But to answer this purpose, those surfaces must be finely polished; an advantage hardly procureable to the internal surface of this furnace, which can be made of nothing but earth; besides, if it were possible to give it a polish, the violent action of the fire that must be employed in this furnace would presently destroy it. Yet the elliptical figure must not be entirely disregarded; for, if care be taken to keep the internal surface of the furnace as smooth as possible, it will certainly reflect the heat pretty strongly, and collect it about the center.

The fire-place of this furnace ought to have but four apertures.

First that of the lower grate, which communicates with the ash-hole.

Secondly, a door in it fore-side, through which may be introduced coals, crucibles, and tongs for managing them; this aperture should be made to shut exactly with a plate of iron, having its inside coated with earth, and turning on two hinges fixed to the furnace.

Thirdly, over this door a hole slanting downwards towards the place where the crucible is to stand. The use of this hole is to give the operator an opportunity of examing the condition of the matters contained in his crucible, without opening the door of the fire-place; this hole should be made to open and shut easily, by means of a stopple of earth.

Fourthly, a circular aperture of about three inches wide in the upper part or vault of the furnace, which should gradually lessen and terminate, like that of the dome of the reverberating furnace, in a short conical funnel of about three inches long, and fitted to enter the conical pipe before described, which is applied when the activity of the fire is to be increased.

When this furnace is to be used, and a crucible to be placed in it, care must be taken to set on the grate a cake of baked earth somewhat broader than the foot of the crucible. The use of this stand is to support the crucible, and raise it above the grate, for which purpose it should be two inches thick. Were it not for this precaution, the bottom of the crucible, which would stand immediately on the grate, could never be thoroughly heated, because it would be always exposed to the stream of cold air which enters by the ash-hole. Care should also be taken to heat this earthen bottom red-hot before it be placed in the furnace, in order to free it from any humidity, which might otherwise happen to be driven against the crucible during the operation, and occasion its breaking.

We omitted to take notice, in speaking of the ash-hole, that, besides its door, it should have about the middle of its height a small hole, capable of receiving the nosel of a good perpetual bellows, which is to be introduced into it and worked, after the door is exactly shut, when it is thought proper to excite the activity of the fire to the utmost violence.

The forge is only a mass of bricks of about three foot high, along whose upper surface is directed the nose or pipe of a pair of large perpetual bellows, so placed that the operator may easily blow the fire with one hand. The coals are laid on the hearth of the forge near the nose of the bellows; they are confined, if necessary, to prevent their being carried away by the wind of the bellows, within a space knclosed by bricks; and then by pulling the bellows in fire is continually kept up in its greatest activity. The forge is of use when there is occasion to apply a great degree of heat suddenly to any substance, or when it is necessary that the operator be at liberty to handle frequently the matters which he proposes to fuse or calcine.

The cupelling furnace is that in which gold and silver are purified, by the means of lead, from all alloy of other metallic substances. This furnace must give a heat strong enough to vitrify lead, and therewith all the alloy which the perfect metals may contain. This furnace is to be built in the following manner.

First, of thick iron-plates, or of some such composition of earth as we recommended for the construction of furnaces, must be formed a hollow quadrangular prism, whose sides may be about a foot broad, and from ten to eleven inches high; and extending from thence upwards may converge towards the top, so as to form a pyramid truncated at the height of seven or eight inches, and terminated by an aperture of the width of seven or eight inches every way. The lower part of the prism is terminated and closed by a plate of the same materials of which the furnace is constructed.

Secondly, in the fore-side or front of this prism there is an opening of three or four inches in height by five or six inches in breadth; this opening, which should be very near the bottom, is the door of the ash-hole. Immediately over this opening is placed an iron grate, the bars of which are quadrangular prisms of half an inch square, laid parallel to each other, and about eight or nine inches asunder, and so disposed that two of their angles are laterally opposite, the two others looking one directly upwards, and the other downwards. As in this situation the bars of the grate present to the fire-place very oblique surfaces, the ashes and very small coals do not accumulate between them, or hinder the free entrance of the air from the ash-hole. This grate terminates the ash-hole at its upper part, and serves for the bottom of the fire-place.

Thirdly, three knches, or three and a half, above the grate, there is in the fore-side of the furnace another opening terminated by an arch for its upper part, which consequently has the figure of a semi-circle; it ought to be four inches wide at bottom, and three inches and an half high at its middle. This opening is the door of the fire-place; yet it is not intended for the same uses as the door of the fire-place in other furnaces; the purpose for which it is actually destined shall be explained when we come to shew how the furnace is to be used. An inch above the door of the fire-place, still in the foreside of the furnace, are two holes of about an inch diameter, and at the distance of three inches and a half from each other, to which answer two other holes of the same size, made in the hinder part, directly opposite to these. There is, moreover, a fifth hole of the same width about an inch above the door of the fire-place. The design of all these holes shall be explained when we describe the manner in which these furnaces are to be used.

Fourthly, the fore-part of the furnace is bound by three iron braces, one of which is fixed just below the door of the ash-hole; the second occupies the whole space between the ash-hole door and the door of the fire-place, and has two holes in it, answering to those which we directed to be made in the furnace itself about this place; and the third is placed immediately over the door of the fire-place. These braces must extend from one corner of the front of the furnace to the other, and be fastened thereto with iron pins, in such a manner that their sides next to the doors may not lie quite close to the body of the furnace, but form a kind of grooves for the iron plates to slide in, that are designed to shut the two doors of the furnace when it is necessary. Each of these iron plates should have a handle, by which it may be conveniently moved; and to each door there should be two plates, which meeting each other, and joining exactly in the middle of the door-place, may shut it very close. Each of the two plates belonging to the door of the fire-place ought to have a hole in its upper part; one of these holes should be a slit of about two lines wide, and half an inch long; the other may be a semi-circular opening of one inch in height and two in breadth. These holes should be placed so that neither of them may open into the fire-place when the two plates are joined together in the middle of the door to shut it close.

Fifthly, to terminate the furnace above, there must be a pyramid, formed of the same materials with the furnace, hollow, quadrangular, three inches high, on a base of seven inches, which base must exactly fit the upper opening of the furnace; the top of this pyramidal cover must end in a tube of three inches in diameter and two in height, which must be almost cylindrical, and yet a little inclining to the conical form. This tube serves, as in the furnaces already described, to carry the conical funnel, which is fitted to the upper part when a fire of extraordinary activity is wanted.

The furnace thus constructed is fit to serve all the purposes for which it is designed; yet, before it can be used, another piece must be provided, which, though it does not properly belong to the furnace, is nevertheless necessary in all the operations performed by it; and that is a piece contrived to contain the cupels, or other vessels which are to be exposed to the fire in this furnace. It is called a muffle, and is made in the following manner.

On an oblong square, of four inches in breadth, and six or seven in length, a concave semi-cylinder is erected, in the form of a vault, which makes a semi-circular canal, open at both ends. One of these is almost entirely closed, except that near the bottom two small semi-circular holes are left. In each of its sides likewise two such holes are made, and the other end is left quite open.

The muffle is intended to bear and communicate the fiercest heat; and therefore it must be made thin, and of an earth that will resist the violence of fire, such as that of which crucibles are made. The muffle being thus constructed, and then well baked, is fit for use.

When it is to be used, it must be put into the furnace by the upper opening, and set upon two iron bars, introduced through the holes made for that purpose below the door of the fire-place. The muffle must be placed on these bars in the fire place, in such a manner that its open end shall stand next to and directly against the door of the fire-place, and may be joined to it with lute. Then the cupels are ranged in it, and the furnace is filled up, to the height of two or three inches above the muffle, with small coals not bigger than a walnut, to the end that they may lie close round the muffle, and procure it an equal heat on every side. The chief use of the muffle is to prevent the coals and ashes from falling into the cupels, which would be very prejudicial to the operations carrying on in them; for the lead would not vitrify as it ought, because the immediate contact of the coals would continually restore its phlogiston; or else the glass of lead, which ought to penetrate and pass through the cupels, would be rendered incapable of so doing; because the ashes mixing therewith would give it such a consistence and tenacity as would destroy that property, or at least considerably lessen it. The openings, therefore, which are left in the lower part of the muffle, should not be so high as to admit coals or ashes to get into the cupels; the use of them is to procure an easier passage for the heat and the air to those vessels. The muffle is left quite open in its fore-part, that the operator may be at liberty to examine what passes in the cupels, to stir their contents, to remove them from one place to another, to convey new matters into them, etc. and also to promote the free access of the air, which must concur with the fire towards the evaporation necessary to the vitrification of lead; which air, if fresh were not often enough admitted, would be incapable of producing that effect; because it would soon be loaded with such a quantity of vapours that it could not take up any more.

The government of the fire in this furnace is founded on the general principles above laid down for all furnaces. Yet as there are some little differences, and as it is very essential to the success of the operations for which this furnace is intended, that the artist should be absolutely master of his degree of heat, we shall in a few words shew how that may be raised or lowered.

When the furnace is filled with coals and kindled, if the door of the ash-hole be set wide open, and that of the fire place shut very close, the force of the fire is increased; and if, moreover, the pyramidal cover be put on the top, the conical funnel added to it, the fire will become still more fierce.

Seeing the matters contained in this furnace are encompassed with fire on all sides, except in the forepart opposite to the door of the fire place, and as there are occasions which require that the force of the fire should be applied to this part also, an iron box, of the shape and size of the door, hath been contrived to answer that purpose. This box is filled with lighted coals, and applied immediately to the door-place, by which means the heat there is considerably augmented. This help may be made use of at the beginning of the operation, in order to accelerate it, and bring the heat sooner to the desired degree; or in case of a very fierce heat be required; or at a time when the air being hot and moist will not make the fire burn with the necessary vigour.

The heat may be lessened, by removing the iron box, and shutting the door of the fire-place quite close. It may be still further and gradually diminished, by taking off the conical funnel from the top; by shutting the door of the fire-place with one of its plates only, that which has the least, or that which has the greatest aperture in it; by taking off the pyramidal cover; by shutting the ash-hole door wholly or in part; and lastly, by setting the door of the fire-place wide open; but, in this last case, the cold air penetrates into the cavity of the muffle, and refrigerates the cupels more than is almost ever necessary. If it be observed, during the operation, that the muffle grows cold in any particular part, it is a sign there is a vacuity left by the coals in that place; in this case an iron wire must be thrust into the furnace, through the hole which is over the door of the fire-place, and the coals stirred therewith, so as to make them fall into their places and fill up the vacant interstices.

It is proper to observe, that, besides what has been said concerning the ways of increasing the activity of the fire in the cupelling furnace, several other causes also may concur to procure to the matters contained in the muffle a greater degree of heat; for example, the smaller the muffle is, the wider and more numerous the holes in it are; the nearer to its bottom, or further end, the cupels are placed, the more will the matters therein contained be affected with heat.

Besides the operations to be performed by the cupel, this furnace is very useful, and even necessary, for many chemical experiments; such, for instance, as those relating to sundry vitrifications and enamelling. As it is pretty low, the best way is to place it, when it is to be used, on a base of brick-work that may raise it to a level with the operator's hand.

A lamp-furnace is exceedkng useful for all operations that require only a moderate, but long continued degree of heat. The furnace for working with a lamp heat is very simple; it consists only of a hollow cylinder, from fifteen to eighteen inches high, and five or six in diameter, having at its bottom an aperture large enough for a lamp to be introduced and withdrawn with ease. The lamp must have three or four wicks, to the end that by lighting more or fewer of them a greater or less degree of heat may be produced. The body of the furnace must moreover have several small holes in it, in order to supply the flame of the lamp with air enough to keep it alive.

On the top of this furnace stands a bason five or six inches deep, which ought to fill the cavity of the cylinder exactly, and to be supported at its circumerence by a rim which may entirely cover and close the furnace: The use of this bason is to contain the sand through which the lamp heat is usually conveyed.

Besides this, there must be a kind of cover or dome made of the same material with the furnace, and of the same diameter with the sand-bath, without any other opening than a hole, nearly circular, cut in its lower extremity. This dome is a sort of reverberatory, which serves to confine the heat and direct it towards the body of the retort; for it is used only when something is to be distilled in a vessel of this fashion; and then the hole at its bottom serves for a passage to the neck of the retort. This dome should have an ear or handle, for the conveniency of putting it on and taking it off with ease.

OF LUTES. Chemical vessels, especially such as are made of glass, and the earthen vessels commonly called stoneware, are very subject to break when exposed to sudden heat or cold; whence it comes that they often crack when they begin to heat, and also when being very hot they happen to be cooled, either by fresh coals thrown into the furnace, or by the access of cold air. There is no way to prevent the former of these accidents, but by taking the pains to warm your vessel very slowly, and by almost insensible degrees. The second may be avoided by coating the body of the vessel with a paste or lute, which being dried will defend it against the attacks of cold.

The fittest stuff for coating vessels is a composition of fat earth, Windsor-loam, fine sand, filings of iron, or powdered glass, and chopped cow's hair, mixed and made into a paste with water. This lute serves also to defend glass vessels against the violence of the fire, and to prevent their melting easily.

In almost all distillations it is of great consequence, as hath been said, that the neck of the distilling vessel be exactly joined with that of the receiver into which it is introduced, in order to prevent the vapours from escaping into the air and so being lost; And this junction is effected by means of a lute.

A few slips of paper, applied round the neck of the vessels with common size, will be sufficient to keep in such vapours as are aqueous, or not very spirituous.

If the vapours are more acrid and more spirituous, recourse may be had to slips of bladder long steeped in water, which, containing a sort of natural glue, close the junctures of the vessels very well.

If it be required to confine vapours of a still more penetrating nature, it will be proper to employ a lute that quickly grows very hard; particularly a paste made with quick-lime and any sort of jelly, whether vegetable or animal; such as the white of an egg, stiff size, etc. This is an excellent lute, and not easily penetrated. It is also used to stop any cracks or fractures that happen to glass vessels. But it is not capable of resisting the vapours of mineral acid spirits, especially when they are strong and smoking: For that purpose it is necessary to incorporate the other ingredients thoroughly with fat earth softened with water; and even then it frequently happens that this lute is penetrated by acid vapours, especially those of the spirit of salt, which of all others are confined with the greatest difficulty.

In such cases its place may be supplied with another, which is called fat lute, because it is actually worked up with fat liquors. This lute is composed of a very fine cretaceous earth, called tobacco-pipe clay, moistened with equal parts of the drying oil of lint-seed, and a varnish made of amber and gum copal. It must have the consistence of a stiff paste. When the joints of the vessels are closed up with this lute, they may, for greater security, be covered over with slips of linen smeared with the lute made of quick-lime and the white of an egg.

Chemical vessels are liable to be broken in an operation by other causes besides the sudden application of heat or cold. It frequently happens that the vapours of the matters, exposed to the action of fire, rush out with such impetuosity, and are so elastic, that finding no passage through the lute with which the joints of the vessels are closed, they burst the vessels themselves, sometimes with explosion and danger to the operator.

To prevent this inconvenience, it is necessary, that in every receiver there be a small hole, which being stopped only with a little lute may easily be opened and shut again as occasion requires. It serves for a vent-hole to let out the vapours when the receiver begins to be too much crowded with them. Nothing but practice can teach the artist when it is requisite to open this vent. If he hits the proper time, the vapours commonly rush out with rapidity, and a considerable hissing noise; and the vent should be stopped again as soon as the hissing begins to grow faint. The lute employed to stop this small hole ought always to be kept so ductile, that by taking the figure of the hole exactly it may entire stop it. Besides, if it should harden upon the glass, it would stick so fast, that it would be very difficult to remove it without breaking the vessel. This danger is easily avoided by making use of the fat lute, which continues pliant for a long time, when it is not exposed to an excessive heat.

This way of stopping the vent-hole of the receiver has yet another advantage: For if the hole be of a proper width, as a line and half, or two lines, in diameter, then when the vapours are accumulated in too great a quantity, and begin to make a great effort against the sides of the receiver, they push up the stopple, force it out, and make their way through the vent-hole: So that by this means the breaking of the vessels may always be certainly prevented. But great care must be taken that the vapours be not suffered to escape in this manner, except when absolute necessity requires it; for it is generally the very strongest and most subtile part of a liquor which is thus dissipated and lost.

Heat being the chief cause that puts the elasticity of the vapours in action, and prevents their condensing into a liquor, it is of great consequence in distillation that the receiver be kept as cool as possible. With this view a thick plank should be placed between the receiver and the body of the furnace, to intercept the heat of the latter, and prevent its reaching the former. As the vapours themselves rise very hot from the distilling vessel, they soon communicate their heat to the receiver, and especially to its upper part, against which they strike first. For this reason it is proper, that linen cloths dipt in very cold water be laid over the receiver, and frequently shifted. By this means the vapours will be considerably cooled, their elasticity weakened, and their condensation promoted.

By what hath been said in this first part, concerning the properties of the principal agents in chemistry, the construction of the most necessary vessels and furnaces, and the manner of using them, we are sufficiently prepared for proceeding directly to the operations, without being obliged to make frequent and long stops, in order to give the necessary explanations on those heads.

Nevertheless, we shall take every proper occasion to extend the theory here laid down, and to improve it by the addition of several particulars, which will find their places in our treatise of chemical operations.

EXPLANATION OF PLATE LXIV.

Fig. 1. A COPPER ALEMBIC. A, The cucurbit or body. B, the neck. C, the head. D, The beak, nose, or spout. E, The refrigeratory, or cooler. F, Its cock. G, The receiver.

Fig. 2. A GLASS ALEMBIC. A, The cucurbit. B, The head. C, The gutter within the head. D, The beak.

Fig. 3. A LONG NECKED GLASS ALEMBIC. A, The body of the matrass. B, The neck. C, The head.

Fig. 4. A GLASS ALEMBIC OF ONE PIECE. A, The cucurbit. B, The head. C, The aperture in the head. D, Its stopple. E, The mouth of the cucurbit.

Fig. 5. A PELICAN. A, The cucurbit. B, The head. C, The aperture in the head, with its stopple. D D, The two curved spouts.

Fig. 6. A ROW OF ALUDELS.

Fig. 7. A RETORT. A, Its bowl. B, Its neck.

Fig. 8. AN ENGLISH RETORT.

Fig. 9. A REVERBERATING FURNACE. A, The ash-hole door. B, The fire-place door. C C C C, Registers. D, The dome, or reverberatory. E, The conical funnel. F, The retort in the furnace. G, The receiver. H H, Iron bars to sustain the retort.

Fig. 10. THE CONICAL FURNACE BY ITSELF.

Fig. 11. BACK VIEW OF A MUFFLE. A, The bottom of the muffle. B, Its arch. C C C, Lateral apertures.

Fig. 12. FORE-VIEW OF A MUFFLE.

Fig. 13. A MELTING FURNACE. A A, The base of the furnace. B, The ash-hole. C D, The grate for the fire. E, The fire-place. F G H, Curvature of the inside of the upper part of the fire-place. I, The shaft, or chimney.

PLATE LXV. Fig. 1. A CUPELLING FURNACE. A, The ash-hole. B B, Its sliding doors. C, The fire-place. D D, Its sliding doors. E F, Small apertures in the sliders. G G, Holes for bars to bear the muffles. H H H, Iron braces in the fore-part of the furnace, which form grooves for the doors of the fire-place and ash-hole to slide in. I, The upper pyramidal part of the furnace. K, An aperture therein for managing the coals. L, The opening at top. M, The pyramidal cover. N, The chimney, or end of the shaft, on which the conical funnel may be fitted. O O O O, Handles for moving the sliding doors. P P, Ears of the pyramidal covers.

PART II. PRACTICE OF CHEMISTRY

OF THE VITRIOLIC ACID. TO EXTRACT VITRIOL FROM THE PYRITES. Take any quantity you please of iron pyrites; leave them for some time exposed to the air: They will crack, split, lose their brightness, and fall into powder. Put this powder into a glass cucurbit, and pour upon it twice its weight of hot water; stir the whole with a stick, and the liquor will grow turbid. Pour it while it is yet warm into a glass funnel lined with brown filtering paper; and having placed your funnel over another glass cucurbit, le the liquor drain into it. Pour more hot water on the powdered pyrites, filter as before, and so go on, every time lessening the quantity of water, till that which comes off the pyrites appears to have no astringent vitriolic taste.

Put all these waters together into a glass vessel that widens upwards; set it on a sand bath, and heat the liquor till a considerable smoke arises; but take care not to make it boil. Continue the same degree of fire till the surface of the liquor begins to look dim, as if some dust had fallen into it; then cease evaporating, and remove the vessel into a cool place: In the space of four and twenty hours there will be formed therein a quantity of crystals of a green colour and a rhomboidal figure: These are vitriol of Mars, or copperas. Decant the remaining liquor; add thereto twice its weight of water; filter, evaporate, and crystallize as before; repeat these operations till the liquor will yield no more crystals, and keep by themselves the crystals obtained at each crystallisation.

In large works for extracting vitriol from the pyrites, they proceed thus. They

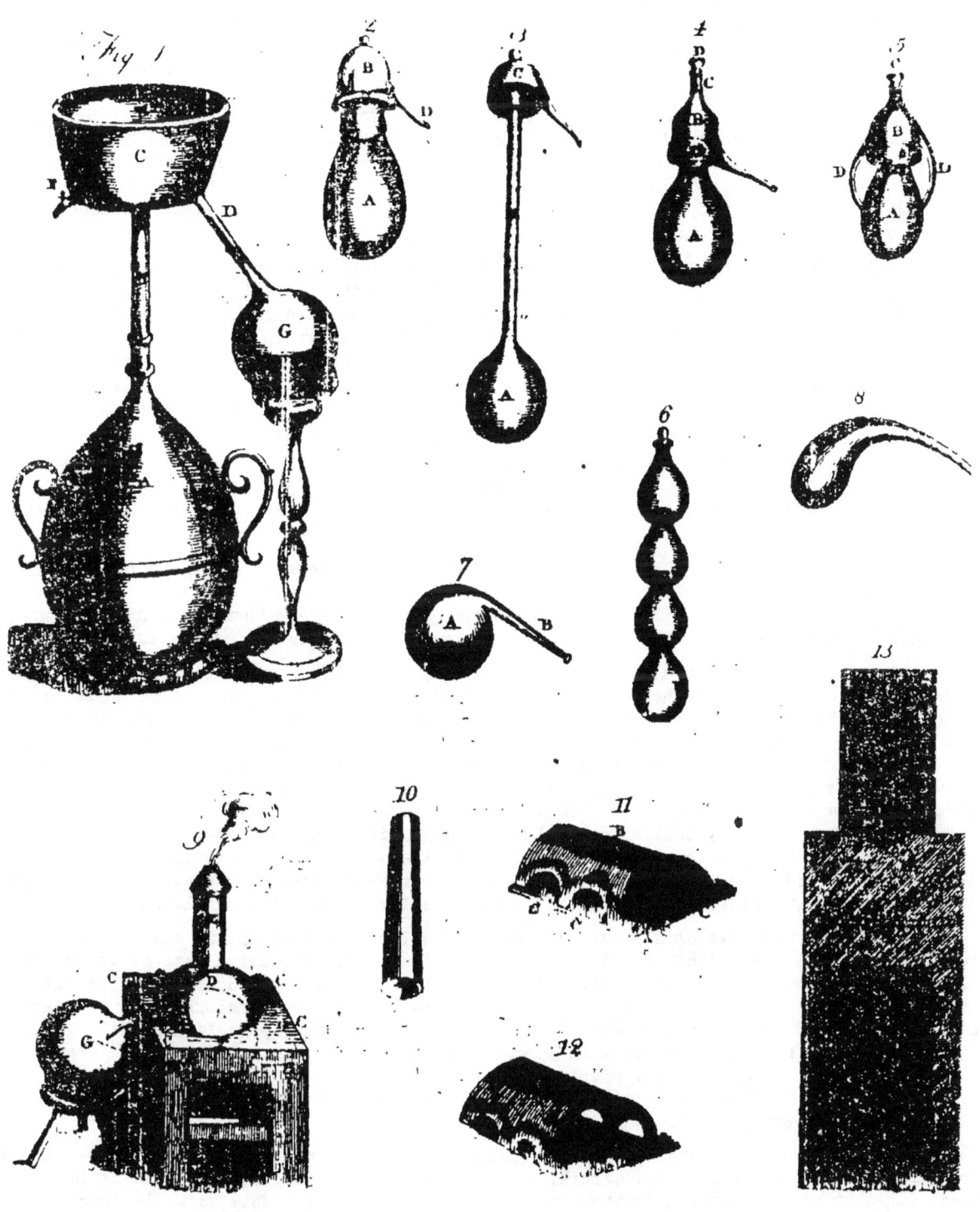

collect a great quantity of pyrites on a piece of ground exposed to the air, and pile them up in heaps of about three foot high. There they leave them exposed to the action of the air, sun, and rain, for three years together; taking care to turn them every six months, in order to facilite the efflorescence of those which at first lay undermost. The rain water which has washed those pyrites is conveyed by proper channels ito a cistern; and when a sufficient quantity thereof is gathered, they evaporate it to a pellicle in large leaden boilers, having first put into it a quantity of iron, some part of which is dissolved by the liquor, because it contains a vitriolic acid that is not fully saturated therewith. When it is sufficiently evaporated, they draw if off into large leaden or wooden coolers, and there leave it to shoot into crystals. In these last vessels several sticks are placed, crossing each other in all manner of directions, in order to multiply the surfaces on which the crystals may fasten.

TO EXTRACT SULPHUR FROM THE PYRITES, AND OTHER SULPHUREOUS MINERALS. Reduce to a coarse powder any quantity of yellow pyrites, or other mineral containing sulphur. Put this powder into an earthen or glass retort, having a long wide neck, and so large a body that the matter may fill but two thirds of it. Set the retort in a sand-bath fixed over a reverberating furnace; Fit to it a receiver half full of water, and so placed that the nose of the retort may be about an inch under the water: Give a gradual fire, taking care you do not make it so strong as to melt the matter. Keep the retort moderately red for one hour, or an hour and half, and then let the vessels cool.

Almost all the sulphur, separated by this operation from its matrix, will be found at the extremity of the neck of the retort, being fixed there by the water. You may get it out either by melting it with such a gentle heat as will not set it on fire, or by breaking the neck of the retort.

TO EXTRACT ALUM FROM ALUMINOUS MINERALS. Take such minerals as are known or suspected to contain alum. Expose them to the air, that they may effloresce. It they remain there a year without any sensible change, calcine them, and then leave them exposed to the air, till a bit thereof being put on the tongue imparts an astringent aluminous taste.

When your matters are thus prepared, put them into a leaden or glass vessel; pour upon them thrice their weight of hot water; boil the liquor; filter it, and repeat these operations till the earth be so edulcorated that the water which comes off it hath no taste. Mix all these solutions together, and let them stand four and twenty hours, that the gross and earthy parts may settle to the bottom; or else filter the liquor; then evaporate till it will bear a new-laid egg. Now let it cool, and stand quiet four and twenty hours; in that time some crystals will shoot, which are most commonly vitriolic; for alum is rarely obtained by the first crystallisation. Remove these vitriolic crystals; if any crystals of alum be found amongst them, these must be dissolved anew, and set to crystallise a second time in order to their purification; because they partake of the nature as well as of the colour of vitriol. By this method extract all the alum that the liquor will yield.

If you get no crystals of alum by this means, boil your liquor again, and add to it a twentieth part of its weight of a strong alkaline lixivium, or a third part of its weight of putrefied urine, or a small quantity of quick-lime. Experience and repeated trials must teach you which of these three substances is to be preferred, according to the particular nature of the mineral on which you are to operate. Keep your liquor boiling, and if there be any alum in it, there will appear a white precipitate; in that case let it cool and settle. When the white precipitate is entirely fallen, decan the clear, and leave the crystals of alum to shoot at leisure, till the liquor will yield no more; it will then be exceeding thick.

Alum is obtained from several sorts of minerals. In some parts of Italy, and in sundry other places, it effloresces naturally on the surface of the earth. There it is swept together with brooms, and thrown into pits full of water. This water is impregnated therewith till it can dissolve no more. Then it is filtered, and set to evaporate in large leaden vessels; and when it is sufficiently evaporated, and ready to shoot crystals, it is drawn off into wooden coolers, and there left for the salt to crystallise.

In aluminous soils there are often found springs strongly impregnated with alum; so that to obtain it the water need only be evaporated.

In the country about Rome there is a very hard stone, which is hewn out of the quarry, just like other stones for building; stine stone yields a great deal of alum. In order to extract it, the stones are calcined for twelve or fourteen hours; after which they are exposed to the air in heaps, and carefully watered three or four times a day for forty days together. In that time they begin to effloresce, and to throw out a reddish matter on their surface. Then they are boiled in water, which dissolves all the alum they contain, and being duly evaporated gives it back in crystals. This is the alum called Roman alum.

Several sorts of pyrites also yield a great deal of alum. The English have a stone of this kind, which in colour is very like a slate. This stone contains much sulphur, which they get rid of by roasting it. After this they steep the calcined stone in water, which dissolves the alum it contains, and to this solution they add a certain quantity of a lye made of the ashes of sea-weeds.

TO EXTRACT THE VITRIOLIC ACID FROM GREEN VITRIOL. Take any quantity of green vitriol; put it in an unglazed earthen vessel, and heat it gradually. Vapours will soon begin to rise. Increase the fire a little, and it will liquify by means of the water contained in it, and acquire what we called an aqueous fluor. Continue the calcination, and it will become less and less fluid, grow thick, and turn of a greyish colour. Now raise your fire, and keep it up till the salt recover its solidity, acquire an orange colour, and begin to grow red where it immediately touches the sides of the vessel. Then take it out and reduce it to powder.

Put the bitriol thus calcined and pulverised into a good earthen retort, of which one half at least must remain empty. Set the retort in a reverberatory furnace: Fit thereto a large glass receiver, and, having luted the joint well, give fire by degrees. You will soon see white clouds rise into the receiver, which will render it opaque and heat it. Continue the same degree of fire till these clouds disappear: They will be succeeded by a liquor which will trickle down the sides of the receiver in veins. Still keep up the fire to the same degree as long as these veins appear. When they begin to abate, encrease the fire, and push it to the utmost extremity: Upon this there will come over a black, thick liquor: It will even be found congealed, and prove the icy oil of vitriol, if care hath been taken to change the receiver, keep the vessels perfectly close, and give a sufficient degree of heat. Proceed thus till nothing more comes over, or at least very little. Let the vessels cool, unlute them, pour the contents of the receiver into a bottle, and seal it hermetically.

TO DECOMPOSE SULPHUR, AND EXTRACT ITS ACID, BY BURNING IT. Take any quantity of the purest sulphur; fill therewith a crucible or other earthen dish; heat it till it melts; then set it on fire, and when its whole surface is lighted, place it under a large glass head, so that the flame of the sulphur do not touch either its sides or bottom; that the air have free access, in order to make the sulphur burn clear; that the head incline a little toward the side on which its beak is, that as the vapours condense therein the liquor may run off with ease. To the beak of this vessel fit a receiver: The fumes of the lighted sulphur will be condensed, and gather into drops in the head, out of which they will run into the receiver. There, when the sulphur has done burning, you will find an acid liquor, which is the spirit of sulphur.

TO CONCENTRATE THE VITRIOLIC ACID. Take the vitriolic acid you intend to concentrate, that is, to dephlegmate and make stronger: Pour it into a good glass retort of such a size that your quantity of acid may but half fill it: Set this retort in the sand-bath of a reverberating furnace; fit it to a receiver; lute it on, and give a gradual fire. There will come over into the receiver a clear liquor, the first drops of which will be but faintly acid: This is the most aqueous part.

When the drops begin to follow one another much more slowly, raise your fire, till the liquor begin to bubble a little in the middle. Keep it thus gently boiling, till one half or two thirds thereof be come over into the receiver. Then let your vessels cool; unlute them; what remains in the retort pour into a crystal bottle, and stop it exactly with a glass stopple rubbed with emery.

TO DECOMPOSE VITRIOLATED TARTAR BY MEANS OF THE PHLOGISTON: OR TO COMPOSE SULPHUR BY COMBINING THE VITRIOLIC ACID WITH THE PHLOGISTON. Take equal parts of vitriolated tartar, and very dry salt of tartar, separately reduced to powder; add an eighth part of their weight of charcoal dust; and mix the whole together very accurately. Throw this mixture into a red-hot crucible, placed in a furnace filled with burning coals. Cover it very close, and keep it very hot, till the mixture melt, which may be known by uncovering the crucible from time to time. There will then appear a bluish flame, accompanied with a pungent smell of sulphur.

Take the crucible out of the fire; dissolve its contents in hot water; filter the solution through brown paper supported by a glass funnel; drop into the filtered liquor by little and little any acid whatever. As you add the acid, the liquor will grow more and more turbid, and let fall a grey precipitate. Continue dropping in more acid till the liquor will yield no more precipitate: What remains on the filter is a true inflammable sulphur, which you may either melt or sublime into flowers.

OF THE NITROUS ACID. TO EXTRACT NITRE OUT OF NITROUS EARTHS AND STONES. THE PURIFICATION OF SALT PETRE. MOTHER OF NITRE. MAGNESIA. Take any quantity of nitrous earths or stones; reduce them to powder; and therewith mix a third part of the ashes of green wood and quick-lime. Put this mixture into a barrel or vat, and pour on it hot water to about twice the weight of the whole mass. Le it stand thus for twenty four hours, stirring it from time to time with a stick. Then filter the liquor through brown paper, or pass it through a flannel bag, till it come clear; it will then have a yellowish colour. Boil this liquor, and evaporate till you perceive that a drop of it let fall on any cold body coagulates. Then stop the evaporation, and set your liquor in a cool place. In the space of four and twenty hours crystals will be formed in it, the figure of which is that of a hexagonal prism, having its opposite planes generally equal, and terminated at each extremity by a pyramid of the same number of sides. These crystals will be of a brownish colour, and deflagrate on a live coal.

Decant the liquor from these crystals; mix it with twice its weight of hot water; evaporate and crystallise as before. Repeat the same operation till the liquor will yield no more crystals; it will then be very thick, and goes by the name of mother of nitre.

Earths and stones that have been impregnated with animal or vegetable juices susceptible of putrefaction, and have been long exposed to the air, but sheltered from the sun and rain, are those which yield the greatest quantity of nitre. But all sorts of earths and stones are not equally fit to produce it. None is ever found in flints or sands of a crystalline nature.

Some earths and stones abound so with nitre, that it effloresces spontaneously on their surface, in the form of a crystalline down. This nitre may be collected with brooms, accordingly has the name of salt-petre sweepings. Some of this sort is brought from India.

The process by which our salt-petre makes extract nitre in quantities, out of rubbish and nitrous earths, is very nearly the same with that here set down; so that we shall not enter into a particular account of it. We shall only take notice of one thing, which is of some consequence to know; namely, that there is no nitrous earth which does not contain sea-salt also. The greatest quantities of this salt are to be found in those earths which have been drenched with urine or other animal excrements. Now, as the rubbish of old houses in great cities is in this class, it comes to pass, that when the salt-petre workers evaporate a nitrous lixivium drawn from that rubbish, as soon as the evaporation is brought to a certain pitch, a great many little crystals of sea-salt form in the liquour, and fall to the bottom of the vessel.

The salt-petre workers in France call these saline particles the grain, and take great care to separate them from the liquor, (which as long as it continues hot keeps the salt-petre dissolved) before they set it to crystallise. This fact seems a little singular, considering that sea-salt dissolves in water more easily than salt-petre, and crystallises with more difficulty.

In order to discover the cause of this phenomenon, we must recollect, first, that water

can keep but a determinate quantity of any salt in solution, and that if water fully saturated with a salt be evaporated, a quantity of salt will crystallise in proportion of
water evaporated. Secondly, that those salts which are the most soluble in water, particularly those which run in the air, will dissolve in cold and in boiling water equally:
whereas much greater quantities of the other salts will dissolve in hot and boiling water than in cold water. These things being admitted, when we know that sea-salt is one
of the first sort, and salt-petre of the second, the reason why sea-salt precipitates in
the preparation of salt-petre appears at once. For,

When the solution of salt-petre and sea salt comes to be evaporated to such a degree
that it contains as much sea-salt as it possibly can, this salt must begin to crystallise, and continue to do so gradually as the evaporation advances. But because at the
same time it does not contain as much salt-petre as it can hold, seeing it is capable of
dissolving a much greater quantity thereof when it is boiling hot than when it is cold,
this last named salt will not crystallise so soon. If the evaporation were continued
till the caseof the salt-petre came to be the same with that of the sea-salt, then the
salt-petre also would begin to crystallise gradually in proportion to the water evaporated, and the two salts would continue crystallising promiscuously together; but it is
never carried so far; nor is it ever necessary; for as the water cools it becomes more
and more incapable of holding in solution the same quantity of salt-petre as when it was
boiling hot.

And then comes the very reverse, with regard to the crystallising of the two salts;
for then the salt-petre shoots, and not the sea-salt. The reason of this fact also is
founded on what has just been said. The sea-salt, of which cold water will dissolve as
much as boiling water, and which owed it crystallising before only to the evaporation,
now ceases to crystallise as soon as the evaporation ceases; while the salt-petre, which
the water kept dissolved only because it was boiling hot, is forced to crystallise merely by the cooling of the water.

When the solution of salt-petre has yielded as many crystals of that salt as it can
yield by cooling, it is again evaporated, and being then suffered to cool yields more
crystals. And thus they continue evaporating and crystallising till the liquor will afford no more crystals. It is plain, that as the salt-petre crystallises the proportion
of sea-salt to the dissolving liquor increases; and as a certain quantity of water evaporates also during the time employed in crystallising the salt-petre, a quantity of sea-
salt, proportioned to the water so evaporating, must crystallise in that time; and this
is the reason why salt-petre is adulterated with a mixture of sea-salt. It likewise follows, that the last crystals of nitre, obtained from a solution of salt-petre and sea-
salt, contain much more sea-salt than the first.

From all that has been said concerning the crystallisation of salt-petre and sea-salt,
it is easy to deduce the proper way of purifying the former of these two salts from a
mixture of the latter. For this purpose the salt-petre to be refined need only be dissolved in fair water. The proportion between the two salts in this second solution is
very different from what it was in the former; for it contains no more sea-salt than what
had crystalized along with the salt-petre under favor of the evaporation, the rest having
been left dissolved in the liquor that refused to yield any more nitrous crystals.

As there is therefore a much greater quantity of salt-petre than of sea-salt in this
second solution, it is easy to evaporate it to such a degree that a great deal of salt-
petre than of sea-salt in this second solution, it is easy to evaporate it to such a degree that a great deal of salt-petre shall crystallise, while much more of the water must
necessarily be evaporated before any of the sea-salt will crystallise.

However, the salt-petre is not yet entirely freed from all mixture of sea-salt by this
first purification; for the crystals obtained from this liquor, in which sea-salt is dissolved, are still incrusted, and, as it were, infected therewith; hence it comes that,
to refine the salt-petre thoroughly, these crystallisations must be repeated four or five
times.

The salt-petre men commonly content themselves with crystallising it thrice, and call the produce salt-petre of the first, second, or third shoot, according to the number of crystallisations it has undergone. But their best refined salt-petre, even that of the third shooting, is not yet sufficiently pure for chemical experiments that require much accuracy; so that it must be further purified, but still by the same method.

The nitrous acid is not pure in the earths and stones from which it is extracted. It is combined partly with the very earth in which it is formed, and partly with the volatile alkali produced by the putrefaction of the vegetable or animal matters that concurred to its generation. A fixed alkali and quick-lime are added to the lixivium of a nitrous earth, in order to decompose the nitrous salts formed in that earth, and to separate the acid from the volatile alkali and the absorbent earth with which it is united; thence comes that copious sediment which appears in the lye at the beginning of the evaporation. These matters form with that acid a true nitre, much more capable than the original nitrous salts of crystallisation, detonation, and the other properties which are essential thereto. The basis of nitre is therefore a fixed alkali mixed with a little lime.

The mother of nitre, which will yield no more crystals, is brown and thick; by evaporation over a fire it is further inspiffated, and becomes a dry, solid body; which however being left to itself soon gives, and runs into a liquor. This water still contains a good deal of nitre, sea-salt, and the acids of these salts united with an absorbent earth. It contains moreover a great deal of a fat, viscid matter, which prevents its crystallising.

All saline solutions in general, after having yielded a certain quantity of crystals, grow thick, and refuse to part with any more, though they still contain much salt. They are all called mother-waters, as well as that which hath yielded nitre. The mother-waters of different salts may prove the subjects of curious and useful enquires.

If a fixed alkali be mixed with the mother of nitre, a copious white precipitate immediately falls, which being collected and dried is called magnesia. This precipitate is nothing but the absorbent earth that was united with the nitrous acid, together with a good deal of the lime that was added, and was also united with that acid, from which they are now separated by the fixed alkali, according to the usual laws of affinities or elective attractions.

The vitriolic acid poured upon mother of nitre causes many acid vapours to rise, which are a compound of the nitrous and marine acids, that is, an aqua regia. On this occasion also there falls a large quantity of a white powder, which is still called magnesia; yet it differs from the firmer in that it is not, like it, a pure absorbent earth, but combined with the vitriolic acid.

An aqua regis may also be drawn from nitrous earths by the force of fire only, without the help of any additament.

TO DECOMPOSE NITRE BY MEANS OF THE PHLOGISTON. NITRE FIXED BY CHARCOAL. CLYSSUS OF NITRE. SAL POLYCHRESTUM. Take the purest salt petre in powder; put it into a large crucible, which it may but half fill; set the crucible in a common furnace, and surround it with coals. When it is red hot the nitre will melt, and become as fluid as water. Then throw in to the crucible a small quantity of charcoal dust; the nitre and the charcoal will immediately deflagrate with violence; and a great commotion will be raised, accompanied with a considerable hissing, and abundance of black smoke. As the charcoal wastes, the detonation will abate, and cease entirely as soon as the coal is quite consumed.

Then throw into the crucible the same quantity of charcoal-dust as before, and the same phenomena will be repeated. Let this coal also be consumed; then add more, and go on in the same manner till you can excite no further deflagration; always observing to let the burning coat be entirely consumed before you add any fresh. When no deflagration ensues, the matter contained in the crucible will have lost much of its fluidity.

Nitre will not take fire, unless the inflammable matter added to it be actually burning, or the nitre itself red hot, and so thoroughly ignited as immediately to kindle it.

Therefore, if you would procure the detonation of nitre with charcoal, and make use of cold charcoal, as in the process, the nitre in the crucible must be red hot, and in perfect fusion; but you may also use live coals; and then the nitre need not be red hot.

The matter remaining in the crucible after the operation, is a very strong fixed alkali. Being exposed to the air, it quickly extracts the moisture thereof, and runs into a liquor. It is called alkalizated nitre, or to distinguish it from nitre alkalizated by other inflammable matters, nitre fixed by charcoal.

The nitrous acid is not only dissipated during the deflagration of the nitre, but is even destroyed, and perfectly decomposed. The smoke that rises during the operation has not the least odour of an acid.

In order to collect the vapours discharged by the deflagration of nitre, fit to a tubulated earthen retort two or three large adopters; set the retort in a furnace; and under it make a fire sufficient to keep its bottom moderately red. Then take a small quantity, two or three pinches for example, of a mixture of three parts of nitre with one of charcoal-dust, and drop it into the retort through its tube, which must be uppermost, and immediately stopped close. A detonation instantly ensues, and the vapours that rise from the inflamed mixture of nitre and charcoal, passing out through the neck of the retort into the adopters, circulate therein for a while, and at last condense into a liquor.

When the detonation is over, and the vapours condensed, or nearly so, drop into the retort another equal quantity of the mixture; and repeat this till you find there is liquor enough in the recipients to be examined with ease and accuracy. This liquor is almost insipid, and shews no tokens of acidity; or at most but very slight ones. It is called clyssus of nitre.

Nitre is also decomposed and takes fire by the means of sulphur; but the circumstances and the result differ widely from those produced therewith by charcoal or any other inflammable body.

Nitre deflagrates with sulphur on account of the phlogiston which the latter contains. If one part of sulphur be mixed with two or three parts of nitre, and the mixture thrown by little and little into a red-hot crucible, upon every projection there arises a detonation accompanied with a vivid flame.

The vapours discharged on this occasion have the mingled smell of a sulphureous spirit and spirit of nitre; and if they be collected by means of a tubulated retort, and such an apparatus of vessels as was used in the preceding experiment, the liquor contained in the recipients is found to be an actual mixture of the acid of sulphur, the sulphureous spirit, and the acid of nitre; the first being of greater quantity than the other two, and the second greater than the last.

Nor is the remainder after detonation a fixed alkali, as in the former experiments; but a neutral salt, consisting of the acid of sulphur combined with the alkali of nitre; a sort of vitriolated tartar, known in medicine by the name of sal polychrestum.

TO DECOMPOSE NITRE BY MEANS OF THE VITRIOLIC ACID. THE SMOKING SPIRIT OF NIYTR. SAL DE DUOBUS. THE PURIFICATION OF SPIRIT OF NITRE.

Take equal parts of well purified nitre and green vitriol; dry the nitre thoroughly, and bruise it to a fine powder. Calcine the vitriol to redness; reduce it likewise to a very fine powder; and mingle these two substances well together. Put the mixture into an earthen long neck, or a good glass retort coated, of such a size that it may be but half full.

Set this vessel in a reverberating furnace covered with its dome; apply a large glass receiver, having a small hole in its body, stopped with a little lute. Let this receiver be accurately luted to the retort with the fat lute, and the joint covered with a slip of canvas smeared with lute made of quick-lime and the white of an egg. Heat the vessels very gradually. The receiver will soon be filled with very dense red vapours, and drops will begin to distill from the nose of the retort.

Continue the distillation, increasing the fire a little when you observe the drops to follow each other but slowly, so that above two thirds of a minute passes between them; and, in order to let out the redundant vapours, open the small hote in the receiver from time to time. Towards the end of the operation raise the fire so as to make the retort red. When you find that, even when the retort is red-hot, nothing more comes over, unlute the receiver, and without delay pour the liquor it contains into a crystal bottle, and close it with a crystal stopple rubbed in its neck with emery. This liquor will be of a reddish yellow colour, smoking exceedingly, and the bottle containing it will be constantly filled with red fumes like those observed in the receiver.

By the process here delivered, a very strong, perfectly dephlegmated, and vastly smoking spirit of nitre is obtained.

When the operation is over, you will find a red mass at the bottom of the retort, cast as it were in a mould. This is a neutral salt of the nature of vitriolated tartar, resulting from the union of the acid of the vitriol with the alkaline basis of the nitre.

The ferruginous basis of the vitriol, which is mixed with this salt, gives it the red colour. To separate it therefrom, you must pulverise it, dissolve it in boiling water, and filter the solution several times through brown paper; because the ferruginous earth of the vitriol is so fine, that some of it will pass through the first time. When the solution is very clear, and deposites no sediment, let it be set to shoot, and it will yield crystals of vitriolated tartar; to which chemists have given the peculiar title of sal de duobis.

Nitre may also be decomposed, and its acid obtained, by the interposition of any of the other vitriols, alums, gypsums, boles, clays; in short, by means of any compound in which the vitriolic acid is found, provided it have not a fixed alkali for its basis.

The distiller of aqua fortis, who make large quantities at a time, and who use the least chargeable methods, do their business by the means of earths impregnated with the vitriolic acid; such as clays and boles. With these earths they accurately mix the nitre from which they intend to draw their spirit; this mixture they put into large oblong earthen pots, having a very short curved neck, which enters a recipient of the same matter and form. These vessels they place in two rows opposite to each other in long furnaces, and cover them over with bricks cemented with Windsor-loam, which serves for a reverberatory; then they light the fire in the furnace, making it at first very small, only to warm the vessels; after which they throw in wood, and raise the fire till the pots grow quite red-hot, in which degree they keep it up till the distillation is entirely finished.

Most experiments require the spirit of nitre to be absolutely pure; and if it be intended for such, it must be perfectly cleansed from the vitriolic taint.

This is easily effected by mixing your spirit with very pure nitre, and distilling it a second time. The vitriolic acid, with which this spirit of nitre is adulterated, coming in contact with a great quantity of undecomposed nitre, unites with its alkaline basis, and expels a proportionable quantity of the nitrous acid.

OF THE MARINE ACID. TO EXTRACT SEA-SALT FROM SEA-WATER, AND FROM BRINE-SPRINGS. EPSOM SALT. Filter the salt-water from which you intend to extract the salt; evaporate it by boiling, till you see on its surface a dark pellicle; this consists wholly of little crystals of salt just beginning to shoot; now slacken the fire, that the brine may evaporate more slowly, and without any agitation. The crystals, which at first were very small, will become larger, and form hollow truncated pyramids, the apices whereof will point downwards, and their bases be even with the surface of the liquor.

These pyramidal crystals are only collection of small cubical crystals concreted into this form. When they have acquired a certain magnitude they fall to the bottom of the liquor. When they come to be in such heaps as almost to reach the surface of the liquor, decant it from them, and continue the evaporation till no more crystals of sea-salt will shoot.

The acid of sea-salt is scarce ever found, either in sea-water or in the earth, otherwise than united with a fixed alkali of a particular kind, which is its natural basis; and consequently it is in the form of a neutral salt. This salt is plentifully dissolved in the waters of the ocean, and when obtained therefrom bears the name of sea-salt. It is also found in the earth in vast crystalline masses, and is then called sal-gem; so that sea-salt and sal-gem are but one and the same sort of salt; differing very little from each other, except as to the places where they are found.

In the earth are also found springs and fountains, whose waters are strong brines, a great deal of sea-salt being dissolved in them. These springs either rise directly from the sea, or run through some mines of sal-gem, of which they take up a quantity in their passage.

As the same, or at least nearly the same quantity of sea-salt will continue dissolved in cold water as boiling water will take up, it cannot shoot, as nitre does, by the mere cooling of the water in which it is dissolved; it crystallises only by means of evaporation, which continually lessens the proportion of the water to tye salt; so tht it is always capable of containing just so much the less sea-salt the more there is crystallised.

The brine should not boil after you perceive the pellicle of little crystals beginning to form on its surface; for the calmness of the liquor allows them to form more regularly, and become larger. Nor after this should the evaporation be hurried on too fast; for a saline crust would form on the liquor, which, by preventing the vapours from being carried off, would obstruct the crystallisation.

If the evaporation be continued after the liquor ceases to yield any crystals of sea-salt, other crystals will be obtained of an oblong four-sided form, which have a bitter taste, and are almost always moist. This sort of salt is known by the name of Epsom salt, which it owes to a salt spring in England, from the water of which it was first extracted. This salt, or rather saline compound, is a congeries of Glauber's salt and sea-salt, in a manner confounded together, and mixed with some of the mother of sea-salt, in which is contained a kind of bituminous matter. These two neutral salts, which constitute the Epsom salt, may be easily separated from each other, by means of crystallisation only. Epsom salt is purgative and bitter; and therefore named sal catharii cum amarum, or bitter purging salts.

There are different methods used in great works for obtaining sea-salt out of water in which it is dissolved. The simplest and easiest is that practised in France, and in all those countries which are not colder. On the sea-shore they lay out a sort of broad shallow pits, pans, or rather ponds, which the sea fills with the tide of flood. When the ponds are thus filled, they stop their communication with the sea, and leave the water to evaporate by the heat of the sun; by which means all the salt contained in it necessarily crystallises. These pits are called salt ponds. Salt can be made in this way in the summer-time only, at least in France, and other countries of the same temperature; for during the winter, when the sun has less power, and rains are frequent, this method is not practicable.

For this reason, as it often rains in the province of Normandy, the inhabitants take another way to extract salt from sea-water. The labourers employed for this purpose raise heaps of sand on the shore, so that the tide waters and drenches them when it flows, and leaves the sand dry when it ebbs. During the interval between two tides of flood the sun and the air easily carry off the moisture that was left, and so the sand remains impregnated with all the salt that was contained in the evaporated water. Thus they let it acquire as much salt as it can by several returns of flood, and then wash it out with fresh water, which they evaporate over a fire in leaden boilers.

To obtain the salt from brine-springs, the water need only be evaporated; but as several of these springs contain too little salt to pay the charges that would be incurred, if the evaporation were effected by the force of fire only, the manufacturers have fallen upon a less expensive method of getting rid of the greatest part of the water, and preparing the brine for crystallisation, in much less time, and with much less fire, than would otherwise have been necessary.

The method consists in making the water fall from a certain height on a great many small spars of wood, which divide it into particles like rain. This is performed under sheds open to all the winds, which pass freely through this artificial shower. By this means the water presents to the air a great extent of surface, being indeed reduced almost entirely to surface, and the evaporation is carried on with great ease annd expedition. The water is raised by pumps to the height from which it is intended to fall.

EXPERIMENTS CONCERNING THE DECOMPOSITION OF SEA-SAKTM BT MEANS OF THE PHLOGISTON. KUNCKEL'S PHOSPHORUS. Of pure urine that has fermented five or six days take a quantity in proportion to the quantity of phosphorus you intend to make; it requires about one third part of a hogshead to make a dram of phosphorus. Evaporate it in iron pans, till it become clotted, hard, black, and nearly like chimney soot; at which time it will be reduced to about a sixtieth part of its original weight before evaporation.

When the urine is brought to this condition, put it inseveral portions into so many iron pots, under which you must keep a pretty brisk fire so as to make their bottoms red, and stir it incessantly until the volatile salt and the fetid oil be almost wholly dissipated, till the matter cease to emit any smoke, and till it smell like peach-blossoms. Then put out the fire, and pour on the matter, which will now be reduced to a powder, somewhat more than twice its weight of warm water. Stir it about in this water, and leave it to soak therein for twenty-four hours. Pour off the water by inclination; dry the drenched matter, and pulverise it. The previous calcination carries off from the matter about a third of its weight, and the lixiviation washes out half the remainder.

With what remains thus calcined, washed, and dried, mix half its weight of gravel, or yellow free-stond rasped, having sifted out and thrown away all the finest particles. River-sand is not proper on this occasion, because it flies in a hot fire. Then add to this mixture a sixteenth part of its weight of charcoal, made of beech, or of any other wood except oak, because that also flies. Moisten the whole with as much water as will bring it to a stiff paste, by working and kneading it with your hands: Now introduce it into your retort, taking care not to daub its neck. The retort must be of the best earth, and of such a size, that when your matter is in it, a full third thereof shall still be empty.

Place your retort, thus charged, in a reverberating furnace, so proportioned, that there may be an interval of two inches all round between the sides of the furnace and the bowl of the retort, even where it contracts to form the neck, which should stand inclined at an angle of sixty degrees. Stop all the apertures of the furnace, except the doors of the fire-place and ash-hote.

Fit on to the retort a large glass ballon two thirds full of water, and lute them together, as in distilling the smoking spirit of nitre. In the hinder part of this ballon, a little above the surface of the water, a small hote must be bored. This hole is to be stopped with a small peg of birch-wood, which must slip in and out very easily, and have a small knob to prevent its falling into the ballon. This peg is to be pulled out from time to time, that by applying the hand to the hole it may be known whether the air rarefied by the heat of the retort, issues out with too much or too little force.

If the air rushes out with too much rapidity, and with a hissing noise, the door of the ash-hole must be entirely shut, in order to slacken the fire. If it do not strike pretty smartly against the hand, that door must be opened wider, and large coals thrown into the fire-place to quicken the fire immediately.

The operation usually lasts four and twenty hours; and the following signs shew that it will succeed, provided the retort resist the fire.

You must begin the operation with putting some unlighted charcoal in the ash-hole, and a little lighted charcoal at the door thereof, in order to warm the retort very slowly. When the whole is kindled, push it into the ash-hole, and close the door thereof with a tile. This moderate heat brings over the phlegm of the mixture. The same degree of heat must be kept up four hours, after which some coals may be laid on the grate of the fire-place, which the fire underneath will kindle by degrees. With this second heat brought nearer the retort, the ballon grows warm, and is filled with white vapours which have the smell of fetid oil. In four hours after, this vessel will grow cool and clear; and then you must open the door of the ash-hole one inch, throw fresh coals into the fire-place every three minutes, and every time shut the door of it, lest the cold air from without should strike against the bottom of the retort and crack it.

When the fire has been kept up to this degree for about two hours, the inside of the ballon gegins to be netted over with a volatile salt of a singular nature, which cannot be driven up but by a very violent fire, and which smells pretty strong of peach-kernels. Care must be taken that this concrete salt do not stop the little hole in the ballon; for in that case it would burst, the retort being then red-hot, and the air exceedingly rarefied. The water in the ballon, being heated by the vicinity of the furnace, exhales vapours which dissolve this sprigged salt, and the ballon clears up in half an hour after it has ceased rising.

In about three hours from the first appearance of this salt, the ballon is again filled with new vapours, which smell like sal ammoniac thrown upon burning coals. they condense on the sides of the receiver into a salt which is not branched like the former, but appears in long perpendicular streaks, which the vapours of the water do not dissolve. These white vapours are the fore-runners of the phosphorus; and a little before they cease to rise they lose their first smell of sal ammoniac, and acquire the odour of garlick.

As they ascend with great rapidity, the little hote must be frequently opened, to observe whether the hissing be not too strong; for in that case it would be necessary to shut the door of the ash-hole quite close. These white vapours continue two hours. When you find they cease rising, make a small passage through the dome, by opening some of its registers, that the flame may just begin to draw. Keep up the fire in this mean state till the first volatile phosphorus begin to appear.

This appears in about three hours after the white vapours first begin to rise. In order to discover it, pull out the little birchen peg once every minute, and rub it against some hot part of the furnace, where it will leave a trail of light, if there be any phosphorus upon it.

Soon after you observe this sign, there will issue out through the little hole of the ballon a stream of bluish light, which continues of a greater or shorter extent to the end of the operation. This stream or spout of light does not burn. If you hold your finger against it for twenty or thirty seconds, the light will adhere to it; and if you rub that finger over your hand, the light will besmear it, and render it luminous.

But from time to time this streamer darts out to the length of seven or eight inches, snapping and emitting sparks of fire; and then it burns all combustible bodies that come in its way. When you observe this, you must manage the fire very warily, and shut the door of the ash-hole quite close, yet without ceasing to throw coals into the fire-place every two minutes.

The volatile phosphorus continues two hours; after which the little spout of light contracts to the length of a line or two; and now is the time for pushing your fire to the utmost; Immediately set the door of the ash-hole wide open, throw billets of wood into it, unstop all the registers of the reverberatory, supply the fire-place with large coals every minute; In short, for six or seven hours all the inside of the furnace must be kept of a white heat, so that the retort shall not be distinguishable.

In this fierce extremity of heat the true phosphorus distills like an oil, or like melted wax: One part thereof floats on the water in the recipient, the other falls to the bottom. At last the operation is known to be quite over when the upper part of the ballon, in which the volatile phosphorus appears condensed in a blackish film, begins to grow red: For this shews that the phosphorus is burnt where the red spot appears. You must now stop all registers, and shut all the doors of the furnace, in order to smother the fire; and then close up the little hole in the ballon with fat lute or bees-wax. In this condition the whole must be left for two days; because the vessels must not be separated till they are perfectly cold, lest the phosophorus should take fire.

As soon as the fire is out, the ballon, which is then in the dark, presents a most a-greeable object: All the empty part thereof above the water seems filled with a beau-tiful blue light; which continues for seven or eight hours, or a long as the ballon keeps warm, never disappearing till it is cooled.

When the furnace is quite cold, take out the vessels, and separate them from each other as neatly as possible. With a linen cloth wipe away all the black stuff you find in the mouth of the ballon; for if that filth should mix with the phosphorus, it would hinder it from being transparent when moulded. This must be done with great expedition: After which pour into the ballon two or three quarts of cold water, to accelerate the precipitation of the phosphorushat swims at top. Then agitate the water in the ballon, to rinse out all the phosphorus that may stick to the sides; pour out all the water thus shaken and turbid, into a very clean earthen pan, and let it stand till it grows clear. Then decant this first useless water, and on the blackish sediment left at the bottom of the pan pour some boiling water to melt the phosphorus; which thereupon unites with the fuliginous matter, or volatile phosphorus, that precipitated with it, both together for-ming a mass of the colour of slate. When this water in which you have melted the phos-phorus is cool enough, take out the phosphorus, throw it into cold water, and therein break it into little bits in order to mould it.

Then take a matras, having a long neck somewhat wider next the body than at its mouth: Cut off half the body, so as to make a funnel of the neck part, the smaller end of which must be stopped with a cork. The first mould being thus prepared, plunge it end-wise, with its mouth uppermost, in a vessel full of boiling water, and fill it with that water. Into this funnel throw the little bits of your slate-like mass, which will melt again in this hot water, and fall so melted to the bottom of the tube. Stir this melted matter with an iron wire, to promote the separation of the phosphorus from the fuligin-ous matter with which it is fouled, and which, being less ponderous than the phosphorus, will gradually rise above it towards the upper part of the cylinder.

Keep the water in the vessel as hot as at first, till on taking out the tube you see the phosphorus clean and transparent. Let the clear tube cool a little, and then set it in cold water, where the phosphorus will congeal as it cools. When it is perfectly con-gealed, pull out the cork, and with a small rod near as big as the tube, push the cylin-der of phosphorus towards the mouth of the funnel, where the seculency lies. Cut off the black part of the cylinder, and keep it apart: For when you have got a quantity thereof, you may melt it over again in the same manner, and separate the clean phosphor-us which it still contains. As to the rest of the cylinder which is clean and transpar-ent, if you intend to mould it into smaller cylinders, you may cut it in slices, and melt it again by the help of boiling water in glass tubes of smaller dimensions.

It is proper to observe, in the first place, that one of the most usual causes of mis-carriage in this operation is a defect of the requisite qualities in the retort employed. It is absolutely necessary to have that vessel made of the best earth, and so well made that it shall be capable of resisting the utmost violence of fire, continued for a very long time.

We shall, in the second place, observe with M. Hellot, "that, before you set your re-tort in the furnace, it is proper to make an essay of your matter, to see if there be reason to hope for success. For this purpose put about an ounce thereof into a small crucible, and heat it till the vessel be red. The mixture, after having smoked, ought to chop and crack without puffing up, or even rising in the least. From these cracks will issue undulated flames, white and bluish, darting upwards with rapidity. This is the first volatile phosphorus, which occasions all the danger of the operation. When these first flashes are over, increase the heat of your matter by laying a large live coal upon the crucible. You will then see the second phosphorus, like a luminous, stea-dy vapour, of a colour inclining to violet, covering the whole surface of the matter: It continues for a very long time, and diffuses a smell of garlick, which is the distin-guishing odour of the phosphorus you are seeking.

"When this luminous vapour is entirely gone, pour the red hot matter out of the cru-cible upon an iron plate. If you do not find one drop of salt in fusion, but that, on the contrary, the whole falls readily into powder, it is a proof that your matter was sufficiently lixiviated, and that it contains no more fixed salt, or sea-salt, if you will, than is requisite. If you find on the plate a drop of salt coagulated, it shews that there is too much left in it, and that there is danger of your miscarrying in the operation because the redundant salt would corrode and eat through the retort. In this case your matter must be washed again, and then sufficiently dried."

The furnace must be so constructed, that within a narrow compass it may give a heat at least equal to that of a glass-house furnace, or rather greater, especially during the last seven or eight hours of the operation. M. Hellot, in his Memoir, gives an exact description of such a furnace.

"As certain accidents may happen in the course of the operation, some precautions are to be taken against them. For instance, if the ballon should break while the phosphorus is distilling, and any of it should fall on combustible bodies, it would set them on fire, and probably burn the laboratory, because it is not to be distinguished without the greatest difficulty. The furnace must therefore be erected under some vault, or upon a bed of brick-work, raised under some chimney that draws well: Nor must any furniture or utensil of wood be left near it. If a little flaming phosphorus should fall on a man's legs or hands, in less than three minutes it would burn its way to the very bone. In such a case nothing but urine will stop its progress.

"If the retort crack while the phosphorus is distilling there is an unsuccessful end to your operation. It is easy to perceive this by the stink of garlick which you will smell about the furnace; and moreover, the flame that issues through the apertures of the reverberatory will be of a beautiful violet colour. The acid of sea-salt always gives this colour to the flame of such matters as are burnt along with it. But if the retort break before the phosphorus hath made its appearance, its contents may be saved by throwing a number of cold bricks into the fire-place, and upon them a little water to quench the fire at once." All these useful observations we owe also to M. Hellot.

The phosphorus here described was first discovered by a citizen of Hamburg named Brandt, who worked upon urine in search of the philosopher's stone. Afterwards two other skilful chemists, who knew nothing more of the process than that phosphorus was obtained from urine, or in general from the human body, likewise endeavoured to discover it; and each of them separately did actually make the discovery. These two chemists were Kunckel and Boyle.

The former perfected the discovery, and found out a method of making it in considerable quantities at a time; which occasioned it to be called Kunckel's phosphorus. The other, who was an English gentleman, had not time to bring his discovery to perfection, and contented himself with lodging a voucher of his having discovered it in the hands of the secretary of the Royal Society of London, who gave him a certificate thereof.

"Though Brandt, who had before this sold his secret to a chemist named Krafft, sold it afterwards to several other persons, and even at a very low rate; and though Mr. Boyle published the process for making it; yet it is extremely probable that both of them kept in their own hands the master-key: I mean, the particular management necessary to make the operation succeed: For till Kunckel found it out, no other chemist ever made any considerable quantity thereof, except Mr. Godfrey Hanwitz, and English chemist, to whom Mr. Boyle revealed the whole mystery.

"And thus it came to pass, that, after Kunckel and Boyle died M. Godfrey Hankwitz was the only chemist that could supply Europe therewith; on which account it is likewise very well known by the name of English phosphorus."

Almost all the chemists consider phosphorus as a substance consisting of the acid of sea-salt combined with the phlogiston, in the same manner as sulphur consists of the vitriolic acid combined with the phlogiston. This opinion is founded on the following principles.

First, urine abounds with sea-salt, and contains also a great deal of phlogiston; now these are the ingredients of which they conjecture phosphorus to be composed.

Secondly, phosphorus has many of the properties of sulphur; such as being soluble in oils; melting with a gentle heat; being very combustible; burning without any soot; giving a vivid and bluish flame; and lastly, leaving an acid liquor when burnt; sensible proofs that it differs from sulphur in nothing but the nature of its acid.

Thirdly, this acid of phosphorus, being mixed with a solution of silver in spirit of nitre, precipitates the silver; and this precipitate is a true luna cornea, which appears to be more volatile even than the common sort. This fact proves more incontesably that the acid of phosphorus is of the same nature with that of sea-salt.

Fourthly, M. Stahl observes, that if sea-salt be cast on live coals, they instantly burn with great activity; that they emit a vivid flame, and are much sooner consumed than if none of this salt had touched them; that sea-salt in substance, which will bear the violence of fire a considerable time when fused in a crucible, without sustaining any sensible diminution, yet evaporates very quickly, and is reduced to white flowers, by the immediate contact of burning coals; and lastly, that the flame which rises on this occasion is of a blue colour inclining to violet, especially if it be not thrown directly on the coals themselves, but kep in fusion amidst burning coals, in a crucible so placed that the vapour of the salt may join with the inflamed phlogiston as it rises from the coals.

These experiments of Mr. Stahl's prove, that the phlogiston acts upon the acid of sea-salt, even while it is combined with its alkaline basis. The flame that appears on this occasion may be considdred as an imperfect phosphorus; and indeed its colour is exactly like that of phosphorus.

All the facts above related evince, that the acid of phosphorus is akin to that of sea-salt; or rather, that it is the very same. But there are other facts which prove, that this acid undergoes some change at least, some peculiar preparation, before it enters into the composition of a true phosphorus; and that, when extricated therefrom by burning, it is not a pure acid of sea-salt, but is still adulterated with a mixture of some other substance, which makes it considerably different from that acid. For these observations we are obliged to M. Marggraff.

M. Marggraff hath also published a process for making phosphorus, and assures us, that by means thereof we may obtain in less time, with less heat, less trouble, and less expence, a greater quantity of phosphorus than by any other method. His operation is this:

He takes two pounds of sal ammoniac in powder, which he mixes accurately with four pounds of minium. This mixture he puts into a glass retort, and with a graduated fire draws off a very sharp, volatile, urinous spirit.

We observed in Part I, that some metallic substances have the property of decomposing sal ammoniac, and separating its volatile alkali. Minium, which is a calx of lead, is one of those metallic substances. In this experiment it decomposes the sal ammoniac, and separates its volatile alkali; what remains in the retort is a combination of the minium with the acid of sal ammoniac, which is well known to be the same with the marine acid; and consequently the residue of this operation is a sort of plumbum corneum.

The quantity thereof is four pounds eight ounces. Of this he mixes three pounds with nine or ten pounds of urine, that has stood putrefying for two months, evaporated to the consistence of honey. These he mixes by little and little in an iron pan over the fire, stirring the mixture from time to time. Then he adds half a pound of charcoal dust, and evaporates the matter, kept continually stirring till the whole be brought to a black powder. He next distills the mixture in a glass retort with degrees of fire, which he raises towards the end so as to make the retort red-hot, in order to expel all the urinous spirit, superfluous oil, and ammonical salt. The distillation being finished, there remains nothing in the retort but a very friable caput mortuum.

This remainder he pulverises again, and throws a pinch of it on live coals to discover whether or no the matter be rightly prepared for yielding phosphorus. If it be so, it presently emits an arsenical odour, and a blue undulating flame, which passes over the surface of the coals like a wave.

Being thus assured of the success of his operation, he puts one half of his matter, in three equal parts, into three small earthen German retorts, capable of holding about eighteen ounces of water a-piece. These three retorts, none of which is above three quarters full, he places together in one reverberatory furnace, built much like those we have described, except that it is so constructed as to hold the three retorts disposed in one line. To each retort he lutes a recipient something more than half full of water, ordering the whole in such a manner, that the noses of his retorts almost touch the surface of the water.

He begins the distillation with warming the retorts slowly, for about an hour, by a gentle heat. When that time is elapsed he raises the fire gradually, so that in half an hour more the coals begin to touch the bottoms of the retorts. He continues throwing coals into the furnace by little and little, till they rise half way the height of the retorts; and in this he employs another half hour. Lastly, in the next half hour he raises the coals above the bowels of the retorts.

Then the phosphorus begins to ascend in clouds; on this he instantly increases the heat of the fire as much as possible, filling the surface quite up with coals, and making the retorts very red. This degree of fire causes the phosphorus to distill in drops which fall to the bottom of the water. He keeps up this intense heat for an hour and half, at the end of which the operation is finished; so that it last but four hours and a half in all: In the same manner he distills the second moiety of his mixture in three other such retorts.

He purifies and moulds his phosphorus much in the same manner as M. Hellot does. From the quantity of ingredients above mentioned, he obtains two ounces and a half fine crystalline moulded phosphorus.

The acid of phosphorus seems to be more fixed than any other; and therefore if you would separate it by burning from the phlogiston with which it is united, there is no occasion for such an apparatus of vessels as is employed for obtaining the spirit of sulphur. For this acid will remain at the bottom of the vessel in which you burn your phosphorus; indeed, if it be urged by the force of fire, its most subtile part evaporates, and the remainder appears in the form of a vitrified matter.

This acid effervesces with fixed and volatile alkalis, and therewith forms neutral salts; but very different from sea-salt, and from sal ammoniac. That which has a fixed alkali for its basis does not crackle when thrown on burning coals; but swells and vitifies like borax. That which has a volatile alkali for its basis shoots into long pointed crystals; and, being urged by fire in a retort, lets go its volatile alkali, a vitrified matter remaining behind.

We shall conclude this article with an account of certain properties of phosphorus which have not yet been mentioned.

Phosphorus dissolves by lying exposed to the air. What water cannot effect, says M. Hellot, or at least requires eight or ten years to bring about, the moisture of the air accomplishes in ten or twelve days; whether it be that the phosphorus takes fire in the air, and the inflammable part evaporating, almost entirely, leaves the acid of the phosphorus naked, which like all other acids, when exceedingly concentrated, is very greedy of moisture; or else that the moisture of the air, being water divided into infinitely fine particles, is so subtile as to find its way through the pores of the phosphorus, into which the grosser particles of common water can by no means insinuate themselves.

Phosphorus heated by the vicinity of fire, or by being any way rubbed, soon takes fire and burns fiercely. It is soluble in all oils, and in aether, giving to those liquors the property of appearing luminous, when the bottle containing the solution is opened. Being boiled in water, it likewise communicates thereto this luminous quality.

The late Mr. Groffe observed, that phosphorus being dissolved in essential oils crystallises therein. These crystals take fire in the air, either when thrown into a dry vessel, or wrapt up in a piece of paper. If they be dipped in spirit of wine, and taken out immediately, they do not afterwards take fire in the air; they smoke a little, and for a very short time, but hardly waste at all. Though some of them were left in a spoon for a fortnight, they did not seem to have lost any thing of their bulk; but when the spoon was warmed a little they took fire, just like common phosphorus that had never been dissolved and crystallised in an essential oil.

M. Marggraff, having put a dram of phosphorus with an ounce of highly concentrated spirit of nitre into a glass retort, observed, that, without the help of fire, the acid dissolved the phosphorus; that part of the acid came over into the recipient which was luted to the retort; that at the same time the phosphorus took fire, burnt furiously, and burst the vessels with explosion. Nothing of this kind happens when any of the other acids, though concentrated, are applied to phosphorus.

TO DECOMPOSE SEA SALT BY MEANS OF THE VITRIOLIC ACID. GLAUBER'S SALT. THE PURIFICATION AND CONCENTRATION OF SPIRIT OF SALT. Put the sea-salt from which you mean to extract the acid into an unglazed earthen pipkin, and set it amidst live coals. The salt will decrepitate, grow dry, and fall into a powder. Put this decrepitated salt into a tubulated glass retort, leaving two thirds thereof empty. Set the retort in a reverberating furnace; apply a receiver like that used in distilling the smoking spirit of nitre, and lute it on in the same manner, or rather more exactly if possible. Then through the hole in the upper convexity of the retort pour a quantity of highly concentrated oil of vitriol, equal in weight to about a third part of your salt, and immediately shut the hole very close with a glass stopple, first rubbed therein with emery so as to fit it exactly.

As soon as the oil of vitriol touches the salt, the retort and receiver will be filled with abundance of white vapours; and soon after, without lighting any fire in the furnace, drops of a yellow liquor will distill from the nose of the retort. Let the distillation proceed in this manner without fire, as long as you perceive any drops come; afterwards kindle a very small fire under the retort, and continue distilling and raising the fire by very slow degrees, and with great caution, to the end of the distillation; which will be finished before you have occasion to make the retort red-hot. Unlute the vessels, and without delay pour the liquor, which is a very smoking spirit of salt, out of the receiver into a crystal bottle, like that directed for the smoking spirit of nitre.

When the operation is finished, we find a white, saline mass at the bottom of the retort as in a mould. If this mass be dissolved in water, and the solution crystallized, it yields a considerable quantity of sea-salt that hath not been decomposed, and a neutral salt consisting of the vitriolic acid united with the alkaline basis of that part which hath been decomposed. This neutral salt, which bears the name of Glauber its inventor, differs from vitriolated tartar, or the Sal de duobus, which remains after distilling the nitrous acid, especially in that it is more fusible, more soluble in water, and hath its crystals differently figured. But as in these two salts the acid is the same, the differences that appear between them must be attributed to the peculiar nature of the basis of sea-salt.

Spirit of salt drawn by the process above described is tainted with a small mixture of the vitriolic acid, carried up by the force of fire before it had time to combine with the alkali of the sea-salt; which happens likewise to the nitrous acid procured in the same manner. If you desire to have it pure, and absolutely free from the acid of vitriol, it must be distilled a second time from sea-salt, as the acid of nitre was before directed to be distilled again from fresh nitre, in order to purify it from any vitriolic taint.

TO DECOMPOSE SEA-SALT BY MEANS OF NITROUS ACID. AQUA REGIS. QUADRANGULAR NITRE. Take dried sea-salt; bruise it to powder; put it into a glass retort, leaving one half of the vessel empty. Pour upon it a third of its weight of good spirit of nitre. Place your retort in the sand-bath of a reverberating furnace; put on the dome; lute to the retort a receiver having a small hole in it, and heat the vessels very slowly. There will come over into the receiver some vapours, and an acid liquor. Increase the fire gradually till nothing more rises. Then unlute the vessels, and pour the liquor out of the receiver into a crystal bottle, stopped like others containing acid spirits.

The nitrous acid hath a greater affinity than the marine acid with fixed alkalis. When therefore spirit of nitre and sea-salt are mixed together, the same consequences will follow as when the vitriolic acid is mixed with that salt; that is, the nitrous acid will, like the vitriolic, decompose it, by dislodging its acid from its alkaline basis, and assuming its place. But as the nitrous acid is considerably weaker, and much lighter, than the vitriolic acid, a good deal of it rises along with the acid of sea-salt during the operation. The liquor found in the receiver is therefore a true aqua regis.

If decrepitated salt, and a right smoking spirit of nitre, be employed in this process, the aqua regis obtained will be very strong.

The operation being finished, there is left in the retort a saline mass, containing sea-salt not decomposed, and a new species of nitre, which having for its basis the alkali of sea-salt, that is, an alkali of a peculiar nature, differs from the common nitre, 1. In the figure of its crystals; which are solids of four sides, formed like lozenges: 2. In that it crystallizes with more difficulty, retains more water in its crystals, attracts the moisture of the air, and dissolves in water with the same circumstances as sea-salt.

OF BORAX. TO DECOMPOSE BORAX BY THE MEANS OF ACIDS, AND TO SEPARATE FROM IT THE SEDATIVE SALT BY SUBLIMATION AND BY CRYSTALLISATION. Reduce to a fine powder the borax from which you intend to extract the sedative salt. Put this powder into a wide-necked glass retort. Pour upon it an eighth part of its weight of common water, to moisten the powder; and then add concentrated oil of vitriol, to the weight of somewhat more than a fourth part of the weight of the borax. Set the retort in a reverberatory, make a moderate fire at first, and augment it gradually till the retort become red-hot.

A little phlegm will first come over, and then , with the last moisture that the heat expels, the sedative salt will rise; by which means some of it will be dissolved in this last phlegm, and pass therewith into the receiver; but most of it will adhere in the form of saline flowers to the fore-part of the neck of the retort, just where it is clear of the groove of the furnace. There they collect into a heap, which the succeeding flowers push insensibly forward till they slightly stop the passage. Those which rise after the neck is thus stopped stick to the after part of it which is hot, vitrify in some measure, and form a circle of fused salt. In this state the flowers of the sedative salt seem to issue out of the circle, as from their basis: They appear like very thin, light, shining scales, and must be brushed off with a feather.

At the bottom of the retort will be left a saline mass: Dissolve this in a sufficient quantity of hot water; filter the solution, in order to free it from a brown earth which it deposites; set the liquor to evaporate, and crystals of sedative salt will form in it.

Though borax is of great use in many chemical operations, especially in the fusion of metals, as we shall have occasion to see, yet, till of late years, chemists were quite ignorant of its nature, as they still are of its origin; concerning which we know nothing with certainty, but that it comes rough from the East Indies, and is purified by the Dutch.

OF OPERATIONS ON METALS. OF GOLD. TO SEPARATE GOLD, BY AMALGAMATION WITH MERCURY, FROM THE EARTH AND STONES WITH WHICH IT IS FOUND MIXED. Pulverise the earths and stones containing gold. Put the powder into a little wooden tray; dip this tray in water, gently shaking it and its contents. The water will grow muddy by taking up the earthy parts of the ore. Continue washing it in this manner till the water cease to appear turbid. Upon the ore thus washed pour strong vinegar, having first dissolved therein, by the help of heat, about a tenth part of its weight of alum. The powder must be quite drenched and covered with this liquor, and so left to stand for twice twenty-four hours.

Decant the vinegar, and wash your powder with warm water till the last that comes off hath no taste; then dry it; and put it into an iron mortar, with four times its weight of quick-silver; triturate the whole with a heavy wooden pestle, till all the powder be of a blackish colour; then pour in a little water, and continue rubbing for some time

time longer. More earthy and heterogeneous particles will be separated from the metalline parts by means of this water, which will look dirty; it must then be decanted, and more fair water added. Repeat this several times; then dry what remains in the mortar with a sponge, and by the help of a gentle heat; you will find it an almalgam of the mercury with the gold.

Put this almalgam into a chamoy bag; tie a knot on its neck, and squeeze it hard between your fingers, over some wide-mouthed vessel; there will issue through the pores of the leather numberless little jets of mercury, forming a sort of shower, that will collect into large globules in the vessel placed underneath. When you can force out no more mercury by this means, open the bag, and in it you will find the amalgam freed from the superfluous mercury; the gold retaining only about as much thereof as nearly equals itself in weight.

Put this amalgam into a glass retort; set this retort in the sand-bath of a reverberating furnace; cover it quite over with sand; apply a glass receiver half full of water, so that the nose of the retort may be under the water. The receiver need not be luted to the retort. Give a gradual heat, and raise the fire till drops of the sublimed mercury appear in the neck of the retort, and fall into the water with a hissing noise. If you hear any noise in the retort, slacken your fire a little. Lastly, when you observe, that, though you raise the fire still higher than before, nothing more will come over, take out your retort, break it, and there you will find the gold, which must be melted in a crucible with borax.

TO DISSOLVE GOLD IN AQUA REGIS, AND BY THAT MEANS TO SEPARATE IT FROM SILVER. Take gold that is perfectly pure, or alloyed with silver only. Reduce it to little thin plates, by hammering it on an anvil. If it be not sufficiently tough, neal it till it be red in a moderate, clear fire, quite free from smoking coals, and then let it cool gradually, which will restore its ductility.

When the plates are thin enough, make them red-hot once more, and cut them into small bits with a pair of sheers. Put these bits into a tall, narrow-mouthed cucurbit, and pour on them twice their weight of good aqua regis, made of one part sal ammoniac, or spirit of salt, and four parts spirit of nitre. Set the cucurbit in a sand-bath moderately heated, stopping its orifice slightly with a paper coffin, to prevent any dirt from falling in. The aqua regis will presently begin to smoke. Round the little bits of gold will be formed an infinite number of small bubbles, which will rise to the surface of the liquor. The gold will totally dissolve, if it be pure, and the solution will be of a beautiful yellow colour; if the gold be alloyed with a small quantity of silver, the latter will remain at the bottom of the vessel in the form of a white powder. If the gold be alloyed with much silver, when the gold is dissolved the silver will retain the form of the little metalline plates put into the vessel.

When the dissolution is completed, gently pour off the liquor into another low, widemouthed, glass cucurbit, taking care that none of the silver, which lies at the bottom in the form of a powder escape with the liquor. On this powder of silver pour as much fresh aqua regis as will cover it entirely; and repeat this till you are sure that nothing more can be taken up by it. Lastly, having decanted the aqua regis from the silver, wash the silver with a little spirit of salt weakened with water, and add this spirit of salt to the aqua regis in which your gold is dissolved. Then to the body containing these liquors fit a head and a receiver, and distill with a gentle heat, till the matter contained in the cucurbit become dry.

Mix together equal parts of common brinstone, and a very strong fixed alkali; for instance, nitre fixed by charcoal. Put them in a crucible, and melt the mixture, stirring it from time to time with a small rod. There is no occasion to make the fire brick, because the sulphur facilitates the fusion of the fixed alkali. Some sulphureous vapours will rise from the crucible; the two substances will mix intimately together, and form a reddish compound. Then throw into the crucible some little pieces of gold beat into thin plates, so that the whole do not exceed in weight one third part of the liver of sulphur; raise the fire a little. As soon as the liver of sulphur is perfectly melted, it will begin to dissolve the gold with ebullition; and will even emit some flashes of fire. In the space of a few minutes the gold will be entirely dissolved, especially if it was cut and flatted into small thin leaves.

The process here delivered is taken from M. Stahl. The design of his inquiries was to discover how Moses could burn the golden calf, which the Israelites had set up and worshipped while he was on the mount; how he could afterwards reduce that calf to powder, throw it into the water which the people used, and make all who had apostatized drink thereof, as related in the book of Exodus, and he concludes, that Moses must have performed this operation by means of liver of sulphur.

TO SEPARATE GOLD FROM ALL OTHER METALLIC SUBSTANCES BY MEANS OF ANTIMONY. Having put the gold you intend to purify into a crucible, set it in a melting furnace, cover it, and make the gold flow. When the metal is in fusion, cast upon it, by a little at a time, twice its weight of pure crude antimony in powder, and after each projection cover the crucible again immediately; this done keep the matter in fusion for a few minutes. When you perceive that the metallic mixture is perfectly melted, and that its surface begins to sparkle, pour it out into a hollow iron cone, previously heated, and smeared on the inside with tallow. Immediately strike with a hammer the floor on which the cone stands; and when all is cold, or at least sufficiently fixed, invert the cone and strike it; the whole metallic mass will fall out, and the under part thereof, which was at the point of the cone, will be a regulus more or less yellow as the gold was more or less pure. On striking the metallic mass, the regulus will freely part from the sulphureous crust at top.

Return this regulus into the crucible, and melt it. Less fire will do now than was required before. Add the same quantity of antimony, and proceed as at first. Repeat the same operation a third time, if your gold be very impure.

Then put your regulus into a good crucible, much larger than is necessary to hold it. Set your crucible in a melting furnace, and heat the matter but just enough to make it flow, with a smooth, brilliant surface. When you find it thus conditioned, point towards it the nose of a longpsnouted pair of bellows, and therewith keep gently and constantly blowing. There will arise from the crucible a considerable smoke, which will abate greatly when you cease to blow, and increase as soon as you begin again. You must raise the fire gradually as you approach towards the end of the operation. If the surface of the metal lose its brilliant polish, and seem covered with a hard crust, it is a sign the fire is too weak; in which case it must be increased, till the surface recover its shining appearance. And last, when no more smoke rises, and the surface of the gold looks neat and greenish, cast on it, by little and little, some pulverized nitre, or a mixture of nitre and borax. The matter will swell up. Continue thus adding more nitre gradually, till no commotion is thereby produced in the crucible; and then let the whole cool. If you find, when the gold is cold, that it is not tough enough, melt it over again; when it begins to melt cast it in the same salts as before; and repeat this till it be perfectly ductile.

TO SEPARATE SILVER FROM ITS ORE, BY MEANS OF SCORIFICATION WITH LEAD. Beat to powder in an iron mortar the ore from which you mean to separate the silver, having first roasted it well in order to free it from all the sulphur and arsenic that it may contain. Weigh it exactly; then weigh out by itself eight times as much granulated lead. Put one half of this lead into a test, and spread it equally thereon; upon this lead lay your ore, and cover it quite over with the remaining half of the lead.

Place the test thus loaded under the further end of the muffle in a cupelling furnace. Light your fire, and increase it by degrees. If you look through one of the apertures in the door of the furnace, you will perceive the ore, covered with calcined lead, swim upon the melted lead. Presently afterwards it will grow soft, melt, and be thrown towards the sides of the vessel, the surface of the lead appearing in the midst thereof bright and shining like a luminous disc; the lead will then begin to boil, and emit fumes. As soon as this happens, the fire must be a little checked, so that the ebullition of the lead may almost entirely cease for about a quarter of an hour. After this it must be excited to the degree it was at before, so that the lead may begin again to boil and smoke. Its thinning surface will gradually lessen, and be covered with scoria. Stir the whole with an iron hook, and draw in towards the middle what you observe towards the sides of the vessel; to the end that, if any part of the ore should still remain un-dissolved by the lead, it may be mixed therewith.

When you perceive that the matter is in perfect fusion, that the greatest part of what sticks to the iron hook, when you dip it in the melted matter, separates from it again, and drops back into the vessel; and that the extremity of this instrument, when grown cold, appears varnished over with a thin, smooth, shining crust; you may look on these as marks that the business is done; and the more uniform and evenly the colour of the crust is, the more perfect may you judge the scorification to be.

Matters being brought to this pass, take the test with a pair of tongs from under the muffle, and pour its whole contents into an iron cone, first heated and greased with tallow. The whole operation lasts about three quarters of an hour. When all is cold, the blow of a hammer will part the regulus from the scoria; and as it is not possible, how perfect soever the scorification be, to avoid leaving a little lead containing sil-ver in the scoria, it is proper to pulverise this scoria, and separate therefrom what-ever extends under the hammer, in order to add it to the regulus.

THE REFINING OF SILVER BY THE CUPEL. Take a cupel capable of containing one third more matter than you have to put into it; set it under the muffle of a furnace like that described in our theoretical elements, as peculiarly appropriated to this sort of operation. Fill the furnace with charcoal; light it; make the cupel red-hot, and keep it so till all its moisture be evaporated; that is, for about a good quarter of an hour if the cupel be made wholly of the ashes of burnt bones; and for a whole hour, if there be any washed wood-ash in its composition.

Reduce the regulus which remained after the preceding operations to little thin pla-tes, flatting them with a small hammer, and separating them carefully from all the ad-herent scoria. Wrap these in a bit of paper, and with a small pair of tongs put them gently into the cupel. When the paper is consumed, the regulus will soon melt, and the scoria, which will be gradually produced by the lead as it turns to litharge, will be driven to the sides of the cupel, and immediately absorbed thereby. At the same time the cupel will assume a yellow, brown, or blackish colour, according to the quantity and nature of the scoria imbibed by it.

When you see the matter in the cupel in a violent ebullition, and emitting much smoke, lower the fire by the methods formerly prescribed. Keep up such a degree of heat only that the smoke which ascends from the matter may not rise very high, and that you may be able to distinguish the colour which the cupel acquires from the scoria.

Increase the fire by degrees, as more and more litharge is formed and absorbed. If the regulus examined by this assay contain no silver, you will see it turn wholly into scoria, and at last disappear. When it contains silver, and the quantity of lead is much diminished, you will perceive little vivid irised or beautiful rain-bow colours, shooting swiftly along the surface, and crossing each other in many different directions. At last, when all the lead is destroyed, the thin dark skin, that is continually protru-ded by the lead while it is turning into litharge, and which hitherto covered the sil-ver, suddenly disappears; and, if at this moment the fire happen not to be strong en-ough to keep the silver in fusion, the surface of that metal will at once dart out a dazzling splendor; but, if the fire be strong enough to keep the silver in fusion, though freed from all mixture of lead, this change of colour, which is called its ful-guration, will not be so perceptible, and the silver will appear like a bead of fire.

These phenomena shew that the operation is finished. But the cupel must still be left a minute or two under the muffle, and then drawn slowly out with the iron hook to-wards the door of the furnace. When the silver is so cooled as to be but moderately red, you may take the cupel from under the muffle with your little tongs, and in the middle of its cavity you will find an exceeding white bead of silver, the lower part whereof will be unequal, and full of little pits.

TO PURIFY SILVER BY NITRE. Granulate the silver you intend to purify, or reduce it to thin plates; put it into a good crucible; add thereto a fourth part in weight of very dry pulverised nitre, mixed with half the weight of the nitre of calcined wine-lees, and about a sixth part of the same weight of common glass in powder. Cover this crucible with another crucible inverted; which must be of such a size that its mouth may enter a little way into that of the lower one, and have its bottom pierced with a hole of about two lines in diameter. Lute the two crucibles together with clay and Windsor-loam. When the lute is dry, place the crucibles in a melting furnace. Fill the furnace with charcoal, taking care however that they do not rise above the upper crucible.

Kindle the fire, and make your vessels of a middling red-heat. When they are so, take up with the tongs a live coal, and hold it over the hole of the upper crucible. If you immediately perceive a vivid splendor round the coal, and at the same time hear a gentle hissing noise, it is a sign that the fire is of a proper strength; and it must be kept up at the same degree till this phenomenon cease.

Then increase the fire to the degree requisite to keep pure silver in fusion and immediately take your vessels out of the furnace. You will find the silver at the bottom of the lower crucible covered with a mass of alkaline scoria of a greenish colour. If the metal be not rendered perfectly pure and ductile by the operation, it must be repeated a second time.

TO DISSOLVE SILVER IN AQUA FORTIS, AND THEREBY SEPARATE IT FROM EVERY OTHER METALLINE SUBSTANCE. The silver you intend to dissolve being beaten into thin plates, put it into a glass cucurbit; pour on it twice its weight of good precipitated aqua fortis; cover the cucurbit with a paper, and set it on a sand-bath moderately heated. The aqua fortis will begin to dissolve the silver as soon as it comes to be a little warm. Red vapours will rise; and from the upper surfaces of the silver there will seem to issue streams of little bubbles, ascending to the top of the liquor, between which and the silver they will form, as it were, a number of fine chains: This is a sign that the dissolution proceeds duly, and that the degree of heat is such as it ought to be. If the liquor appear to boil and be agitated, a great many red vapours rising at the same time, it is a sign that the heat is too great, and should be lessened till it be reduced to the proper degree indicated above; having obtained that, keep it equally up till no more bubbles or red vapours appear.

If your silver be alloyed with gold, the gold will be found, when the dissolution is finished, at the bottom of the vessel in the form of a powder. The solution must now be decanted while it is yet warm; on the powder pour half as much fresh aqua fortis as before, and make it boil; again decant this second aqua fortis, and repeat the same a third time; then with fair water wash the remaining powder well: It will be of a brown colour inclining to red.

TO SEPARATE SILVER FROM THE NITROUS ACID BY DISTILLATION. CRYSTALS OF SILVER. THE INFERNAL STONE. Into a large, low, glass body, put the solution of silver from which you intend to separate the silver by distillation. To this body fit a tubulated head provided with its stopple. Set this alembic in a sand-bath, so that the body may be almost covered with sand; apply a receiver, and distill with a moderate heat, so that the drops may succeed each other at the distance of some seconds. If the receiver grow very hot, check the fire. When red vapours begin to appear, pour into the alembic, through the hole in its head, a fresh quantity of your solution of silver, first made very hot. Continue distilling in this manner, and repeating the addition of fresh liquor, till all your solution be put into the alembic. When you have no more fresh solution to put in, and when, the phlegm being all come over, red vapours begin again to appear, convey into the alembic half a dram or a dram of tallow, and distill to driness; which being done, increase your fire so as to make the vessel containing the sand-bath red-hot. In the alembic you will find a calx of silver, which must be melted in a crucible with some soap and calcined wine-lees.

- If the distillation be stopped when part of the phlegm is drawn off, and the liquor be then suffered to cool, many crystals will shoot therein, which are a neutral salt constituted of the nitrous acid and silver. If the distillation be carried further, and stopped when near its conclusion, the liquor being then suffered to cool will wholly coagulate into a blackish mass called the infernal stone.

TO SEPARATE SILVER FROM THE NITROUS ACID BY PRECIPITATION. LUNA CORNEA. LUNA CORNEA REDUCED. Into your solution of silver pour about a fourth part in weight of spirit of salt, solution of sea-salt, or solution of sal ammoniac. The liquor will instantly become turbid and milky. Add twice or thrice its weight of fair water, and let it stand some hours to settle. It will deposite a white powder. Decant the clear liquor, and on the precipitate pour fresh aqua fortis, or spirit of salt, and warm the whole on a sand bath with a gentle heat for some time. Pour off this second liquor; and boil your precipitate in pure water, shifting it several times, till the precipitate and the water both quite insipid. Filter the whole, and dry the precipitate, which will be a luna cornea, and must be reduced in the following manner.

Smear the inside of a good crucible well with soap. Put your luna cornea into it; cover it with half its weight of salt of tartar, thoroughly dried and pulverised; press the whole hard down; pour thereon as much oil, or melted tallow, as the powder is capable of imbibing; set the crucible thus charged, and close covered, in a melting furnace, and, for the first quarter of an hour, kindle no more fire than is necessary to make the crucible moderately red; after that raise it so as to melt the silver and the salt, throwing into the crucible from time to time little bits of tallow. When it ceases to smoke, let the whole cool; or pour it into a hollow iron cone, warmed and tallowed.

TO DISSOLVE SILVER, AND SEPARATE IT FROM GOLD, BY CEMENTATION. Mix thoroughly together fine brick-dust four parts, vitriol calcined to redness one part, and sea-salt or nitre one part. Moisten this powder with a little water. With this cement cover the bottom of a crucible half an inch thick; on this first bed lay a thin plate of the mass of gold and silver you intend to cement, and which you must previously take care to beat into such thin plates. Cover this plate with a second layer of cement, of the same thickness as the former; on this second bed lay another plate of your metal; cover it in like manner with cement; and so proceed till the crucible be filled to within half an inch of its brim. Fill up the remaining space with cement, and close the crucible with a cover, luted with a paste made of Windsor-loam and water. Set your crucible thus charged in a furnace, whose fire-place is deep enough to let it be entirely surrounded with coals, quite up to its mouth. Light some coals in the furnace, taking care not to make the fire very brisk at first; increase it by degrees, but only so far as to make the crucible moderately red; keep up the fire in this degree for eighteen or twenty hours; Then let the fire go out; open the crucible when it is cold, and separate the cement from your plates of gold. Boil the gold repeatedly in fair water, till the water comes off quite insipid.

OF COPPER. TO SEPARATE COPPER FROM ITS ORE. Beat your copper ore to a fine powder, having first freed it as accurately as possible, by washing and roasting, from all stoney, earthy, sulphureous, and arsenical parts. Mix your ore thus pulverised with thrice its weight of the black flux, put the mixture into a crucible; cover it with common salt to the thickness of half an inch, and press the whole down with your finger. With all this the crucible must be but half full. Set it in a melting furnace; kindle the fire by degrees, and raise it insensibly till you hear the sea-salt crackle. When the decrepitation is over, make the crucible moderately red-hot for half a quarter of an hour. Then give a considerable degree of heat, exciting the fire with a pair of good perpetual bellows, so that the crucible may become very red-hot, and be perfectly ignited. Keep the fire up to this degree for about a quarter of an hour; then take out the crucible, and with a hammer strike a few blows on the floor on which you set it. Break it when cold. If the operation hath been rightly and successfully performed, you will find at the bottom of the vessel a hard regulus, of a bright yellow colour, and semi-malleable; and over it a scoria of a yellowish brown colour, hard, and shining, from which you may separate the regulus with a hammer.

TO PURIFY BLACK COPPER, AND RENDER IT MALLEABLE. Break into small bits the black copper you intend to purify; mix therewith a third part in weight of granulated lead, and put the whole into a cupel set under the muffle in a cupelling furnace, and previously heated quite red. As soon as the metals are in the cupel raise the fire considerably;

making use, if it be needful of a pair of perpetual bellows, to melt the copper speedily When it is thoroughly melted, lower the fire a little, and continue it just high enough to keep the metalline mass in perfect fusion. The melted matter will then boil, and throw up some scoria; which will be absorbed by the cupel.

When most of the lead is consumed, raise the fire again till the face of the copper become bright and shining, thereby shewing that all its alloy is separated. As soon as your copper comes to this state, cover it with charcoal dust conveyed into the cupel with an iron laddle: Then take the cupel out of the furnace, and let it cool.

TO DEPRIVE COPPER OF ITS PHLOGISTON BY CALCINATION. Put your copper in filings into a test, and set it under the muffle of a cupelling furnace; light the fire, and keep up such a degree of heat as may make the whole quite red, but not enough to melt the copper. The surface of the copper will gradually lose its metalline splendor, and put on the appearance of a reddish earth. From time to time stir the filings with a little rod of copper or iron; and leave your metal exposed to the same degree of fire till it be always calcine.

TO RESUSCITATE THE CALX OF COPPER, AND REDUCE IT TO COPPER, BY RESTORING ITS PHLOGISTON. Mix the calx of copper with thrice as much of the black flux; put the mixture into a good crucible, so as to fill two thirds thereof, and over it put a layer of seasalt a finger thick. Cover the crucible, and set it in a melting furnace; heat it gradually, and keep it moderately red till the decrepitation of the sea-salt be over. Then raise the fire considerably by means of a good pair of perpetual bellows; satisfy yourself that the matter is in perfect fusion, by dipping into the crucible an iron wire; continue the fire in this degree for half a quarter of an hour. When the crucible is cold, you will find at its bottom a button of very fine copper, which will easily separate from the saline scoria at top.

TO DISSOLVE COPPER IN THE MINERAL ACIDS. On a sand-bath, in a very gentle heat, set a matras containing some copper filings; pour on them twice their weight of oil of vitriol. That acid will presently attack the copper. Vapours will rise, and issue out of the neck of the matras. A vast number of bubbles will ascend from the surface of the metal to the top of the liquor, and the liquor will acquire a beautiful blue colour. When the copper is dissolved, put a little and a little more, till you perceive the acid no longer acts upon it. Then decant the liquor, and let it stand quiet in a cool place. In a short time great numbers of beautiful blue crystals will shoot in it. These crystals are called vitriol of copper, or blue vitriol. They dissolve easily in water.

OF IRON. TO SEPARATE IRON FROM ITS ORE. Pound into a coarse powder the martial stones or earths out of which you design to extract the iron; Roast this powder in a test under the muffle for some minutes, and let your fire be brisk. Then let it cool, beat it very fine, and roast it a second time, keeping it under the muffle till it emit no more smell.

Then mix with this powder a flux composed of three parts of nitre fixed with tartar, one part of fusile glass, and half a part of borax and charcoal-dust. The dose of this reducing flux must be thrice the weight of the ore.

Put this mixture into a good crucible; cover it with about half a finger thick of seasalt; over the crucible put its cover, and lute it on with Windsor-loam made into a paste with water. Having thus prepared your crucible, set it in a melting furnace, which you must fill up with charcoal. Light the fire, and let it kindle by gentle degrees, till the crucible become red-hot. When the decrepitation of the sea-salt is over, raise your fire to the highest by the blast of a pair of perpetual bellows, or rather several. Keep up this intense degree of heat for three quarters of an hour, or a whole hour, taking care that during all this time the furnace be kept constantly filling up with fresh coals as the former consume. Then take your crucible out of the furnace; strike the pavement on which you set it several times with a hammer, and let it stand to cool; Break it, and you will find therein a regulus of iron covered with slag.

In smelting-houses iron ore is fused amidst charcoal, the phlogiston of which combines with the martial earth, and gives it the metalline form. The iron thus melted runs down to the bottom of the furnace; from whence it is let out into large moulds, in which it takes the shape of oblong blocks, called pigs of iron. This iron is still very impure, and quite unmalleable. Its want of ductility after the first melting arises partly from hence, that, notwithstanding the previous roasting which the ore underwent, there still remains, after this first fusion, a considerable quantity of sulphur or arsenic combined with the metal.

A certain quantity of quick-lime, or of stones that will burn to lime, is frequently mixed with iron ore on putting it into the smelting furnace. The lime being an absorbent earth, very apt to unite with sulphur and arsenic, is of use to separate those minerals from the iron.

It is also of use to mix some such matters with the ore, when the stones or earths which naturally accompany it are very fusible; for, as the iron is of difficult fusion, it may happen that the earthy matters mixed with the iron shall melt as easily as the metal, or perhaps more easily. In such a case there is no separation of the earthy from the metalline part, both of which melt and precipitate together promiscuously: Now quick-lime, being extremely refractory, serves on this occasion to check the melting of those matters which are too fusible.

Yet quick-lime, notwithstanding its refractory quality, may sometimes be of use as a flux for iron: This is the case when the ore happens to be combined with substances which, being united with lime render it fusible: Such are all arsenical matters, and even some earthy matters, which, being combined with quick-lime, make a fusible compound.

When the ore of an iron mine is found difficult to reduce, it is usually neglected even though it be rich; because iron being very common, people chuse to work those mines only whose ores are smelted with the most ease, and require the least consumption of wood.

Yet refractory ores are not to be altogether rejected, when another iron ore of a different quality is found near them. For it often happens, that wo several iron ores, which being worked separately are very difficult to manage, and yield at last but bad iron, become very tractable, and yield excellent iron, when smelted together: And accordingly such mixtures are often made at iron-works.

The iron obtained from ores by the first fusion may be divided into two sorts. The one, when cold, resists the hammer, doth not easily break, and is in some measure extensible on the anvil; but if struck with a hammer, when red-hot, flies into many pieces: This sort of iron hath always a mixture of sulphur in it. The other sort, on the contrary, is brittle when cold, but somewhat ductile when red-hot. This iron is not sulphurated, is naturally of a good quality, and its brittleness arises from its metalline parts not being sufficiently compacted together.

Iron abounds so much, and is so universally diffused through the earth, that it is difficult to find a body in which there is none at all: And this hath led several chemists into the error of thinking, that they had transmuted into iron several sorts of earths in which they suspected no iron, by combining them with an inflammable matter; whereas, in fact, all they did was to give the metalline form to a true martial earth which happened to be mixed with other earths.

TO RENDER PIG-IRON AND BRITTLE IRON MALLEABLE. Into an earthen vessel widening upwards, put some charcoal-dust, and thereon lay the pig-iron which you propose to render ductile; cover it all over with a quantity of charcoal; excite the fire violently with a pair, or more, of perpetual bellows till the iron melt. If it do not readily flow and form a great deal of slag on its surface, add some flux, such as a very fusible sand.

When the matter is in fusion, keep stirring it from time to time, that all the parts thereof may be equally acted on by the air and the fire. On the surface of the melted iron scoria will be formed, which must be taken off as they appear. At the same time you will see a great many sparkles darted up from the surface of the metal, which will form a sort of fiery shower. By degrees, as the iron grows purer, the number of these sparkles diminishes, though they never vanish entirely. When but few sparkles appear, remove the coals which cover the iron, and let the slag run out of the vessel; whereupon the metal will grow solid in a moment. Take it out while it is still red-hot, and give it a few strokes with a hammer, to try if it be ductile. If it be not yet malleable, repeat the operation a second time, in the same manner as before. Lastly, when it is thus sufficiently purified by the fire, work it for a long time on the anvil, extending it different ways, and making it red-hot as often as there is occasion. Iron thus brought to the necessary degree of ductility, so as to yield to the hammer, and suffer itself to be extended every way, either hot or cold, without breaking to bits, or even cracking in the least, is very good and very pure. If it cannot be brought to this degree by the method here prescribed, it is a proof, that the ore from which this iron was extracted, ought to be mixed with other ores; but it frequently requires a great number of trials to obtain an exact knowledge of the quality and proportion of those other ores with which it is to be mixed.

TO CONVERT IRON INTO STEEL. Take small bars of best iron; that is, of such as is malleable both hot and cold; set them on their ends in a cylindrical earthen vessel, whose depth is equal to the length of the bars, and in such a manner that they may be an inch distant from each other, and from the sides of the crucible. Fill the vessel with a cement compounded of two parts of charcoal, one part of bones burnt in a close vessel till they become very black, and one half part of the shes of green wood; having first pulverised and thoroughly mixed the whole together. Take care to lift up the iron bars a little, to the end that the cement may cover the bottom of the vessel, and so that there be about the depth of half-an inch thereof under every bar: Cover the crucible and lute on the cover.

Set the crucible thus prepared in a furnace, so contrived, that the crucible may be surrounded with coals from top to bottom: For eight or ten hours keep up such a degree of fire that the vessel may be moderately red; after this take it out of the furnace; plunge your little iron bars into cold water, and you will find them concerted into steel.

The principal difference between iron and steel consists in this, that the latter is combined with a greater quantity of phlogiston than the former.

It appears by this experiment, that, to make iron unite with an inflammable matter, it is necessary it should be in fusion; it is sufficient that it be so red-hot as to be opened and softened by the fire.

Every kind of charcoal is fit to be an ingredient in the composition of the cement employed to make steel, provided it contain no vitriolic acid. However, it hath been observed that animal coals produce a speedier effect than others; for which reason it is proper to mix something of that kind with charcoal-dust, as above directed.

The following signs shew that the operation hath succeeded, and that the iron is changed into good steel.

This metal being quenched in cold water as proposed above, acquires such an extraordinary degree of hardness, that it will by no means yield to any impression of the file or hammer, and will sooner break in pieces than stretch upon the anvil. And here it is proper to observe, that the hardness of steel varies with the manner in which it is quenched. The general rule is, that the hotter the steel is when quenched, and the colder the water is in which you quench it, the harder it becomes. It may be deprived of the temper thus acquired, by making it red-hot, and letting it cool slowly; for it is thereby softened, rendered malleable, and the file will bite upon it. For this reason the artisans who work in steel begin with untempering it, that they may with more ease shape it into the tool they intend to make. They afterwards new-temper the tool when finished, and by this second temper the steel recovers the same degree of hardness it had acquired by the first temper.

The colour of steel is not so white as that of iron, but darker, and the grains, facets, or fibres, which appear on breaking it, are finer than those observed in iron.

If the bars of iron thus cemented, in order to convert them into steel, be too thick, or not kept long enough in cementation, they will not be turned into steel throughout their whole thickness; their surfaces only will be steel to a certain depth, and the centre will be mere iron; because the phlogiston will not have thoroughly penetrated them. On breaking a bar of this sort, the difference in colour and grain between the steel and the iron is very visible.

It is easy to deprive steel of the superabundant quantity of phlogiston which constitutes it steel, and thereby reduce it to iron. For this purpose it need only be kept red-hot for some time, observing that no matter approach it all the while that is capable of refunding to it the phlogiston which the fire carries off. The same end is still sooner obtained by cementing it with meagre hungry matters, capable of absorbing the phlogiston; such as bones calcined to whiteness, and cretaceous earths.

THE CALCINATION OF IRON. SUNDRY SAFFRONS OF MARS. Take filings of iron, what quantity you please; put them into a broad unglazed earthen vessel, set under the muffle of a cupelling furnace; make it red-hot; stir the filings frequently; and keep up the same degree of fire till the iron be wholly turned into a red powder.

Iron easily loses its phlogiston by the action of fire. The calx that remains after its calcination is exceeding red; which makes this be thought the natural colour of the earth of that metal. It hath accordingly been observed, that all the earths and stones, which either are naturally red, or acquire that colour by calcination, are ferruginous.

The yellowish red colour which every calx of iron hath, in whatever manner it be prepared, hath procured the name of crocus, or saffrom, to every preparation of this kind. That made in the manner above directed is called in medicine crocus martis astringent.

The rust produced on the surface of iron, is a sort of calx of iron made by way of dissolution. The moisture of the air acts upon the metal, dissolves it, and robs it os some of its phlogiston. This rust is called in medicine crocus martis aperiens; because it is thought that the saline parts, by means whereof the humidity dissolves the iron, remain united with the metal after its dissolution, and give it an aperitive virtue. The apothecaries prepare this sort of saffrom of mars by exposing iron filing to the dew till they be turned entirely to rust; which is then called saffron of mars by dew.

Another saffrom of mars is also prepared in a much shorter manner, by mixing filings of iron with pulverised sulphur, and moistening the mixture, which after some time ferments and grows hot. It is then set on the fire; the sulphur burns away, and the mass is kept stirring till it become a red matter. This saffron is nothing but iron dissolved by the acid of sulphur, which is known to be of the same nature with that of vitriol; and consequently this saffron of mars is no way different from vitriol calcined to redness.

IRON DISSOLVED BY THE MINERAL ACIDS. Put any mineral acid whatever into a matras with some water; set the matras on a sand-bath gently heated; drop into the vessel some filings of iron; the phenomena which usually accompany metalline dissolutions will immediately appear. Add more filings, till you observe the acid hath lost all sensible action upon them; then remove your matras from the sand-bath; you will find in it a solution of iron.

OF TIN. TO EXTRACT TIN FROM ITS ORE. Break your tin ore into a coarse powder, and by washing carefully, separate from it all the heterogeneous matters and ores of a different kind that may be mixed therewith. Then dry it, and roast it in a strong degree of fire, till no more arsenical vapour rise from it. When the ore is roasted, reduce it to a fine powder, and mix it thoroughly with twice its weight of the black flux well dried, a fourth part of its weight of clean iron filings, together with as much borax and pitch; put the mixture into a crucible; over all put sea-salt to the thickness of four fingers, and cover the crucible close.

Set the crucible thus prepared in a melting furnace; apply at first a moderate and slow degree of fire, till the flame of the pitch, which will escape through the joint of the cover, disappear entirely. Then suddenly raise your fire, and urge it with rapidity to the degree necessary for melting the whole mixture. As soon as the whole is in fusion , take the crucible out of the furnace, and separate the regulus from the scoria.

All tin ores contain a considerable quantity of arsenic, and no sulphur at all, or at most very little. Hence, though tin be the lightest of all metals, its ore is nevertheless much heavier than any other; arsenic being much heavier than sulphur, of which the ores of every other kind always contain a pretty large proportion. This ore is moreover very hard, and is not brought to a fine powder with so much ease as the rest.

These properties of tin ore furnish us with the means of separating it easily by lotion, not only from earthy and stony parts, but even from the other ores which may be mixed with it. And this is of the greater advantage on two accounts, viz. because tin cannot endure, without the destruction of a great part thereof, the degree of fire necessary to scorify the refractory matters which accompany its ore; and again, because this metal unites so easily with iron and copper, the ores of which are pretty commonly blended with tin ore, that after the reduction it would be found adulterated with a mixture of these two metals, if they were not separated from it before the fusion.

Into an unvarnished earthen dish put the quantity of tin you intend to calcine; melt it, and keep stirring it from time to time. Its surface will be covered with a greyish white powder: Continue the calcination till all your tin be converted into such a powder, which is the calx of tin.

THE DISSOLUTION OF TIN BY ACIDS. Put into a glass vessel what quantity you please of fine tin cut into little bits. Pour on it thrice as much aqua regis, compounded of two parts aqua fortis weakened with an equal quantity of very pure water, and one part spirit of salt. An ebullition will arise, and the tine will be very rapidly dissolved; especially if the quantities of metal and aqua regis be considerable.

TO EXTRACT LEAD FROM ITS ORE. Having roasted your lead-ore, reduce it to a fine powder; mix it with twice its weight of the black flux, and one fourth of its weight of clean iron filings and borax; put the whole into a crucible capable of containing at least thrice as much; over all put sea-salt four fingers thick; cover the crucible; lute the juncture; dry the whole with a gentle heat, and set it in a melting furnace.

Make the crucible moderately red; you will hear the sea-salt decrepitate, and after the decrepitation a small hissing in the crucible. Keep up the same degree of fire till that be over.

Then throw in as many coals as are necessary to complete the operation entirely, and raise the fire suddenly, so as to bring the whole mixture into perfect fusion. Keep up this degree of fire for a quarter of an hour, which is time sufficient for the precipitation of the regulus.

When the operation is finished, which may be known by the quietness of the matter in the crucible, and by a bright vivid flame that will rise from it, take the crucible out of the furnace, and separate the regulus from the scoria.

TO SEPARATE LEAD FROM COPPER. With luting earth and charcoal-dust make a flat vessel, widening upwards, and large enough to contain your metalline mass. Set it shelving downwards from the back towards the fore-part; and in the fore-part, at the bottom, make a little gutter communicating with another vessel of the same nature, placed near the former and a little lower. Let the mouth of the gutter within inside the upper vessel be narrowed, by means of a small iron plate fixed across it, while the loam is yet soft; so as to leave a very small apperture in the lower part of this canal sufficient to discharge the lead as it melts. Dry the whole by placing lighted coals round it.

When this apparatus is dry, put your mixed mass of copper and lead into the upper vessel; both in that, and in the other vessel, light a very gentle fire of wood or charcoal, so as not to exceed the degree of heat necessary to melt lead. In such a degree of heat the lead contained in the mixed mass will melt, and you will see it run out of the upper vessel into the lower; at the bottom of which it will unite into a regulus. When in this degree of heat no more lead flows, increase the fire a little, so as to make the vessel moderately red.

When no more will run, collect the lead contained in the lower vessel. Melt it over again in an iron ladle, with a degree of fire sufficient to make the ladle red; throw into it a little tallow or pitch, and while it burns keep stirring the metal, in order to reduce any part of it that may be calcined. Remove the pellicle or thin crust which will form on the surface; squeeze out all the lead it contains, and then put it to the mass of copper left in the upper vessel. Cjeck the fire, and in the same manner take off a second skin that will form on the surface of the lead. Lastly, when the metal is ready to fix, take off the skin that will then appear on it. The lead remaining after this will be very pure, and free from all alloy of copper.

With regard to the copper itself, you will find it in the upper vessel covered with a thin coat of lead, and if the lead mixed with it was in the proportion of a fourth or a fifth part only, and the fire applied was gentle and slow, it will retain nearly the same form after the operation that the mixed mass had before.

THE CALCINATION OF LEAD. Take what quantity of lead you please; melt it in one or more unglazed earthen pans; a dark grey powder will be found on its surface. Keep stirring the metal incessantly till it be wholly converted into such a powder, which is the calx of lead.

In the calcination of all metals, and particularly in this of lead, there appears a singular phenomenon which is not easily accounted for. It is this; though these matters lose a great deal of their substance, either by the dissipation of their phlogiston, or because some of the metal perhaps exhales the vapours, yet, when the calcination is over, their calxes are found to be encreased in weight, and this increase is very considerable. An hundred pounds of lead, for example, converted into minium, which is nothing but a calx of lead brought to a red colour by continuing the calcination, are found to gain ten pounds weight; so that for an hundred pounds of lead we have one hundred and ten pounds of minium; a prodigious and almost incredible augmentation, if it be considered that, far from adding any thing to the lead, we have on the contrary dissipated part of it.

TO PREPARE GLASS OF LEAD. Take two parts of litharge, and one part of pure crystalline sand; mingle them together as exactly as possible, adding a little nitre and sea-salt; put this mixture into a crucible of the most solid and most compact earth. Shut the crucible with a cover that may perfectly close it.

Set the crucible thus prepared in a melting furnace; fill the furnace with coals; light the fire gradually, so that the whole may be slowly heated: Then raise the fire so as to make the crucible very red, and bring the matter it contains into fusion; keep it thus melted for a quarter of an hour.

Then take the crucible out of the furnace, and break it: In the bottom thereof you will most commonly find a small button of lead, and over it a transparent glass of a yellow colour nearly resembling that of amber. Separate this glass from the little button of metal, and from the saline matters which you will find above it.

LEAD DISSOLVED BY THE NITROUS ACID. Put into a matras some aqua fortis precipitated like that used to dissolve silver; weaken it by mixing therewith an equal quantity of common water; set the matras in a hot sand-bath; throw into it, little by little, small bits of lead, till you see that no more will dissolve. Aqua fortis thus lowered will dissolve about a fourth of its weight of lead.

There is gradually formed upon the lead, as it dissolves, first a grey powder, and afterwards a white crust, which at last hinder the solvent from acting on the remaining part of the metal; and therefore the liquor should be made to boil, and the vessel should be shaken to remove those impediments, by which means all the lead will be dissolved.

OF MERCURY. TO EXTRACT MERCURY FROM ITS ORE, OR TO REVIVIFY IT FROM CINABAR. Pulverize the cinabar from which you would extract the mercury; with this powder mix an equal part of clean iron filings; put the mixture into a retort of glass or iron, leaving at least one third part thereof empty. Set the retort thus prepared in a sand-bath, so that its body may be quite buried in the sand, and its neck decline considerably downwards; fit on a receiver half filled with water, and let the nose of the retort enter about half an inch into the water.

Heat the vessel so as to make the retort moderately red. The mercury will rise in vapours, which will condense into little drops, and fall into the water in the receiver.

When you see that nothing more comes over with this degree of heat, increase it, in order to raise what mercury may still be left. When all the mercury is thus brought over, take off the receiver, pour out the water contained in it, and collect the mercury.

Mercury is never mineralized in the bowels of the earth by any thing but sulphur; with which if forms a compound of a brownish red colour, known by the name of Cinabar.

The oldest and richest mine of mercury is of Almaden in Spain. It is a singular property of that mine, that though the mercury found in it is combined with sulphur, and in the form of cinabar, yet no additament is required to procure the separation of these two; the earthy and stony matter, with which the particles of the ore are incorporated, being itself an excellent absorbent of sulphur.

In the quick-silver works carried on at this mine they make no use of retorts. They place lumps of the ore on an iron grate, which stands immediately over the furnace. The furnaces which serve for this operation are closed at the top by a sort of dome, behind which stands the shaft of a chimney that communicates with the fireplace, and gives vent to the smoke. These furnaces have in their fore-side sixteen apertures, to each of which is luted an aludel in a horizontal position, communicating with a long row of other aludels placed likewise in an horizontal direction; which aludels so connected together form one long pipe or canal, the further end whereof opens into a chamber destined to receive and condense all the mercurial vapours. These rows of aludels are supported from end to end by a terrass, which runs from the body of the building, wherein the furnaces are erected, to that where the chambers are built that perform the office of receivers.

This is a very ingenious contrivance, and saves much labour, expence, and trouble, that would be unavoidable if retorts were employed.

That part of the furnace which contains the lumps of ore, serves for the body of the retort; the row of aludels for its neck; and the little chambers in which these canals terminate are actual receivers. The terrass of communication, which reaches from the one building to the other, is formed of two inclined planes, the lower edges of which, meeting in the middle of the terrass, rise from thence insensibly; the one quie to the building where the furnaces are, and the other to that which forms the recipient chambers. By this means, when any mercury escapes through the joints of the aludels, it naturally runs down along these inclined planes, and so is collected in the middle of the terrass, where the inferior sides of the planes meeting together form a sort of canal, out of which it is easily taken up.

TO GIVE MERCURY, BY THE ACTION OF FIRE, THE APPEARANCE OF A METALLINE CALX. Put mercury into several little glass matrasses with long and narrow necks. Stop the matrasses with a little paper, to prevent any dirt from falling into them. Set them all in one sand-bath, so that they may be surrounded with sand as high as two thirds of their length. Apply the stongest degree of heat that mercury can bear without subliming; continue this heat without interruption, till all the mercury be turned to a red powder. The operation lasts about three months.

Mercury thus converted to a red powder is known in chemistry and medicine by the name of mercury precipitated per se.

TO DISSOLVE MERCURY IN THE VITRIOLIC ACID. TURBITH MINERAL. Put mercury into a glass retort, and pour on it thrice its weight of good oil of vitriol. Set the retort in a sand-bath; fit on a recipient; warm the bath by degrees till the liquor just simmer. With this heat the mercury will begin to dissolve. Continue the fire in this degree till all the mercury be dissolved.

The vitriolic acid dissolves mercury pretty well; but for this purpose the acid must be very hot, or even boil; and then too it is a very long time before the dissolution is completed. We have directed the operation to be performed in a retort; because this solution is usually employed to make another preparation called turbith mineral, which requires that as much as possible of the acid solvent be abstracted by distillation. Having therefore dissolved your mercury in the vitriolic acid, if you will now prepare the turbith, you must, by continuing to heat the retort, drive over all the liquor into the receiver, and distill till nothing remains but a white powdery matter; then break the

the retort; pulverise its contents in a glass mortar, and there pour common water, which will immediately turn the white matter of a lemon-colour; wash this yellow matter in five or six warm waters, and it will be what is called in medicine a turbith mineral; that is, a combination of the vitriolic acid with mercury, five or six grains whereof is a violent purgative, and also an emetic; qualities which it possesses in common with the vegetable turbith, whose name it hath therefore taken.

TO COMBINE MERCURY WITH SULPHUR. AETHIOPS MINERAL. Mix a dram of sulphur with three drams of quick-silver, by triturating the whole in a glass mortar with a glass pestle. By degrees, as you triturate, the mercury will disappear, and the matter will acquire a black colour. Continue the triture till you cannot perceive the least particle of running mercury. The black matter you will then have in the mortar is known in medicine by the the name of aethiops mineral. An aethiops may also be made by fire in the following manner.

In a shallow unglazed earthen pan melt one part of flowers of sulphur; add three parts of running mercury, making it fall into the pan in the form of small rain, by squeasing it through chamoy leather. Keep stirring the mixture with the shank of a tobacco-pipe all the while the mercury is falling; you will see the matter grow thick and acquire a black colour. When the whole is thoroughly mixed, set fire to it with a match, and let as much of the sulphur burn away as will flame.

TO SUBLIME THE COMBINATION OF MERCURY AND SULPHUR INTO CINABAR. Grind to powder aethiops mineral prepared by fire. Put it into a cucurbit; fit thereto a head; place it in a sand-bath, and begin with applying such a degree of heat as is requisite to sublime sulphur. A black matter will rise, and adhere to the sides of the vessel. When nothing more will rise with this degree of heat, raise the fire so as to make the sand and the bottom of the cucurbit red; and then the remaining matter will sublime in the form of a brownish red mass, which is true cinabar.

TO DISSOLVE MERCURY IN THE NITROUS ACID. SUNDRY MERCURIAL PRECEPITATES. Put into a matras the quantity of mercury you intend to dissolve; pour on it an equal quantity of good spirit of nitre, and set the matras in a sand-bath moderately heated. The mercury will dissolve with the phenomena that usually attend the dissolutions of metals in this acid. When the dissolution is comp;eted, let the liquor cool. You will know that the acid is perfectly saturated, if there remain at the bottom of the vessel, notwithstanding the heat, a little globule of mercury that will not dissolve.

Mercury dissolves in the nitrous acid with much more facility, and in much greater quantity, than in the vitriolic; so that it is not necessary, on this occasion, to make the liquor boil. This solution when cold yields crystals, which are a nitrous mercurial salt. If you desire to have a clear limpid solution of mercury, you must employ an aqua fortis that is not tainted with vitriolic or marine acid; for, the affinity of these two acids with mercury being greater than that of the nitrous acid, they precipitate it in the form of a while powder, when they are mixed with the solvent.

Mercury thus precipitated in a white powder, out of a solution thereof in the spirit of nitre, is used in medicine. To obtain this precipitate, which is known by the name of the white precipitate, sea-salt, dissolved in water, together with a little sal ammoniac is used; and the precipitate is washed several times in pure water, without which precaution it would be corrosive, on account of the great quantity of the marine acid which it would contain.

The preparation known by the name of red precipitate, is also obtained from our solucuib of mercury in spirit of nitre. It is made by abstracting all the moisture of the solution, either by distillation in a retort, or by evaporation in a glass bason set on a sand-bath. When it begins to grow dry, it appears like a white ponderous mass. Then the fire is made strong enough to drive off almost all the nitrous acid, which, being now concentrated, rises in the form of red vapours. If these vapours be catched in a receiver, they condense into a liquor, which is a very strong and vastly smoking spirit of nitre.

By degrees, as the nitrous acid is forced up by the fire, the mercurial mass loses its white colour, and becomes first yellow, and at last very red. When it is become entirely of this last colour, the operation is finished. The red mass remaining is a mercury that contains but very little acid, in comparison of what it did while it was white; and indeed the first white mass is such a violent corrosive, that it cannot be used in medicine; whereas, when it become red, it makes an excellent escharotic, which those who know how to use it properly apply with very great success, particularly to veneral ulcers.

TO COMBINE MERCURY WITH THE ACID OF SEA-SALT. CORROSIVE SUBLIMATE. Evaporate a solution of mercury in the nitrous acid till there remain only a white powder, as mentioned in our observations on the preceding process. With this powder mix as much green vitriol calcined to whiteness, and decrepitated sea-salt, as there was mercury in the solution. Triturate the whole carefully in a glass mortar. Put this mixture into a matrass, so that two thirds thereof may remain empty, having first cut off the neck to half its length; or instead thereof you may use an apothecary's phial. Set your vessel in a sand-bath, and put sand round it as high as the contents reach. Apply a moderate fire at first, and raise it by slow degrees. Vapours will begin to ascend. Continue the fire in the same degree till they cease. Then stop the mouth of the vessel with paper, and increase the fire till the bottom of the sand-bath be red-hot. With this degree of heat a sublimate will rise, and adhere to the inside and upper part of the vessel, in the form of white, semi-transparent crystals. Keep up the fire to the same degree till nothing more sublimes. Then let the vessel cool; break it, and take out what is sublimed, which is corrosive sublimate.

SWEET SUBLIMATE. Take four parts of corrosive sublimate; pulverise it in a glass or marble mortar; add by little and little three parts of mercury revivified from cinabar; triturate the whole carefully, till the mercury be perfectly killed, so that no globule thereof can be perceived. The matter will then be grey. Put this powder into an apothecary's phial, or into a matras, whose neck is not above four or five inches long, leaving two thirds thereof empty. Set the vessel in a sand-bath, and put sand around it to one third of its height. Apply a moderate fire at first; and afterwards raise it gradually till you perceive that the mixture sublimes. Keep it up to this degree till nothing more will rise, and then break the vessel. Reject, as useless, a small quantity of earth which you will find at the bottom; separate also what adheres to the neck of the vessel, and carefully collect the matter in the middle, which will be white. Pulverise it; sublime it a second time, in the same manner as before; and in the same manner separate the earthy matter left at the bottom of the vessel, and what you find sublimed into the neck. Pulverise, and sublime a third time, the white matter you last found in the middle. The white matter of this third sublimation is the sweet sublimate, called also aquila alba.

THE PANACEA OF MERCURY. Pulverise some sweet sublimate, and sublime it in the same manner as you did thrice before. Repeat this nine times. After these sublimations it will make no impression on the tongue. Then pour on it aromatic spirit of wine, and set the whole in digestion for eight days. After that decant the spirit of wine, and dry what remains, which is the panacea of mercury.

OF ANTIMONY. TO SEPARATE ANTIMONY FROM ITS ORE BY FUSION. Having drilled some small holes, of about two lines diameter, in the bottom of a crucible, put into it your antimonial ore broken into little bits, about the size of a hazel nut; lute on its cover; for the crucible thus prepared in the mouth of another crucible, and close the joints with lute.

At the distance of half a foot from this compound vessel place bricks all round, so as to form a furnace; the sides of which must rise as high as the brim of the uppermost crucible.

Let the bottom of this furnace be filled with ashes, up to the top of the lower crucible, and the rest of the furnace with lighted coals. Blow the fire, if it be necessary, with bellows, till the upper crucible become red. Keep it up in this degree for about a quarter of an hour. Then take your vessels out of the furnace, and you will find the antimony collected in the bottom of the lower crucible, having run through the holes of the upper one.

THE COMMON REGULUS OF ANTIMONY. Reduce crude antimony to powder. Mix it with three fourths of its weight of white tartar, and half its weight of refined salt-petre, both pulverised. Into a large crucible, made red-hot in the fire, throw a spoonfull of your mixture, and cover it. There will be a very considerable detonation. When it is over, throw in a second spoonfull of your mixture, and cover the crucible as before; this will produce a second detonation. Go on thus, till you have thrown in all your mixture.

When the whole has thus fulminated, increase the fire so as to bring the matter into fusion; that being done, take the crucible out of the furnace, and immediately pour its contents into an iron cone heated and greased with tallow. Strike the floor and the cone some gentle blows with a hammer, to make the regulus precipitate; and when the matter is fixed and cold, invert the cone, and turn it out. You will see it consist of two distinct substances; the uppermost of which is a saline scoria, and the undermost the reguline part. Strike this mass a blow with a hammer, in the place where these substances join, and you will by this means separate the scoria from the regulus; the latter of which will have the form of a metallic cone, on whose base you will observe the signature of a bright star.

REGULUS OF ANTIMONY PRECIPITATED BY METALS. Put one part of small iron nails into a crucible, and set it amidst burning coals, in a melting furnace. When the iron is thoroughly red-hot, and begins to grow white, add thereto little by little, and at several times, two parts of crude antimony in powder. The antimony will immediately flow and unite with the iron. When the antimony is entirely melted, add thereto, at several times, the fourth of its weight of pulverised nitre; a detonation will ensue, and the whole mixture will be in fusion.

After you have kept the matter in this condition for some minutes, pour it into an iron cone, first heated and tallowed. Strike the sides of the cone with a hammer, that the regulus may fall to the bottom; and, when all is cold, separate it from the scoria by a blow with a hammer. Melt this first regulus again in another crucible, adding a fourth part of its weight of crude antimony. Keep the crucible close shut, and give no more heat than is necessary to melt the matter. When it is in perfect fusion, add to it at several times, as you did before, the sixth part of its weight of pulverised nitre; and, in half a quarter of an hour after this, pour the whole into a cone as you did the first time.

Lastly, Melt your regulus over again a third or even a fourth time, always adding a little nitre, which will detonate as before. If after all these fusion you pour the regulus into an iron cone, you will find it very beautiful, and the star well formed; it will be covered with a semi-transparent, lemon-coloured scoria. This scoria is extremely acrid and caustic.

THE CALCINATION OF ANTIMONY. Take an unglazed earthen vessel, wider at top than at bottom; put into it two or three ounces of crude antimony finely pulverised. Set this vessel over a weak charcoal-fire, and increase the heat till you see the antimony begin to smoke a little. Continue the fire in this degree, and keep incessantly stirring the antimony with the shank of a tobacco-pipe all the while it is upon the fire.

The powder of antimony, which, before calcination, was of a brilliant colour inclining to black, will become dull, and look like an earth. When it comes to have this appearance, raise your fire till the vessel be red-hot, and keep it up in this degree till the matter cease entirely to smoke.

CALX OF ANTIMONY REDUCED TO A REGULUS. Mix the calx of antimony, which you intend to reduce, with an equal quantity of black soap. This mixture will make a thin paste. Put it little by little into a crucible, previously made red-hot amidst live coals. Thus let the soap burn, till it cease to emit an oily smoke. Then cover the crucible; make the fire strong enough to melt the matter, and you will hear it effervesce and boil. When this noise is over, let the crucible cool, and then break it; you will find in it a beautiful scoria, marked with circles of several colours; and under that a button of regulus, which is not yet quite pure, and must be purified in the following manner.

Pound this regulus, and mix it with half its weight of an antimonial calx as perfectly desulphurated as possible. Put it into a crucible, and cover it; melt the whole, so that the surface of the melted matter may be smooth and uniform. Let the crucible cool, and then break it; you will find in it a beautiful button of very pure regulus, covered with a scoria, having the appearance of an opaque glass, or a kind of greyish enamel, moulded on the finely radiated surface of the regulus.

ANTIMONY CALCINED WITH NITRE. LIVER OF ANTIMONY. Pulverise and mix perfectly together equal parts of nitre and antimony; but the mixture into an iron mortar, and cover it with a tila, which however must not shut it quite close. With a live coal set fire to the matter in the mortar, and immediately withdraw it. The mixture will flame, with great detonation; which being over, and the mortar cooled, invert it, and strike its bottom to make all the matter fall out. Then, by a blow with a hammer, separate the scoria from the shining part, which is the liver of antimony.

ANOTHER CALCINATION OF ANTIMONY WITH NITRE. DIAPHORETIC ANTIMONY. Mix one part of antimony with three parts of nitre; project this mixture by spoonfulls into a crucible kept red-hot in a furnace. Each projection will be attended with a detonation. Continue doing this till you have used all your mixture; then raise the fire, and keep it up for two hours; after which throw your matter into a pan full of hot water. Let it lie steeping in water kept hot for a whole day. Then pour off the liquor; wash the white powder you find at the bottom in warm water; and repeat the ablutions till the powder become insipid. Dry it, and you have diaphoretic antimony.

CALX OF ANTIMONY VITRIFIED. Take any quantity you please of calx of antimony, made without addition; put it into a good crucible, which set in a melting furnace; kindle the fire gradually, and leave the crucible uncovered at the beginning.

A quarter of an hour after the matter is red-hot, cover the crucible, and excite the fire vigorously till the calx melt. You may know when it is thoroughly melted, by dipping into the crucible an iron wire, to the end of which a little knob of glass will adhere, if the matter be in perfect fusion. Keep it in fusion for a quarter of an hour, or rather longer if your crucible can bear it. Then take it out of the furnace, and immediately pour out the melted matter on a smooth stone, made very hot for the purpose; it will presently fix into a yellow glass.

KERMES MINERAL. Break any quantity you will of Hungarian antimony into little bits; put it into a good earthen coffee-pot; pour on it twice its weight of rain-water, and a fourth part of its weight of well filtered liquor of nitre fixed by charcoal. Boil the whole briskly for two hours, and then filter the liquor. As it cools it will acquire a red colour, grow turbid, and leave a red powder on the filter.

Return your antimony into the coffee-pot. Pour on it as much rain-water as before, and three fourths of the former quantity of the liquor of fixed nitre. Boil it again for two hours, and then filter the liquor. It will again deposite a red sediment. Return your antimony into the coffee pot; pour on it the same quantity of rain-water, and half the first quantity of the liquor of fixed nitre. Boil it again for two hours, and filter the liquor as formerly. Wash all these sediments with warm water, till they become insipid; then dry them, and you have the kermes mineral.

REGULUS OF ANTIMONY DISSOLVED IN THE MINERAL ACIDS. Compound an aqua regis by mixing together four measures of spirit of nitre, and one measure of spirit of salt; on a sand bath moderately heated place a matras, into which pour sixteen times as much of this aqua regis as you have regulus to dissolve. Break your regulus in little bits; and throw them successively one after another into the matras, observing not to add a new one till that put in before is entirely dissolved; continue this till your regulus be all used. By degrees, as the dissolution advances, the liquor will acquire a beautiful golden colour; which however will insensibly disappear, as the white fumes that continually ascend from it evaporate.

REGULUS OF ANTIMONY COMBINED WITH THE ACID OF SEA-SALT. BUTTER OF ANTIMONY. CINABAR OF ANTIMONY. Pulverise and mix thoroughly six parts of regulus of antimony, and sixteen parts of corrosive sublimate. Put this mixture into a glass retort that hath a wide short neck, and let one half of its body at least be left empty. Set it in a reverberatory furnace, and having fitted a recipient thereto and luted the joint, make a very small fire at first to heat it slowly. Increase it afterwards by degrees, till you see a liquor ascend from the retort that grows thick as it cools. Keep up the fire to this degree as long as you see any of this matter come over.

When no more arises with this degree of fire, unlute your vessels, take off the receiver, and in its place substitute another filled with water. Then increase your fire by degrees till the retort be red-hot. Some running mercury will fall into the water, which you may dry and keep for use; it being very pure.

Soon after mixing the regulus with the corrosive sublimate, the matter sometimes grows considerably hot: This is occasioned by the marine acid's beginning to act on the reguline part, and to desert its mercury.

The butter of animony rises with a very moderate heat; because the acid of sea-salt hath the property of volatilizing, and carrying up along with it, the metallic substances with which it is combined: And for this reason a very gentle heat only is required at the beginning of the operation.

It is absolutely necessary that the neck of the retort be wide and short: for otherwise, if the butter of antimony should fix and be accumulated therein, it might stop up the passage entirely, and occasion the bursting of the vessels. By this operation we obtain eight parts and three quarters of fine butter of antimony, and ten parts of running mercury; there being left in the retort one part and a half of a rarefied matter, black, white, and red. This is probably the most earthy and most impure part of the regulus of antimony.

If crude antimony, instead of regulus of antimony, be mixed with corrosive sublimate, a butter of antimony will be obtained in the same manner; but, instead of having a running mercury after the butter, you will find a cinabar sublimed into the neck and upper concavity of the retort.

The reason of this difference is easily conceived: for, when the regulus is used, the mercury being deserted by its acid, finds no other substance to unite with, and so rises in the form of quick-silver; but when crude antimony is employed instead of its regulus, as the reguline part thereof cannot combine with the acid without quitting its sulphur, so this sulphur, being at liberty, unites with the mercury, which is so likewise, and therewith forms a cinabar; which from its origin is named cinabar of antimony.

BUTTER OF ANTIMONY DECOMPOUNDED BY MEANS OF WATER ONLY. THE PULVIS ALGAROTH, OR MERCURIUS VITAE. Melt with a gentle heat as much butter of antimony was you please. When it is melted, pour it into a large quantity of warm water. The water will immediately grow turbid, but whitish, and let fall a great quantity of white powder. When all the precipitate is settled, decant the water: pour on fresh warm water; and having thus edulcorated it by several ablutions, dry it and you have the pulvis Algaroth, or mercurius vitae.

BEZOAR MINERAL. Melt butter of antimony over warm ashes, and put it into a phial or matras. Gradually pour on it good spirit of nitre, 'till the matter be entirely dissolved. This usually requires as much spirit of nitre as there is butter of antimony. During the dissolution fumes will rise, which must be carefully avoided. Pour your solution, which will be clear and of a reddish colour, into a glass cucurbit, or a pan of stone-ware; set it in a sand-bath, and evaporate to dryness with a moderate heat. There will be left a white mass, weighing a fourth part less than the whole quantity used, both of butter and the spirit of nitre. Let it cool, and again pour on it as much spirit of nitre as you used the first time. Place the vessel again in the sand-bath, and evaporate the moisture as before. You will have a white mass that hath neither gained nor lost in weight. On this pour, for the third time, the same quantity of spirit of nitre as you did the first time. Again evaporate the moisture to perfect dryness: then increase your fire, and calcine the matter for half an hour. You will have left a dry, friable, light white matter, of an agreeable acid taste;

which will fall into a coarse powder, and must be kept in a phial carefully stopt. This is Bezoar mineral: it is neither caustic nor emetic, and has only a fudorific virtue. It obtained the name it bears, because, like the animal bezoar, it was imagined to have the property of resisting poison.

FLOWERS OF ANTIMONY. Take an unglazed earthen pot, having an aperture in its side, with a stopple to shut it close. Set this pot in a furnace, the cavity whereof it may fit as exactly as possible; and fill up with lute the space, if any, left between the vessel and the furnace. Over this vessel fix three aludels with a blind-head at the top; and light a fire in the furnace under the pot.

When the bottom of the pot is thoroughly red, throw into the lateral aperture a small spoonful of powdered antimony. Stir the matter immediately with an iron spatula made a little bending, in order to spread it over the bottom of the vessel, and then stop the hole. The flowers will rise and adhere to the insides of the aludels. Keep up the fire so that the bottom of the pot may always continue red; and when nothing more sublimes, put in a like quantity of antimony, and operate as before. In this manner go on subliming your antimony, till you have as many flowers as you want. Then let the fire go out; and when the vessels are cold unlute them. You will find flowers adhering all around the insides of the aludels and the head, which you may collect with a feather.

REGULUS OF ANTIMONY CONVERTED INTO FLOWERS. Pulverise your regulus of antimony; put the powder into an unglazed earthen pot: three or four fingers breadth above the powder, fit into the pot a little cover, made of the same earth and having a small hole in its middle, so that it may with ease be placed in the pot and taken out when there is occasion: cover the mouth of the pot with a common lid; set it in a furnace, and kindle a fire under it sufficient to make the bottom of the pot red and to melt the regulus. When it hath been thus kept in fusion for about an hour, let the fire go out and the whole cool. Then remove the two covers. You will find adhering to the surface of the regulus, which will be in a mass at the bottom of the pot, white flowers resembling snow, intermixed with beautiful, brilliant silver coloured needles. Take them out, and you will find them make about one part in sixty-two of the whole regulus employed.

Put the covers again in their places, and proceed in the same manner as before: when the vessels are cold, you will find half as many more flowers as you got the first time.

Proceed thus till you have converted all your regulus into flowers. This will require a considerable number of sublimations, which, as you advance, will always yield you a greater portion of flowers; respect, however, being had to the quantity of regulus remaining in the pot.

OF BISMUTH. TO EXTRACT BISMUTH FROM ITS ORE. Break the ore of bismuth into small pieces, and therewith fill a crucible either of earth or of iron. Set the crucible in a furnace, and light such a fire that bits of the ore may become moderately red. Stir the ore from time to time; and if you perceive it crackle and fly, keep the crucible covered. At the bottom you will find a button of bismuth.

BISMUTH DISSOLVED BY ACIDS. MAGISTERY OF BISMUTH. SYMPATHETIC INK. Into a matras put bismuth broken into little bits: pour on it, by little and little, twice as much aqua fortis. This acid will attack the semi-metal briskly, and dissolve it entirely, with heat, effervescence, vapours, and puffing up. The solution will be clear and limpid.

If you would have a magistery of bismuth beautifully white, you must perform the dissolution with an aqua fortis that is not tainted with any mixture of the vitriolic acid; for this gives the precipitate a dirty white colour, inclining to grey.

Bismuth may also be precipitated by the means of fixed or volatil alkalis; but the precipitate is not of so fine a white as when procured by the means of pure water only.

A solution of bismuth prepared with the proper quantity of aqua fortis, that is, with two parts of the acid to one of the semi metal, coalesces into little crystals almost as soon as made.

Aqua fortis not only acts on bismuth when separated from its ore, and reduced to a regulus, but attacks it even in its ore, and likewise dissolves at the same time some portion of the ore itself. With this solution of the ore of bismuth Mr. Hellot makes a very curious sympathetic ink, differing from all that were known before.

Mr. Hellot prepares the liquor in the following manner: "He bruises the ore of bismuth to a coarse powder. On two ounces of this powder he pours a mixture of five ounces of common water with five ounces of aqua fortis. He does not heat the vessel till the first ebullitions are over. He then sets it in a gentle sand-heat, and lets it digest there till he sees no more air-bubbles rise. When none appear in this heat, he increases it so as to make the solvent boil slightly for a full quarter of an hour. It takes up a tincture nearly of the colour of brown beer. The ore that gives the aqua fortis this colour is the best. He then lets the solution cool, laying the matras on its side; that he may decant the liquor more conveniently, when all is precipitated that is not taken up by the solvent.

"The second vessel, into which the liquor is first decanted, he also lays declining; that a new precipitate of the undissolved matters may be obtained; after which he pours the liquor into a third vessel. This liquor must not be filtered, if you would have the rest of the process succeed perfectly; because the aqua fortis would dissolve some of the paper, and that would spoil the colour of your liquor.

"When this solution, which Mr. Hellot calls the impregnation, is thoroughly clarified by being decanted three or four times, he puts it into a glass bason with ten ounces of very pure sea-salt. The fine white salt made by the sun succeeded best with Mr. Hellot. If that can not be had, common bay-salt purified by solution, filtration and crystallisation, may be used instead of it. But it is rare to meet with any of the sort that is not a little tainted with iron, the white bay salt is to be preferred. The glass bason he sets in a gentle sand-heat, and keeps it there till the mixture be reduced by evaporation to an almost dry saline mass.

"If you desire to save the aqua regis, the impregnation must be put into a retort, and distilled with the gentle heat of a sand-bath. But there is an inconvenience as Mr. Hellot observes, in employing a retort; which is that, as the saline mass cannot be stirred while it coagulates in the retort, it is reduced to a compact cake of coloured salt, which presents but one single surface to the water in which it must be dissolved; so that the one solution thereof takes up sometimes no less than five or six days. In the bason, on the contrary, the saline mass is easily brought to a granulated salt, by stirring it with a glass rod; and, when thus granulated, it has a great deal more surface; it dissolves more easily, and yields it tincture to water in four hours time. Indeed one is more exposed to the vapours of the solvent, which would be dangerous, if the operation were to be often performed, without proper precautions.

"When the bason, or little vessel containing the mixture of the impregnation and sea-salt, is heated, the liquor, which was of an orange-coloured red, becomes a crimson red; and, when all the phlegm of the solvent is evaporated, it acquires a beautiful emerald colour. By degrees it thickens, and turns of the colour of a mass of verdegris. It must then be carefully stirred with the glass rod, in order to granulate the salt, which must then be kept over the fire till it be perfectly dry; because you run a risk of losing irrecoverably the colour you are seeking. You may be sure you have lost it, if by this much heat the salt that was of a green colour turn to a dirty yellow. If it be once brought to this state, it will continue without changing when cold; but if care be taken to remove it from the fire while it is still green, you will see it gradually grow pale, and become of a beautiful rose-colour as it cools.

"Mr. Hellot separates it from this vessel, and throws it into another containing distilled rain-water; and the second vessel he keeps in gentle digestion, till he observes that the powder which falls to the bottom is perfectly white. If, after three or four hours digesting, the powder still continues tinged with a rose colour, it is proof that water enough was not added to dissolve all the salt impregnated with the tincture of the solution. In this case, the first tinged liquor must be poured off, and fresh water added in proportion to the quantity of tinged salt that is supposed to remain mixed with the precipitate.

"When the ore is pure, and doth not contain a great deal of fusible stone, commonly called fluor, or quartz, an ounce of it generally yields tincture enough for eight or nine ounces of water, and the liquor is of a beautiful colour, like that of the lilach or pipe-tree blossom. In order to prove the effect of this tincture, you must write with this lilach-coloured liquor on good well-gummed paper, that does not sink: or you may use it to shade the leaves of some tree or plant, having first drawn the outlines thereof lightly with China ink or with a black lead pencil. Let this coloured drawing, or writing, dry in a warm air. You will perceive no colour while it is cold; but, if it be gently warmed before the fire, you will see the writing, or the drawing, gradually acquire a blue or greenish blue colour, which is visible as long as the paper continues a little warm, and disappears entirely when it cools."

The singularity of this sympathetic ink consists in its property of disappearing entirely, and becoming invisible, though it be not touched with any thing whatever: and this distinguishes it from all others; which, when once rendered visible by the application of proper means, do not again disappear, or at least not without touching the strokes on the paper with some other liquor.

OF ZINC. TO EXTRACT ZINC FROM ITS ORE, OR FROM CALAMINE. Take eight parts of calamine reduced to a powder; mix this powder accurately with one part of fine charcoal dust, previously calcined in a crucible to free it from all moisture: put this mixture into a stone retort coated with lute, leaving a third part of it empty: set your retort in a reverberatory furnace, capable of giving a very fierce heat. To the retort apply a receiver, with a little water in it. Kindle the fire, and raise it by degrees till the heat be strong enough to melt copper. With this degree of fire the zinc being metallised will separate from the mixture, and sublime into the neck of the retort, in the form of metallic drops. Break the retort when it is cold, and collect the zinc.

Most of the zinc we have comes from an ore of difficult fusion that is worked at Goslar, and yields, at one and the same time, lead, zinc, and another metallic matter called cadmia fornacum, which also contains much zinc.

The furnace used for smelting this ore is closed on its fore-side with thin plates or tables of stone, not aove an inch thick. This stone is greyish, and bears a violent fire.

In this furnace the ore is melted amidst charcoal, by the help of bellows. Each melting takes twelve hours, during which time the zinc flowing with the lead is resolved into flowers and vapours, great part of which adheres to the sides of the furnace in the form of a very hard crust of earth. The workmen take care to remove this crust from time to time; for it would otherwise grow so thick at last, as to lessen the cavity of the furnace very considerably.

There adheres moreover to the fore-part of the furnace, which is formed, as we said before, of thin plates of stone, a metallic matter, which is the zinc, and is expecially collected at the end of each melting, by removing from this part all the live coals. A quantity of small coal is laid unlighted at the bottom; and on this small-coal, by striking the stone-plates gently with a hammer, the zinc is made to fall out of the other matter, known by the Latin name of cadmia fornacum, among which it appears fixed in a radiated form. To this other matter we may properly enough give the name of furnace-calamine. The zinc falls in the form of a melted metal, all on fire, and in a bright flame. It would soon be entirely burnt and reduced to flowers, if it were not extinguished, and easily cooled and fixed, by being hid under the unlighted small-coal placed below on purpose to receive it.

The zinc adheres to the fore-part of the furnace preferably to any other, because that being the thinnest, is therefore the coolest: and, in order further to promote its fixing on this part, they take care to keep the thin stone-plates cool during the operation, by throwing water on them.

Hence it appears that zinc is not extracted from its ore by fusion and the precipitation of a regulus, like other metallic substances. This is owing to the great volatility of our semi-metal, which cannot, without subliming bear the degree of fire necessary to melt its ore. It is at the same time so combustible, that a great part of it rises in flowers which have not the metalline form.

TO SUBLIME ZINC INTO FLOWERS. Take a very deep, large crucible: place this crucible in a furnace, so that it may stand inclining in an angle of forty-five degrees nearly. Throw some zinc into it, and kindle a fire in the furnace somewhat stronger than would be necessary to keep lead in fusion. The zinc will melt. Stir it with an iron wire, and there will appear on its surface a very bright white flame: two inches above this flame a thick smoke will be formed, and with this smoke exceeding white flowers will rise, and remain some time adhering to the sides of the crucible, in the form of a very fine light down. When the flame slackens, stir your melted matter again with the iron wire: you will see the flame renewed, and the flowers begin again to appear in greater abundance. Go on thus till you observe that the matter will not flame, nor any more flowers rise.

TO COMBINE ZINC WITH COPPER, BRASS, PRINCE'S METAL, ETC. Pound one part and an half of calamine, and an equal quantity of charcoal: mingle these two powders together, and moiston them with a little water. Put this mixture into a large crucible, or some other earthen vessel that will bear a melting heat. Amongst and over this mixture put one part of very pure copper in thin plates, and then put fresh charcoal-dust over all: close the crucible; set it in a melting furnace; put coals all round it, and let them kindle gradually. Raise the fire so as to make the crucible very red hot. When you observe that the flame hath acquired a purple or blueish-green colour, uncover the crucible, and dip into it an iron wire, to examine whether or no the copper be in fusion under the charcoal dust. If you find it is, moderate the force of the fire a little, and let your crucible remain in the furnace for a few minutes. Then take it out and let it cool: you will find your copper of a gold colour, increased in weight a fourth, or perhaps a third part, and yet very malleable.

The lapis calaminaris is not the only substance with which copper may be converted into brass: all other ores containing zinc, the furnace-calamine that sublimes where such ores are worked, tutty, zinc in substance, may be substituted for it, and, like it, will make very fine brass; but, in order to succeed, sundry precautions are necessary.

This process is a part of cementation; for the calamine doth not melt; only the zinc is converted into vapours, and then combines with the copper. On this the success of the operation partly depends, as it is the means of the copper's preserving its purity and malleability; because the other metallic substances that may be united with the ore of zinc, or with the zinc itself, not having the same volatility, cannot be reduced to vapours. If you are apprised that the calamine, or other ore of zinc used on this occasion is contaminated with a mixture of any other metallic matter, you must mingle luting earth with the charcoal-dust and the matter containing the zinc; make it into a stiff paste with water; of this make a bed at the bottom of your crucible, and ram it hard down; lay the copper-plates thereon, cover them with charcoal-dust and then proceed as before. By this means, when the copper melts it cannot fall to the bottom of the crucible, nor mix with the ore; but is borne up by the mixture, and cannot combine with any thing but the zinc that rises in vapours, and, passing through the lute, fixes in the copper.

Lapis Calaminaris, or other ore of zinc, may be also purified before it be used for making brass; especially if adulterated with lead ore, which is often the case. For this purpose the ore must be roasted in a fire strong enough to give a small degree of fusion to the leaden matter; which will thereby be reduced into larger, heavier, and tougher masses. The most subtile particles are dissipated in the torrefaction, together with some of the calamine. The calamine, on the contrary, is by roasting made more tender, lighter, and much more friable. When it is in this condition, put it into a washing tray or pan; dip the tray in a vessel full of water, and bruise the matter it contains. The water will carry off the lightest powder, which is the calamine, and leave nothing at the bottom of the tray but the heaviest substance; that is, the leaden matter, which is to be rejected as useless. The powder of the calamine will settle at the bottom of the vessel, where, after pouring off the water, it may be found, and used as above directed.

In this operation the charcoal-dust serves to prevent both the copper and the zinc from being calcined: and for this reason, when you work on a great quantity of materials at once, it is not necessary to use so much charcoal dust, in proportion, as when you work but on a small quantity; because, the greater the mass of metal, the less easily will it calcine.

Though the copper melts in this operation, yet it is far from being necessary to apply such a strong fire as copper usually requires to melt it; for the accession of the zinc, on this occasion, communicates to it a great degree of fusibility. The increase of its weight is also owing to the quantity of zinc combined with it. Copper acquires still another advantage by its association with this semi-metal; for it remains longer in the fire without calcining.

Brass well prepared ought to be malleable when cold. But in whatever manner it be made, and whatever proportion of zinc there be in it, it is constantly found quite malleable when red-hot.

Brass melted in a crucible, with a fierce heat, takes fire almost like zinc, and from its surface many white flowers ascend, dancing about in flakes like the flowers of zinc. They are indeed the flowers of zinc, and the flame of brass urged by a strong fire is no other than the flame of the zinc that is united with the copper, and then burns. If brass be thus kept long in fusion, it will lose almost all the zinc it contains. It will also lose much of its weight, and its colour will be nearly that of copper. It is therefore necessary, towards performing this operation aright, to seize the moment when the copper is sufficiently impregnated with zinc, when it hath acquired the most weight and the finest colour, with the least detriment to its ductility, that is possible, and that instant to put out the fire; because, if the copper be left longer in fusion, it will only lose the zinc already united with it. Skill acquired by much practice, and an acquaintance with the particular calamine employed, are necessary to guide the artist surely through this operation; for there are very considerable differences between the sundry ores of zinc. Some of them contain lead, and in others there is iron. When these hete--ogeneous metals come to be mixed with the copper, they do indeed augment its weight, but they render it at the same time pale and make it very harsh. Some calamines require to be roasted before they can be used for this purpose, and in the torrefaction emit vapours of a volatile alkali, succeeded by vapours of a sulphureous spirit: others exhale no vapours while roasting, and may be employed without any antecedent preparations. These different qualities must evidently produce great differences in the operation.

Brass may also be made, as prince's metal and other imitations of gold are actually made, by using zinc in substance, instead of the ores that contain it. But these compositions have not, when cold, the ductility of brass prepared with lapis calaminaris, because zinc is seldom pure, or free from a mixture of lead. Perhaps also the different manner in which the zinc unites with the copper may contribute to this variation.

To obviate this inconvenience, the zinc must be refined from all alloy of lead. The property of being indissoluble by sulphur, which this semi-metal possesses, points out a very practicable method of doing it. The zinc must be melted in a crucible, and stirred briefly with a strong iron wire, while tallow and mineral sulphur are alternately projected upon it; but to that the quantity of sulphur may greatly exceed that of the tallow. If the sulphur do not burn entirely away, but form a kind of scoria on the surface of the zinc, it is a sign that your semi-metal contains lead. In this case you must continue throwing in more sulphur, and keep stirring the zinc incessantly, till you perceive that the sulphur ceases to unite any more with a metallic substance, but burns freely on the surface of the zinc. The semi-metal is then refined; because the sulphur, which cannot dissolve it, unites very readily with the lead, or other metallic substance, contained in it.

If zinc thus refined be mixed with pure copper, in the proportion of a fourth or a third part, and the mixture be kept in fusion and constantly stirring for some time, the brass produced will be as ductile, when cold, as that made by cementation with the lapis calaminaris.

With regard to prince's metal, and other imitations of gold, they are made either with copper or brass recombined with more zinc. As it is necessary, for giving them a fine golden colour, to mix with them other proportions of zinc than that required to make brass only, they are generally much less ductile.

ZINC DISSOLVED IN THE MINERAL ACIDS. Weaken concentrated oil of vitriol by mixing with it an equal quantity of water. Into a matras put the zinc you intend to dissolve, first broken to small pieces. Pour on it six times its weight of the vitriolic acid, lowered as above directed, and set the matras in a sand-bath gently heated. The zinc will dissolve entirely, without any sediment. The neutral metallic salt resulting from this dissolution shoots into crystals, which go by the name of white vitriol, or vitriol of zinc.

Zinc is dissolved by the nitrous and marine acids, much in the same manner as by the vitriolic; except that the marine acid does not touch a black, spungy, rarefied matter, which it separates from the zinc. M. Hellot found upon trial that this matter is not mercury, and that it cannot be reduced to a metallic substance.

A solution of zinc in the marine acid, being distilled to dryness, yields a sublimate on applying a violent heat to it.

All the acids dissolve with ease; not only zinc, but its flowers also; and that nearly in the same quantity, and with almost all the same phenomena.

OF ARSENIC. TO EXTRACT ARSENIC FROM ITS MATRICES. ZASSRE OR SMELT. Powder some cobalt, white pyrites, or other arsenical matters. Put this powder into a retort with a short wide neck, leaving a full third thereof empty. Set your retort in a reverberating furnace; lute on a receiver; heat your vessel by degrees, and increase the fire till you see a powder sublime into the neck of the retort. Keep up the fire in this degree as long as the sublimation continues: when this begins to slacken, raise your fire, and make it as strong as the vessels will bear. When nothing more ascends, let it go out. On unluting the vessels, you will find in the receiver a little arsenic in the form of a fine light farina. The neck of the retort will be full of white flowers, not quite so fine, some of which will appear like little crystals; and if a good deal of arsenic be sublimed, a ponderous matter, like a white, semi-transparent glass, will be found adhering to that part of the neck of the retort which is next its body.

When all the arsenic the cobalt will yield is thus separated, the earthy fixed matter left behind is mixed with divers fusible matters and vitrified, and produces a glass of beautiful blue colour. It is called smalt. This glass is to be prepared in the following manner.

Take four parts of fine fusible sand, an equal quantity of any fixed alkali perfectly depurated, and one part of cobalt from which the arsenic hath been sublimed by torrefaction. Pulverise these different substances very finely, and mix them thoroughly together; put the mixture into a good crucible, cover it, and set it in a melting furnace. Make a strong fire, and keep it up constantly in the same degree for some hours. Then dip an iron wire into the crucible; to the end of which a glassy matter will stick, in the form of threads, if the fusion and vitrification be perfect. In this case take the crucible out of the fire; cool it by throwing water on it, and then break it. You will find in it a glass, which will be of an exceeding deep blue, and almost black, if the operation hath succeeded. This glass, when reduced to a fine powder, acquires a much brighter and more lively blue colour.

If you find after the operation that the glass hath too little colour, the fusion must be repeated a second time, with twice or thrice the quantity of cobalt. If, on the contrary, the glass be too dark, less cobalt must be used.

In order to make the essay of a particular cobalt, with a view to know what quantity of blue glass it will yield, it is necessary to perform the operation in the manner here set down; a great deal of time and trouble may be saved by melting one part of cobalt with two or three parts of borax. This salt is very fusible, and turns when melted, into a substance which, for a time, possesses all the properties of glass. In this trial the glass of borax will be nearly of the same colour as the true glass, or smalt, made with the same cobalt.

The ores of bismuth, as well as cobalt, yield a matter that colours glass blue; nay, the smalt made with those ores is more beautiful than that procured from the ore of pure arsenic. Some cobalts yield both arsenic and bismuth. When such cobalts are used, it is common to find at the bottom of the crucible a little button of metallic matter, which is called regulus of cobalt. This regulus is a sort of bismuth, generally adulterated with a mixture of serruginous and arsenical parts.

The heaviest and most fixed flowers of arsenic, procured from cobalt, have likewise the property of giving a blue colour to glass. But this colour is faint: it is owing to a portion of the colouring matter carried up along with the arsenic. These flowers may be made an ingredient in the composition of blue glass, not only because of the colouring principle they contain, but also because they greatly promote fusion; arsenic being one of the most efficacious fluxes known.

In short, all those blue glasses, or smalts, contain a certain quantity of arsenic; for a portion of this semi-metal always remains united with the fixed matter of the cobalt, though roasted for a long time, and in a very hot fire. The portion of arsenic that is thus fixed vitriofied with the colouring matter, and enters into the composition of the smalt.

The blue glass made with the fixed part of cobalt hath several names, according to the condition in which it is.

When it hath undergone the first imperfect degree of fusion only, it is called zaffre It takes the name of smalt when perfectly vitrified: and this again being pulverised is called powder blue; or, if finely levigated, blue enamel; because it is used in enamelling, as well as in painting earthen ware and porcelain.

TO SEPARATE ARSENIC FROM SULPHUR. Powder the yellow or red arsenic which you intend to separate from its sulphur. Moisten this powder with a fixed alkali resolved into a liquor. Dry the mixture gently; put it into a very tall glass cucurbit, and fit on a blind-head. Set this cucurbit in a sand-bath; warm the vessels gently, and increase the fire by degrees, till you perceive that no more arsenic sublimes. The arsenic, which before was yellow and red, rises into the head partly on white flowers, and partly in a compact, white, semi-transparent matter, which looks as if it were vitrified. The sulphur combined with the fixed alkali remains at the bottom of the cucurbit.

TO GIVE ARSENIC THE METALLINE FORM. REGULUS OF ARSENIC. Take two parts of white arsenic in fine powder, one part of the black flux, half a part of borax, and as much clean iron filings. Rub the whole together, in order to mix them thoroughly. Put this mixture into a good crucible, and over it put sea salt three fingers thick. Cover the crucible; set it in a melting furnace; and begin with a gentle fire to heat the crucible equally.

When arsenical vapours begin to ascend from the crucible, raise the fire immediately so as to melt the mixture. Examine whether or no the matter be thoroughly melted, by introducing an iron wire into the crucible; and if the fusion be perfect, take the crucible out of the furnace. Let it cool; break it; and you will find in it a regulus of a white and livid metallic colour, very brittle, scarcely hard, but rather friable.

TO DISTIL THE NITROUS ACID BY THE INTERPOSITION OF ARSENIC. BLUE AQUA FORTIS. Pulverise finely any quantity you please of refined salt-petre. Mix it accurately with an equal weight of white crystalline arsenic well pulverised, or else with very white and and very fine flowers of arsenic. Put this mixture into a glass retort in a reverberating furnace; apply a receiver, having a small hole drilled in it, and containing a little filtered rain-water; lute the receiver to the retort with stiff lute. Begin with putting two or three small live coals in the ashhole of the furnace, and replace them with others when they are ready to go out. Go on thus warming your vessels by insensible degrees, and put no coals in the fire-place till the retort begin to be very warm. You will soon see the receiver filled with vapours of a dark red, inclining to a russet colour. With a bit of lute stop the little hole of the receiver. The vapours will be condensed in the water of this vessel, and give it a very fine blue colour, that will grow deeper and deeper as the distillation advances. If your salt-petre was not very dry, some drops of acid will also come over, and falling from the nose of the retort mix with the water in the receiver. Continue your distillation, increasing the fire little by little as it advances, but exceeding slowly, till you see that when the retort is red-hot nothing more comes off; and then let your vessels cool.

When the vessels are cold, unlute the receiver, and as expeditiously as you can pour the blue aqua fortis it contains into a crystal bottle; which you must seal hermetically, because this colour disappears in a short time when the liquor takes air. You will find in the retort a white saline mass moulded in its bottom, and some flowers of arsenic sublimed to its upper cavity, and into its neck.

Pulverise the saline mass, and dissolve it in warm water. Filter the solution, in order to separate some arsenical parts that will be left on the filter. Let the filtered liquor evaporate of itself in the open air; when it is sufficiently evaporated, crystals will shoot in it representing quadrangular prisms terminated at each extremity by pyramids that are also quadrangular. These crystals will be in confused heaps at the bottom of the vessel: Over them will be other crystals in the form of needles; a saline vegetation creeping along the sides of the vessel; and the surface of the liquor will be obscured by a thin dusty pellicle.

TO ALKALISATE NITRE BY ARSENIC. Melt in a crucible the nitre you intend to aklalisate. When it is melted, and moderately red, project upon it two or three pinches of pulverised arsenic. A considerable effervescence and ebullition will immediately be produced in the crucible, attended with a noise like that which nitre makes when it detonates with an inflammable matter. At the same time a thick smoke will rise, which at first will smell like garlick, the odour peculiar to arsenic; it will also smell afterwards like spirit of nitre. When the effervesence in the crucible is over, throw again upon the nitre as much pulverised arsenic as you did the first time; and all the same phenomena will be repeated. Continue thus throwing in arsenic in small parcels, till it produce no more effervescence; taking care to stir the matter at every projection with an iron wire, the better to mix the whole together. Then increase your fire, and melt what remains. Keep it thus in fusion for a quarter of an hour, and then take the crucible out of the fire. It will contain a nitre alkalised by arsenic.

OF VEGETABLES. OF THE SUBSTANCES OBTAINED FROM VEGETABLES BY EXPRESSION ONLY. TO EXPRESS AND DEPURATE THE JUICE OF A PLANT, CONTAINING ITS ESSENTIAL SALT. THE CRYSTALLISATION OF THAT SALT. Before sun-rise, gather a good quantity of the plant, from which you design to express the juice, in order to obtain its salt. Wash it well in running water, to clean it of earth, insects, and other adventitious matters. Bruise it in a marble mortar; put it into a bag of new, strong, thick linen cloth; tie the bag tight, and commit it to a press. By pressing it strongly you will squeeze out a great quantity of green, thick juice, which will have the same taste as the plant. Dilute this juice with six times as much pure rain water, and filter it repeatedly through a woolen bag, till it pass clear and limpid. Evaporate the filtered juice with a gentle heat, till it be almost as thick as before it was mixed with water. Put this inspissated juice into a jar, or other vessel of earth or glass; on its surface pour olive oil to the depth of a line, and set it in a cellar. Seven or eight months after this pour off gently the liquor contained in the vessel, the inside of which you will find covered with a crystallised salt. Separate the crystals gently; wash them quickly with a little fair cold water, and dry them: this is the essential oil of the plant.

Every plant is not equally disposed to yield its essential salt by the method here proposed. Succulent vegetables only, whose juices are aqueous and not too viscous, are fit for this purpose. Such, for example, as sorrel, brook-lime, succory, fumitory, water-cresses, plantain, etc. An essential salt cannot be procured from those that yield thick, viscid, mucilaginous juices, such as the seeds of flea-wort, unless their juices be previously attenuated by fermentation, and that viscosity destroyed which obstructs the crystallisation of this salt.

Nor can the essential salt be obtained in any quantity from vegetable matters abounding in oil. Most kernels and feeds are of this sort: they all contain a great quantity of fat oil, which so entangles and clogs this salt, that the particles thereof cannot shoot away from the tenacious juices into crystals.

The same is to be said of dry aromatic plants; because they contain much essential oil, or resinous matters that produce the same effect. It is true, the essential salt itself contains a certain portion of oil; for it is no other than the acid of the plant incorporated and crystallised with part of its oil and of its earth: but then the oil must not be in too great a quantity; because it sheaths the acid, renders it clammy, as it were, and hinders it from extricating itself so as to be able to exert its qualities, and appear in the form of salt.

The juice of plants obtained by expression is very thick; because it contains many particles of the bruised plant that are unavoidably squeezed out along with it. In order to clear it of these superfluous parts it is proper to filter it: but as that would be difficult, on account of the thickness of the juice, it must be thinned, by diluting it with a quantity of water, sufficient to give it the requisite degree of fluidity.

Instead of thus diluting the expressed juice, the plant may be ground with water before it is put into the press: it will by this means furnish a more fluid juice, that will easily pass through the filter. This method may be employed with success on dry plants, or such as are not very succulent. For this operation rain-water is to be preferred to any other; because it is the purest.

The juice of the plant, when diluted with the quantity of water sufficient to facilitate its filtration, is too aqueous to let the salt it contains unite into crystals: it must therefore be evaporated till it hath recovered a somewhat thicker consistence. The heat applied for that purpose must be gentle; lest the acid and oily parts that are to form the salt, be spoiled or dissipated, as they are not very fixed.

The oil poured on the liquor prevents its fermenting, putrefying, or growing mouldy, during the long space of time required for the crystallisation of the essential salt.

These salts are excellent medicines, being endued with the same virtues as the plants from which they were obtained.

TO DRAW THE OILS OUT OF KERNELS, SEEDS, AND FRUITS, BY EXPRESSES. Pound in a marble mortar, or grind in a mill, the kernels, seeds, or fruits, out of which you intend to express the oil. If your matters be meagre, and grind to meal, suspend that meal in the steam of boiling water, in order to moisten it a little, and then dry it.

Tie up your matters thus prepared in a new, strong, thick canvass bag, and put it into a press, between two iron plates previously heated in boiling water: squeeze it strongly, and you will see the oil run in streams into the receiving vessel.

TO DRAW THE ESSENTIAL OIL OF CERTAIN FRUITS BY EXPRESSION. Take the rind of a citron, lemon, orange, Bergamot-pear, or other fruit of that kind; cut it in slices, and doubling the slices squeeze them between your fingers over against a polished glass set upright, with its lower end in a vessel of earth or porcelain. Every time you squeeze the peel in a new ply, there will squirt out of it several fine jets of liquor, which, meeting with the surface of the glass, will be condensed into drops, and trickle down in small streams into the recipient. This liquor is the essential oil of the fruit.

OF THE SUBSTANCES OBTAINED FROM VEGETABLES BY TRITURATION. TO MAKE THE EXTRACTS OF A PLANT BY TRITURATION. Bruise the vegetable substance of which you intend to make the extracts; or, if it be hard and dry, grind it to a powder: put the matter thus prepared, together with seven or eight times as much rain water, into an earthen vessel; and into this vessel fit a churning staff so that it may be continually whirled around with a rotary motion, by means of a cord, a wheel, and a winch. Ply this machine for ten or twelve hours; and then filter the liquor through two linen cloths spread on a hair-sieve. Let your filtered liquor stand quiet for twelve hours more. Then pour it off by inclination from the sediment you will find at bottom; and filter it a second time through a flannel bag.

Pour fresh water, but in a smaller quantity, on the mass left after trituration with the machine. Triturate it again for four or five hours. Treat the liquor of this second triture just as you did that of the first, and mix them both together. Distribute all the liquor you now have among a sufficient number of shallow earthen plates. and evaporate by gentle heat, such as that of the sun, or of a vapour-bath, to the consistence of an extract, or even to dryness, as you think proper.

TO EXTRACT FROM SEEDS AND KERNELS, BY TRITURATION, THE MATTER OF EMULSIONS. Blanch the kernels of which you desire to make an emulsion; put them into a marble mortar; add a very little water; and pound them with a wooden pestle. Continue pounding and triturating till the matter become like a white paste. From time to time pour on it, by little and little, more fair water warmed, still continuing the trituration; by which means the paste will grow thinner. Go on thus till every particle of your kernels be crushed to pap. Then add, still rubbing the mixture enough of water to make the whole an actual fluid; and you will have a liquor of a dead-white colour, resembling milk. Strain it through a clean linen cloth: it will leave on the filter some coarse parts, which must be returned to those left in the mortar. Again triturate and rub the remainder of the kernels, with the addition of water as before. This second liquor will not be so white nor so rich as the former; filter it in the same manner, and again grind with water the solid parts remaining. In this manner proceed, repeatedly rubbing and adding fresh water till it appear no longer milky, but come off clear. The white milky waters thus obtained go by the name of an emulsion.

All the matters, from which a fat oil is obtainable by expression, produce emulsions when triturated with water.

An emulsion consists chiefly of two substances. One of these is mucilaginous, and soluble in water. This substance by itself would not give a milky appearance to the emulsion, which with it alone, would be limpid. The other is a fat oil, which of itself is not soluble in water; but being divided by the means of trituration into very small globules, it is dispersed through the whole liquor, and suspended therein by the aid of the mucilaginous part. It is this oily part that gives the emulsion its dead-white milky colour; because it is not actually dissolved in the water, but only diffused through it.

If oil be mixed with water in a phial, and the mixture strongly shaken for some time, with a rapid and continued motion, the oil will be divided into a vast number of little globules, which intervening between the parts of the water will destroy its transparency, and give it a dead-white colour, like that of our emulsion. But, as the oil is so minutely divided by this means as by triturating the matters containing it; and again, there being no mucilage in this liquor, as there is in emulsions, the oil soon separates from the water when it is left at rest, re-unites into round globules, and these joining together rise to the surface of the liquor, which then recovers its transparency.

The case is not exactly the same with emulsions; but something like it happens to them also. If they be left to stand quiet in a long bottle, the liquor, which at first appeared homogeneous, separates into two manifestly different parts. The upper part retains its dead-white colour, but is thicker and more opaque; while the lower part becomes perfectly transparent. This is the beginning of an entire separation of the oily from the aqueous parts. The former, being the lighter, ascend and gain the upper part of the liquor, while the lower, being freed from that which obstructed its translucence, recovers its proper limpidity: but the oily parts do not reunite into masses large enough to form one homogeneous whole, with the appearance and limpidness of oil; their being minutely divided and entangled in the mucilage impeding their natural tendency.

Emulsions first begin to spoil, as they grow old, not by turning rancid and acrimonious like the fat oils drawn by expression, but by turning sour; which is owing to the great quantity of mucilage they contain. As there is a fat oil in their composition, they have the same virtues with that sort of oil: but they are moreover incrassating, cooling, and emollient; qualities which render them extremely useful in acute and inflammatory disorders. They grow sour in a very short time, especially in the heat of summer; nay, they sometimes do so in two hours: and therefore they ought to be prepared from time to time as they are to be used.

The matter that is left when all the substance of the emulsion is extracted, and from which the water comes off clear and limpid, is scarce any thing but the earthy part of the seed or kernel that was triturated; which, however, still retains a portion of tenacious and gross oil, adhering to it so firmly as not to be separable by water.

The chyle and milk of animals resemble an emulsion in several respects, and particularly in their dead-white colour; which arises, in the same manner, from the very minute particles of oil contained in them, and distributed through an aqueous gelatinous fluid, but not dissolved therein. In general, whenever any oil of any kind happens to be lodged in this manner between the parts of an aqueous liquor, it always makes the whole of an opaque white: for oil will not mix with water, so as to produce a liquor that shall appear homogeneous and transparent, unless it be intimately dissolved in the water; which cannot be effected but by means of an union previously contracted between it and some saline matter; it is the case of mucilages, certain saponaceous matters, and some other combinations of which we shall have occasion to treat in the sequel.

The methods we have hitherto proposed, for extracting from vegetable substances all that they will yield without the assistance of fire, are not capable of analysing those substances accurately; since by expression and trituration we obtain only the liquid parts, impregnated indeed with almost all the principles of plants, which however are still combined with each other, and barely separated from the grossest earthy and oily parts. We must therefore necessarily have recourse to a more effectual expedient for carrying our analysis further. This expedient consists in making them undergo the action of fire, successively graduated, from the gentlest to the most violent heat.

But, before we enter on this analysis of vegetables, it is proper to describe the different operations that may be performed on oils, the only pure principle we have been able to obtain without the help of fire.

OF OPERATIONS ON FAT OILS. TO ATTENUATE FAT OILS, AND CHANGE THEIR NATURE, BY EXPOSING THEM TO THE ACTION OF FIRE, AND DISTILLING THEM. Mix thoroughly three or four pounds of any fat oil whatever with twice its weight of lime flaked in the air. Put this mixture into a large earthen retort, leaving a third part of it empty. Set it in a reverberating furnace, and lute on a receiver. Heat the vessel with a very gentle fire. A little flame will rise first, and will soon be followed by an oil that will fall in drops from the nose of the retort. Continue the distillation very slowly, till you perceive the oil that comes over begin to be not quite to fluid as before, but rather a little thicker.

Then unlute your receiver, and put another in its place. Continue the distillation, increasing your fire by degrees. The oil that comes over will grow thicker and thicker, its fluidity will decrease, and it will acquire a dark-brown colour, which at last will become blackish. The oil will then be very thick. Push the operation till nothing more will come off, though the retort be red-hot. During the whole time this distillation lasts, there rises a good deal of water in company with the oil. Keep the second thick oil by itself.

Mix the oil that came over first in this operation with an equal part of fresh lime slaked in the air. Put the mixture into an earthen or glass retort, of a size so proportioned to the quantity, that a third part thereof may remain empty. Distill as before. The same phenomena will appear: a clear oil will first come over, and be succeeded by one a little thicker. Then shift your receiver, and distill off all the rest of the oil with an increased fire. The first oil obtained by this second distillation will be clearer and thinner than that of the first distillation; and the second oil will not be so thick nor of so deep a colour as before.

Distill over again in the same manner the thin oil of this second distillation, and go on thus repeatedly distilling, till the first clear oil come over with a degree of heat not exceeding that of boiling water. Then, instead of mixing your oil with lime, put it with some water into a glass retort, or into a body with its head fitted on, and distill it, keeping the water just in a simmer. Your oil will be more and more attenuated, and, after being thus distilled twice or thrice with water, will be so limpid, so thin, and so clear, that you will scarce be able to distinguish it from water itself.

TO COMBINE FAT OILS WITH ACIDS. Put any fat oil whatever into a glass bason, and set it in a sand-bath very moderately heated. Pour on this oil an equal quantity of concentrated oil of vitriol, which will immediately dissolve it with violence; a considerable ebullition and effervescence will arise, attended with great heat, and a prodigious quantity of black thick vapours, in which may be easily perceived the smell of burnt oil, together with that of a sulphureous acid. The mixture will become of a deep-red, black, and thick, Stir it with a small stick, till you observe that all is quiet.

TO COMBINE FAT OILS WITH FIXED ALKALIS. HARD AND SOFT SOAP. THE DECOMPOSITION OF SOAP. Take a lixivium of alicant kelp made more caustic by lime, as we shall shew when we come to speak of alkalis. Evaporate this lye till it be capable of bearing a new-laid egg. Divide it into two parts; and to one of these put just water enough to weaken it so that a new laid egg will not swim in it, but fall to the bottom. With the lye thus weakened, mix an equal quantity of fresh-drawn olive-oil. Stir and agitate the mixture well till it become very white. Set it over a gentle fire, and continue stirring it incessantly, that the two ingredients of which it is compounded may gradually combine together, as part of the water evaporates. When you perceive they begin to unite, pour into the mixture thrice as much of the first strong lye as you took of olive oil. Continue the coction with a gentle fire, always stirring the matter, till it become so thick that a drop of it fixes, as it cools, into the consistence that soap ought to have. By dissolving a little of this soap in water, you will discover whether or no it contains more oil than ought to be in the composition. If it dissolve therein wholly and perfectly, without the appearance of the least little drop of oil floating on the water, it is a sign that it doth not contain too much oil. If, on the contrary, you perceive any of these little globules, you must pour into the vessel containing your matter a little more of the strong lye, to absorb the redundant oil. If there be too much of the alkali, it may be discovered by the taste. If the soap leave on your tongue the sensation of an alkaline salt, and produce an urinous savour, it is a sign that there is too much salt in proportion to the oil. In this case a little oil must be added to the mixture, to saturate the superabundant alkali. An excess in the quantity of alkali discovers itself likewise by the soap's growing moist in the air, on being exposed to it for some time.

Fixed alkalis, even when resolved into a liquor, that is, when loaded with much water, unite easily with fat oils, as appears from the experiment just recited; and require but a moderate heat to perfect that union. This combination may even be completely effected without the aid of fire, and by the heat of the sun only, provided sufficient time be allowed for that purpose. It only requires the mixture of the oil and alkali to be kept five or six days in digestion, and stirred from time to time. A lixivium of pure alkali, not acuated by lime, may also be used to make soap: but it is observed, that the combination succeeds better, and that the alkali unites sooner and more perfectly with oil, when it is sharpened by lime.

The oil is first mixed with a weaker and more aqueous lye, to the end that the combination may take place too hastily, but that all the particles of the two substances to be compounded together may unite equally. But as soon as the alkali begins to dissolve the oil gradually and quietly, the dissolution may then be accelerated; and that is done by adding the remaining lye. which is stronger and less diluted than the other.

Soap made with olive oil is white, hard, and hath not a very disagreeable smell: but as the oil is dear, others, even the fat and oils of animals, are sometimes substituted for it. The soaps made with most of these other matters are neither so hard, nor so white, as that made of olive oil: they are called soft soaps.

Oils thus associated with fixed alkalis are by that means rendered soluble in water; because the alkaline salts, having a great affinity with water, communicate part thereof to the oils with which they are now incorporated. Yet the oil is not for all that rendered thoroughly miscible with water, or perfectly soluble therein; for the water in which soap is dissolved hath always a milky cast: now there is no other criterion of a perfect solution but transparency.

Alkalis also lose part of their affinity with water, by the union they thus contract with oils: for, when the combination is properly made, they no longer attract the moisture of the air, nor doth water dissolve them in such quantities as before. The composition of soap is plainly a saturation of an alkali with an oil; and, in order to make perfect soap, we are forced, as was said in the process to grope, in a manner, by repeated trials, for this point of saturation; just as when we prepare a neutral salt by saturating an alkali with an acid. The union which the oil contracts with the alkali makes it lose in part, the readiness with which it naturally takes fire; because the salt is not inflammable: the water also, which enters, in pretty considerable quantities, into the composition of soap, contributes a good deal to hinder the accension of the oil.

Soap may be decompounded either by distilling it, or by mixing it with some substance that hath a greater affinity than oil with alkalis.

If we decompound it by distillation, a phlegm, or transparent spirit, of a somewhat yellowish colour, first comes over. This liquor is the aqueous part of the soap, quickened by a little of its alkali, which gives it an acrid taste. It is followed by a red oil, which at first is pretty thin and limpid, but thickens as the distillation advances, grows black, and has a very disagreeable empyreumatic smell. This oil is soluble in spirit of wine.

When the distillation is finished, that is, when the retort being kept red-hot for some time will discharge no more, there is left in it a saline mass; which is the alkali of the soap, crusted over with some of the most fixed parts of the oil, that are charred to a coal. This salt may be restored to the same degree of purity it had before its combination with the oil, by calcining it in a crucible with a naked fire, that may consume this burnt part of the oil, and reduce it to ashes.

It is plain, that the oil contained in soap is affected by distillation, much in the same manner as that which we mixed with lime and distilled.

Mr. Geoffroy, by analysing soap with care, discovered that two ounces thereof contain ninety-six grains of salt of kelp, freed from all oil and moisture; or two drams and forty-eight grains of that salt, as it is used in manufacturing soap; that is, containing water enough to make it crystallise; one ounce three drams twenty grains of olive oil; and about two drams four grains of water.

As acids have a greater affinity than any other substance with alkalis, they may be very effectually employed to decompound soap.

If you propose to decompound soap by means thereof, you must first dissolve it in sufficient quantity of water. Mr. Geoffroy, who made this experiment likewise, dissolved two ounces thereof in about three gallons of warm water, and to the solution added oil of vitriol, which he let fall into it drop by drop. Every time a drop of acid falls into it, a coagulum is formed in the liquor. The vessel in which the solution is contained must then be shaken, that the acid may equally attack all the alkali diffused in it.

When no new coagulation is produced by a drop of acid, it is a sign you have added enough. The liquor then begins to grow clear; and if another quart of water be added, in order to facilitate the separation of the oily particles, you will see them rise and unite together on the surface of the liquor.

This is a pure, clear, true olive oil, hath its taste, its smell, and, like it, is fluid in warm weather, and becomes fixed in cold. Yet it differs in some respects from that which hath never been united with an alkali in order to form a soap; for it burns more vividly and more rapidly, and is soluble in spirit of wine. We shall account for these differences when we come to treat of ardent spirits.

Not only the vitriolic acid, but all others, even those obtained from vegetables, are capable of decompounding soap, and separating the oil from the alkali. In the liquor wherein soap is thus decompounded, is found a neutral salt, consisting of the acid made use of, united with the alkali of the soap. If the vitriolic acid be used, you will have a Glauber's salt; a quadrangular nitre, if the nitrous acid be used; and so of the rest.

The facility with which acids decompound soap is the reason that no water, but what is very pure, will dissolve it, or is fit to be used in washing with it.

Water that doth not dissolve soap well is usually called hard water. Such waters contain a certain quantity of saline matters, washed out of the earths through which they pass. The hardness of most well-waters is owing to a considerable quantity of selenitic gypsum with thich the soil abounds. The selenites are neutral salts consisting of the vitriolic acid united with an earthy basis. If, therefore, soap be put into water in which a salt of this kind is dissolved, it is evident that the vitriolic acid in the selenites, having a greater affinity with the fixed alkali of the soap than with its own earthy basis, will quit the latter to unite with the former; and thus the soap will be decompounded instead of being dissolved. Accordingly we see, that, when we attempt to dissolve soap in our well-water, the surface of the liquor is in a short time covered with a fat oily pellicle. However, this decomposition of soap is not complete; at least but a small part of it is perfectly decompounded; because the great quantity of selenites, with which the water is impregnated hinders the soap from mixing so thoroughly with it, as is requisite to produce a total decomposition thereof.

All mineral waters are likewise hard, with regard to soap; for, as most of them owe their virtues to the efflorescencies they have washed off, from pyrites that have grown hot and begun to be decomposed, they are impregnated with the saline matters produced by pyrites in that state; that is, with aluminous, vitriolic, and sulphureous substances which have the same effect on soap as the selenites hath.

Mineral waters containing neutral salts only, such as sea-salt, Epsom salt, Glauber's salt, are nevertheless hard with regard to soap, though the acids of those salts, being united with fixed alkalis, are incapable of decompounding it. The reason is, that those neutral salts are more soluble in water than soap is; so much indeed as to even exclude it: because each of the two principles that compose them hath a very great affinity with water; whereas only one of the principles of soap, namely, its alkali, hath that affinity; the other, viz. the oily principle, having none at all. Thus water impregnated with an acid, or with any neutral salt, is hard with regard to soap, and incapable of dissolving; and hence it follows, that soap is a sort of touchstone for trying the purity of water.

Wine dissolves soap; but imperfectly, because it contains an acid or tartarous part. Spirit of wine also dissolves it: but neither is this dissolution perfect; because it contains too little water: for its spirituous part can dissolve nothing but the oil of the soap; and the alkali is not at all, or at least in a very small quantity, soluble in this menstruum. The true solvent of soap is therefore a liquor that is partly spirituous, partly aqueous, and not acid.

Brandy has these qualities: and accordingly it is the solvent that unites best with soap, dissolves the greatest quantity, and makes the most limpid solution thereof. Yet even this solution hath something of milky cast, occasioned by its not being entirely free from an acid, or the tartarous principle. This fault may be easily corrected, by mixing with it a little alkali to absorb the acid. A dram of crystallised salt of kelp mixed with three ounces and a half of good brandy, renders it capable of dissolving an ounce and two drams of good hard soap into a perfectly limpid liquor.

Some years ago it was discovered that soap might be used with great success in medicine, and that it possesses the property of dissolving the stony concretions that form in several parts of the body, particularly in the kidneys and bladder. Soap is the basis of the composition known by the name of Mrs. Stephen's remedy; and in this one ingredient its whole virtue resides.

From what hath been said on the nature of this compound, as well as on the cause and phenomena of its dissolution, it plainly appears to be of the last consequence, in administering it to a patient, that his constitution be considered, and a proper regimen ordered. All acids should be absolutely forbid him; as we know they hinder the soap from dissolving, and decompound it: and if the patient have any acidities in the first passages, matters capable of neutralising them should be prescribed him; as prepared crabs eyes, and other absorbents known in medicine: In such cases those with which the soap is compounded in Mrs. Stephen's remedy may be of use.

TO COMBINE FAT OILS WITH SULPHUR. Put any fat oil whatever into an earthen vessel; add to it about a fourth part of its weight of flower of sulphur, and set the vessel on a furnace, with lighted coals under it. When the oil hath acquired a certain degree of heat, the sulphur will melt, and you will see it fall immediately to the bottom of the oil, in the form of a very red fluid. The two substances will remain thus separated, without mixing together, while the heat is no greater than is necessary to keep the sulphur in fusion. Increase it therefore; but slowly, and with circumspection, lest the matter take fire. When the oil begins to smoke, the two liquors will begin to mix and look turbid: at last they will unite so as to appear one homogeneous whole. If you keep up the heat, so that the mixture shall always continue smoking and ready to boil, you may add more sulphur, which will perfectly incorporate with it: and thus may a pretty considerable quantity thereof be introduced into this composition.

TO COMBINE FAT OILS WITH LEAD, AND THE CALXES OF LEAD. THE BASIS OF PLASTERS.- THE DECOMPOSITION OF THIS COMBINATION. Into an earthen vessel put granulated lead, litharge, ceruse, or minium; and pour thereon twice its weight of any fat oil whatever. If you set the vessel over a brisk fire, the lead at bottom will melt before the oil begin to boil. When it boils, stir the matter with a stick: the lead, or the calx of lead, will gradually disappear, and at last be totally dissolved by the oil, to which it will give a very thick consistence.

Fat oils dissolve not only lead, but its calxes also: nay, they dissolve the latter more readily than lead in substance; probably because they are more divided. The result of a combination of these matters i a thick, tenacious mass, that grows in some degree hard in the cold and soft by heat. This composition is known in pharmacy by the name of plaster. It is made up with several drugs into plasters, which partake of the virtues of those drugs; so that it is the basis of almost all plasters.

Lead itself is seldom used to make plasters: ceruse, litharge, or minium, are preferred to it; because these matters unite more readily with oils.

OF THE SUBSTANCES OBTAINED FROM VEGETABLES WITH A DEGREE OF HEAT NOT EXCEEDING THAT OF BOILING WATER. TO OBTAIN FROM PLANTS, BY DISTILLING THEM WITH THE MEAN DEGREE OF HEAT BETWEEN FREEZING AND BOILING WATER, A LIQUOR IMPREGNATED WITH THEIR PRINCIPLE OF ODOUR. In the morning, before sun-rise, gather the plant from which you design to extract its odoriferous water. Chuse the plant in its full vigour, perfectly sound, and free from all adventitious matters, except dew. Put this plant, without squeezing it, into the body of a tinned copper alembic, and set it in a water bath. Fit on its head, and to the nose thereof lute a glass receiver with wet bladder.

Warm the bath to the mean degree between freezing and boiling water. You will see a liquor distill and fall drop by drop into the receiver. Continue the distillation with this degree of heat, till no more drops fall from the nose of the alembic. Then unlute the vessels; and if you have not as much liquor as you want, take out of the cucurbit the plant already distilled, and put a fresh one in its place. Distill as before, and go on thus till you have a sufficient quantity of odoriferous liquor. Put it into a bottle; stop it close; and set it in a cool place.

The liquor obtained from plants, with the degree of heat here prescribed, consists of the dew that was on the plant, and some of the phlegm of the plant itself, further with its odorous principle. Mr. Boerhaave, who examined this odoriferous part of plants with great care, calls it the spiritus rector. The nature of this spirit is not yet thoroughly ascertained; because it is so very volatile, that it cannot easily be subjected to the experiments that are necessary to analise it, and to discover all its properties. If the bottle containing the liquor, which may be considered as the vehicle of this spirit, be not exceeding carefully stopped, it flies quite off: so that in a few days nothing will be found but an insipid inodorous water.

Great part of the virtue of plants resides in their principle of odour; and to it must be ascribed the most singular and the most wonderful effects we every day see produced by them. Every body knows that a great number of odorous plants affect, in a particular manner, by their scent only, the brain and the genus nervosum, of such especially whose nerves are very sensible, and susceptible of the slightest impression; such as hypochondriacal or melancholy men and hysterical women. The smell of the tuberose, for instance, is capable of throwing such persons into fits, so as to make them drop down and swoon away. The smell of rue again, which is equally strong and penetrating, but of a different kind, is a specific remedy against the ill effects of the tuberose; and brings those persons to life again, with as quick and as surprising an efficacy as that by which they were reduced to a state not unlike death. This is Mr. Boerhaave's observation.

The odorous exhalations of plants must be considered as a continual emanation of their spiritus rector; but as growing plants are in a condition to repair, every instant, the losses they sustain by their means, as well as by transpiration, it is not surprising that they are not soon exhaulted while they continue in vigour. Those, on the contrary, which we distill, having no such resource, are very soon entirely exhausted of their principle.

The separation of the spiritus rector from plants requires but a very gentle heat, equally distant from the free ing point, and from the heat of boiling water. Accordingly the heat of the sun in summer is sufficient to dissipate it almost entirely. This shews why it is dangerous to stay long in fields, or woods, where many noxious plants grow. The virtues of plants residing chiefly in their exhalations, which the heat of the sun increases considerably, a sort of atmosphere is formed around them, and carried by the air and the wind to very great distances.

For the same reason the air of a country may be rendered salutary and medicinal, by the exhalations of wholesome plants growing therein. From the facility with which the odorous principle of plants evaporates, we learn what care ought to be taken in drying those intended for medical uses, so as to preserve their virtues. They must by no means be exposed to the sun, or laid in a warm place: a cool, dry place, into which the rays of the sun never penetrate, is the properest for drying plants with as little loss of their virtue as possible.

Though there is reason to believe that every vegetable matter hath a spiritus rector, seeing each hath its particular scent, yet this principle is not very perceptible in any but those which have a very manifest odour: and accordingly it is extracted chiefly from aromatic plants, or the most odoriferous parts of plants.

TO EXTRACT THE FAT OILS OF PLANTS BY THE DECOCTION IN BOILING WATER. CACAO-BUTTER. Pound or bruise in a marble mortar your vegetable substances abounding with the fat oil which you intend to extract by decoction: tie them up in a linen cloth: put this packet into a pan with seven or eight times as much water, and make the water boil. The oil will be separated by the ebullition, and float on the surface of the water. Skim it off carefully with a ladle, and continue boiling till no more oil appear.

The heat of boiling water is capable of separating the fat oils from the vegetable matters that contain any: but this is to be effected by actual decoction only, and not by distillation; because these oils will not rise in an alembic with the heat of boiling water. We are therefore necessitated to collect them from the surface of the water, as above directed.

The water used in this coction generally becomes milky, like an emulsion. Nevertheless this way of obtaining the fat oils is not generally practised; because the heat, to which they are exposed in the operation, occasions their being less mild than they generally are: but it is an excellent method, and indeed the only one that can be employed, for extracting from particular vegetables certain concrete oily matters, in the form of butter or wax; which matters are no other than fat oils in a fixed state. The cacao yields, by this means, a very mild butter; and in the same manner is a wax obtained from a certain shrub in America.

TO EXTRACT THE ESSENTIAL OILS OF PLANTS BY DISTILLATION WITH THE HEAT OF BOILING WATER. DISTILLED WATERS. Put into a cucurbit the plant from which you design to extract the essential oil. Add as much water as will fill two thirds of your vessel, and dissolve therein half an ounce of sea-salt for every quart of water you use. To this body fit on an alembic head, and to the nose thereof lute a receiver with fixed paper or wet bladder. Set it in a furnace, and let the whole digest together, in a very gentle warmth, for twenty-four hours.

This being done, light a wood-fire under your vessel, brisk enough to make the water in it boil immediately. Then slacken your fire, and leave it just strong enough to keep the water simmering. There will come over into the receiver a liquor of a whitish colour, somewhat milky; on the surface of which, or at the bottom, will be found an oil, which is the essential oil of the vegetable you put into the cucurbit. Continue your distillation with the same degree of heat, till you perceive the..liquor come off clear, and accompanied with an oil.

When the distillation is finished, unlute the receiver; and, if the essential oil be of that sort that is lighter than water, fill the vessel up to the top with water. On this occasion a long-necked matras should be used for a receiver; that the oil which floats on the water may collect together in its neck, and rise up to its mouth. Then in the neck of this vessel put the end of a thread of cotton twine, so that the depending part without the vessel may be longer than that in the oil, and the extremity thereof hang within the mouth of a little phial, just big enough to contain your quantity of oil. The oil will rise along the yarn as in a siphon filter through it, and fall drop by drop into the little phial. When all the oil is thus come over, stop your little bottle very close, with a cork coated over with a mixture of wax and a little pitch.

If your oil be ponderous and of the sort that sinks in water, pour the whole contents of the receiver into a glass funnel, the pipe of which must terminate in a very small aperture that may be stopped with your fore-finger. All the oil will be collected in the lower part of the funnel: then remove your finger, and let the oil run out into a little bottle through another small funnel. When you see the water ready to come, stop the pipe of the funnel, and cork the bottle containing your oil.

TO EXTRACT THE ESSENTIAL OILS OF PLANTS BY DISTILLATION PER DESCENSUM. Reduce to a powder, or a paste, the vegetable substances from which you intend to extract the essential oil by the method proposed. Lay this matter about half an inch thick on a fine, close, linen cloth. If it be dry and hard, expose the cloth containing it to the steam of boiling water, till the matter become moist and soft. Then lay the cloth, with its contents, over the mouth of a very tall cylindrical glass vessel, which is to do the office of a receiver in this distillation; and, by means of a piece of small pack-thread, fallen down the extremities of the cloth, by winding the thread several times over them and round the vessel; in such a manner, however, that the cloth be not tight, but may yield to a small weight, and sink about five or six lines deep into the vessel over which it is fastened. Set this recipient in a larger vessel, containing so much cold water as will reach half way up the cylindrical vessel, which, having little in it but air, must be ballasted with as much lead as will sink it to the bottom of the water.

On the cloth, containing the substance to be distilled, set a flat pan of iron or copper, about five or six lines deep, that may just fit the mouth of the glass vessel over which the cloth is fastened, so as to shut it quite close. Fill this pan with hot ashes, and on these lay some live coals. Soon after this you will see vapours descend from the cloth, which will fill the recipient, and drops of liquor will be formed on the under side of the cloth, from whence they will fall into the vessel. Keep up an equal gentle heat, till you perceive nothing more discharged. Then uncover the recipient: you will find in it two distinct liquors; one of which is the phlegm, and the other the essential oil of the substance distilled.

INFUSIONS, DECOCTIONS, AND EXTRACTS OF PLANTS. Make some water boiling-hot, and then take it off the fire. When it ceases to boil, pour it on the plant of which you desire to have the infusion; taking care there be enough of it to cover the plant entirely. Cover the vessel, and let your plant lie in the hot water for the space of half an hour, or longer if it be of a firm close texture. Then pour off the water by inclination: it will have partly acquired the colour, the smell, the taste, and the virtues of the plant. This liquor is called an infusion.

To make the decoction of a vegetable substance, put it into an earthen pan, or into a tinned copper vessel, with a quantity of water sufficient to bear being boiled for several hours without leaving any part of the plant dry. Boil your plant more or less acco ing to its nature; and then pour off the water by inclination. This water is impregnated with several of the principles of the plant.

If the infusions and decoctions of plants be altered, and evaporated in a gentle heat, they become extracts, that may be kept for whole years, especially if they be evaporated to a thick consistence; and better still if they be evaporated to dryness.

OF OPERATIONS ON ESSENTIAL OILS. THE RECTIFICATION OF ESSENTIAL OILS. Put into a cucurbit the essential oil you propose to rectify. Set the cucurbit in a balneum maria; fit to it a head of tin, or of copper tinned, together with its refrigeratory; and lute on a receiver. Make the water in the bath boil, and keep up this degree of heat till nothing more will come over. When the distillation is finished, you will find in the receiver a rectified essential oil, which will be clearer, thinner, and better scented than before it was thus before re-distilled; and in the bottom of the cucurbit will be left a matter of a deeper colour, more tenacious, more resinous, and of a less grateful smell.

Essential oils, even the purest, the best prepared, and the thinnest, suffer great changes; and are much impaired by growing old: they gradually turn thick and resinous; their sweet, grateful scent is lost, and succeeded by a more disagreeable smell, somewhat like that of turpentine. The cause of these changes is, that their finest and most volatile part, that which contains most of the odorous principle, is dissipated and separated from that which contains least of it; which therefore grows thicker, and comes so much the nearer to the nature of a resin, as the quantity of acid, that was distributed through the whole oil before the dissipation of the more volatile part, is, after such dissipation united and concentrated in the heaviest part; the acid in oils being much less volatile than the odorous part, to which alone they owe their levity.

Hence it appears what precautions are to be used for preserving essential oils as long as possible without spoiling. They must be kept in a bottle perfectly well stopped, and always in a cool place, because heat quickly dissipates the volatile parts. Some authors direct the bottle to be kept under water.

TO FIRE OILS BY COMBINING THEM WITH HIGHLY CONCENTRATED ACIDS: INSTANCED IN OIL OF TURPENTINE. Mix together in a glass equal parts of concentrated oil of vitriol, and highly smoking fresh-drawn spirit of nitre: pour this mixture at several times, but suddenly, on three parts of oil of turpentine, set for that purpose in a glass bason. By a part here must be understood at dram at least. A most violent commotion, accompanied with smoke, will immediately be raised in the liquors, and the whole will take fire in an instant, flame, and be consumed.

There is not in chemistry a phenomenon more extraordinary, and more surprising, than the firing of oils by mixing them with acids. It could never have been suspected, that a mixture of two cold liquors would produce a sudden, violent, bright, and lasting flame, like that we are at present considering.

TO COMBINE ESSENTIAL OILS WITH MINERAL SULPHUR. BALSAM OF SULPHUR. Put into a matras one part of flowers of sulphur; pour on them six parts of the essential oil of turpentine, for instance; set the matras in a sand-bath, and heat it gradually till the oil boil. The sulphur, which at first lay at the bottom of the matras, will begin to melt and appear to dissolve in the oil. When it hath boiled in this manner for about an hour, take the matras from the fire, and let the liquor cool. A great deal of the sulphur that was dissolved therein will separate from it as it cools, and fall to the bottom of the vessel in the form of needles, much like a salt shooting in water.

When the liquor is perfectly cold, decant it from the sulphur that lies at the bottom of the vessel: to that sulphur put fresh oil of turpentine, and proceed as before: the sulphur will again disappear, and be dissolved in the oil; but when the mixture is cold you will find new crystals of sulphur deposited at the bottom. Decant once more this oil from the crystals, and pour on fresh oil to dissolve them: continue the same method, and you will find, that about sixteen parts of essential oil are required to keep one part of sulphur dissolved when cold. This combination is called balsamum sulphuris terebinthinatum, if made with oil of turpentine; anisatum, if with oil of anise-seed; and so of others.

TO COMBINE ESSENTIAL OILS WITH FIXED ALKALIS. SHARKEY'S SOAP. Take salt of tartar, or any other alkali, thoroughly calcined. Heat it in a crucible till it be red, and in that condition throw it into a hot iron mortar: rub it quickly with a very hot iron pestle; and as soon as it is powdered, pour on it, little by little, nearly an equal quantity of oil of turpentine. The oil will enter into the salt, and unite intimately with it, so as to form a hard paste. Continue rubbing this composition with a pestle, in order to complete the union of the two substances; and, as your oil of turpentine disappears, add more, which will unite in the same manner, and give a softer consistence to the soapy mass. You may add still more oil, according to the consistence you intend to give your soap.

Starkey, the first chemist who found the means of making soap with an essential oil, and by whose name this kind of soap is therefore called, made use of a much more tedious method than that proposed in our process. He began with mixing a very small quantity of oil with his salt, and waited till all the oil united therewith of its own accord, so as to disappear entirely, before he added any more; and thus protracted his operation exceedingly, though in the main it was the same with ours. The method here proposed is more expeditious, and was invented by Dr. Geoffroy.

Starkey's soap dissolves in water much as common soap does, without any separation of the oil: and by this mark it is known to be well made. It may also be decompounded, either by distillation, or by mixing it with an acid: and its decomposition, in either of these ways, is attended with nearly the same phenomena as the decomposition of common soap.

OF THE SUBSTANCES OBTAINED FROM VEGETABLES BY MEANS OF A GRADUATED HEAT, FROM THAT OF BOILING WATER, TO THE STRONGEST THAT CAN BE APPLIED TO THEM IN CLOSE VESSELS. TO ANALISE VEGETABLE SUBSTANCES THAT YIELD NEITHER A FAT NOR AN ESSENTIAL OIL. INSTANCED IN GUAIACUM-WOOD. Take thin shavings of Guaiacum-wood, and put them into a glass or stone retort, leaving one half thereof empty. Set your retort in a reverberating furnace, and lute on a large glass receiver having a small hole drilled in it, such as is used for distilling the mineral acids. Put a live coal or two in the furnace, to warm the vessels gently and slowly.

With a degree of heat below that of boiling water, you will see drops of a clear insipid phlegm fall into the receiver. If you raise the fire a little, this water will come slightly acid, and begin to have a pungent smell. With a degree of fire somewhat stronger, a water will continue to rise which will be still more acid, smell stronger, and become yellowish. When the heat comes to exceed that of boiling water, the phlegm that rises will be very acid, high coloured, have a strong pungent smell, like that of matters long smoked with wood in a chimney, and will be accompanied with a red, light oil, that will float on the liquor in the receiver.

And now it is necessary, that the operation be carried on very cautiously and vent frequently given to the rarefied air by opening the small hole in the receiver; such an incredible quantity thereof rushing out ot the wood, with this degree of heat, as may burst the vessels to pieces, if not discharged from time to time.

When this red, light oil is come over, and the air ceases to rush out impetuously, raise your fire gradually, till the retort begin to redden. The receiver will be filled with dense vapours; and together with the watery liquor, which will then be extremely acid, there will rise a black, thick, ponderous oil, which will fall to the bottom of the receiver and lie under the liquor.

Then give the utmost degree of heat; that is, the greatest your furnace will allow, and your vessels bear. With this excessive heat a little more oil will rise, which will be very ponderous, as thick and black as pitch; and the vessels will continue full of vapours that will not condense.

At last, when you have kept the retort exceeding red for a long time in this extremity of heat, so that it begins to melt if it be of glass, and you perceive nothing more come over, let the fire go out and the vessel cool. Then take off your receiver; from the black oil at the bottom decant the acid liquor with the red oil floating on it, and pour them both into a glass funnel, lined with brown filtering paper, and place over a bottle. The acid liquor will pass through the filter into the bottle, and the oil will be left behind, which must be kept by itself in a separate bottle. Lastly, into another funnel, prepared as the former, pour the thick oil remaining with a little of the acid liquor at the bottom of the receiver. The liquor will filter off in the same manner, and thus be separated from the heavy oil.

In the retort you will find your Guaiacum shavings not in the least altered as to their figure, but light, friable, very black, scentless and tasteless, easily taking fire, and consuming without flame or smoke: in short you will find them charred to a perfect coal.

Hitherto we have examined the substances that may be obtained from vegetables, either without the help of fire, or with a degree of heat not exceeding that of boiling water. The analysis of plants can be carried no further without a greater degree of heat: for, when the principle of odour and the essential oil of an aromatic plant are wholly extracted by the preceding processes, if the distillation be afterward continued without increasing the heat, nothing more will be obtained but a little acid; which will soon cease, as a small part only of the quantity contained in the plant will be elevated; the rest being either too ponderous, or too much entangled with the other principles of the body, to rise with so small a degree of heat.

In order therefore to carry on the decomposition of a plant, from which you have, by the methods before proposed, extracted all the principles it is capable of yielding when treated; or, in order to analise a vegetable matter, which affords neither an expressed nor an essential oil, it must be distilled in a retort with a naked fire, as directed in the process, and be made to undergo all the degrees of heat sucessively, from that of boiling water to the highest that can be raised in a reverberating furnace.

A heat inferior to that of boiling water, with which we must begin in order to warm the vessel gradually, brings nothing over, but an insipid water, destitute of all acidity. By increasing it nearly to the degree of boiling water, the distilled water comes to be slightly acid.

When the heat is made a little stronger than that which is necessary for the elevation of an essential oil, the acidity of the water that comes off is much more considerable. It hath now both colour and smell, and there rises with it a red, light oil, that floats on the liquor in the receiver. This is not an essential oil; it hath none of the odour of the plant. Though so light as to float on water, yet it will not rise with the degree of heat that raises essential oils, even those that much surpass it in gravity, and will not swim on water as they do. This proves, that the ease or difficulty with which a particular degree of heat raises any substance in distillation doth not depend altogether on its gravity: its dilatability, or the volatile nature of the matters with which it is so closely united as not to be separated from them by distillation, may probably contribute greatly to produce this effect.

It is very surprising, that a substance so hard, so compact, so dry in appearance, as Guaiacum-wood, should yield such a large quantity of water by distillation; and it is equally so, that it should discharge so much air, and with so much impetuosity, as nothing but experience could render credible.

It hath been remarked, that the heaviest and most compact woods yield the most air in distillation: and accordingly Guaiacum-wood, as exceeding almost all others in hardness and weight, discharges a vast quantity of air when analised.

The thick, burnt, empyreumatic oil, that comes over last in this distillation, is heavier than water; on account, probably, of the great quantity of acid with which it is replete. The two kinds of oil obtained in this analysis may be rectified, by distilling them a second time, or rather several times; by which means they will become lighter and more fluid. In general, all thick heavy oils constantly owe these qualities to an acid united with them; and it is by being freed from some of that acid in distillation, that they always acquire a greater degree of lightness and fluidity from that operation.

The analysis of a vegetable substance, shews what may be obtained from them when distilled in close vessels, with a graduated heat, from that of boiling water, to that which converts the mixt to a perfect coal; viz. phlegm, an acid, a light oil, much air, and a thick oil. But this analysis is far from being a complete one: it may be carried much farther, and made more perfect.

None of the principles obtained by this analysis are pure, simple, and thoroughly separated from the rest. They are still in some measure blended all together: then separation is but begun; and each requires a second and more accurate analysis, to reduce it to the greatest degree of purity of which it is capable. The oil and the acid chiefly merit so much pains.

A great deal of the acid of the plant remains, combined with the two sorts of oil here obtained; which we have reason to think differ no otherwise from one another; than as there is more or less acid united with each. The best way of freeing these oils from their redundant acid is to distill them frequently from alkalis and absorbents.

The acid is in the same circumstances nearly as the oil. The first that rises is mortified with much water, to which it owes a great deal of its volatility. That which comes over last is much more concentrated, and consequently heavier; yet it is still very aqueous. It might be freed in a great measure from this adventitious water, and so rendered much stronger; which would give us a better opportunity to discover its nature and properties, of which we know but very little.

Water is not the only heterogeneous substance that disguises the vegetable acid: a pretty considerable quantity of the oil of the plant is also combined with it, and contaminates its purity. The proof of this is, that when these acids are kept, in the same condition in which they first come over, for any length of time, in a glass vessel, they gradually deposite, on the bottom and sides of the vessel, an oil incrustation, which grows thicker and thicker the longer it stands; and, as this oily matter separates from it, the acid liquor appears less unctuous and saponaceous.

A very good way to separate this oil more effectually from the acid is to combine the whole with absorbents and abstract the oil again by distillation. By this means a very sensible quantity of oil may be separated that was not perceived before.

The air, that is discharged with impetuosity in the operation, and must be let out, is loaded with many particles of acid and oil reduced to vapours, which it carries off; and by this means the quantity of the principles extracted from the mixt cannot be accurately determined; nor are the vapours, of which the vessels remain full after the operation, any other than particles of acid and oil, which the violence of the fire hath rarefied exceedingly and which do not easily condense.

If we distill in this manner a vegetable aromatic substance, which of course contains an essential oil, provided it hath not been previously extracted by the appropriated process, this essential oil will rise first, as soon as the distilling vessel acquires the heat of boiling water: but its scent will not be near so sweet or grateful, as if it were distilled in the manner before directed as properest for it. On the contrary it will have an empyreumatic smell; because in this way it is impossible to avoid scorching, and half-burning some of the matter distilled; especially that part of it which touches the sides of the retort. Moreover, the very same equable degree of heat can hardly be kept up with a naked fire. The essential oil therefore, though it rises first, will not be pure, but contaminated with a mixture of the empyreumatic oil that first comes over, and will be confounded therewith.

Most vegetable substances, when distilled with a strong fire, yield the same principles with that which we have chosen for an instance. Entire plants of this kind, those from which the odorous principle, the essential oil, or the fat oil, hath been drawn, those of which extracts have been made by infusion or decoction, or the extracts themselves; all such matter being distilled yield phlegm, an acid, a thin oil, air, and a thick oil; and the products of their several analyses differ from each other, only on account of the different quantity or proportion that each contains of the principles here enumerated.

But there are many other plants, which, besides these substances, yield also a considerable quantity of a volatile alkaline salt. This property is possessed chiefly by that tribe of plants which is distinguished by having cruciform flowers, among which there are some that, being analised, greatly resemble animal matters. We shall now analise one of these: mustard-seed, for instance.

TO ANALISE A VEGETABLE SUBSTANCE WHICH YIELDS THE SAME PRINCIPLES AS ARE OBTAINED FROM ANIMAL-MATTERS: INSTANCED IN MUSTARD-SEED. With an apparatus like that of the preceding process, and with the same fire, distill mustard-seed. With a degree of heat, inferior to that of boiling water, there will come over a phlegm somewhat coloured, and impregnated with a volatile alkaline salt. With a degree of heat, greater than that of boiling water, the same kind of phlegm, impregnated with the same salt will continue to come over; but it will be much higher coloured, and will be accompanied with a light oil. At this time a considerable quantity of air is discharged; with regard to which the same precautions must be taken as in distilling Guaiacum.

If the fire be gradually raised, there will come over a black thick oil, lighter however than water; and at the same time vapours will rise, and, condensing on the sides of the receiver, form into springs or ramifications. This is a volatile alkaline salt, in a concrete form, like that of animals, as we shall hereafter see. These vapours are much whiter than those of Guaiacum.

When you have thus drawn off, with a very strong fire, all the volatile alkali and thick oil contained in the subject, there will be nothing left in the retort but a sort of coal, from which a small quantity of phosphorus may be obtained, provided the retort you employ for that purpose be good enough to stand a very violent heat.

Mustard-seed furnishes us with an instance of a vegetable, from which we obtain, by analising it, the very same principles that animal-matters yield. Instead of getting an acid from it, we obtain only a volatile alkali.

We shall not here speak of the manner of separating and depurating the principles obtained by this process; but reserve it for the analysis of animals, which is absolutely the same. We shall content ourselves with observing, that the first volatile alkali, which rises at the beginning of the operation together with the phlegm, in a degree of heat below that of boiling water, differs from that which doth not come over till towards the end of the distillation, when the last thick oil ascends. The different times, and different degrees of heat, in which these two alkalis rise, shew that the former exists actually and perfectly in the plant; but that the latter is generated during the distillation, and is the product of the fire, which combines together the materials whereof it is composed.

Vegetables, that thus yield a volatile alkali with a heat less than that of boiling water, irritate the organ of smelling, affecting it with a sensation of acrimony; and the effluvia, which rise from them when bruised, make the eyes smart so as to draw tears from them in abundance. Several of these matters, being only bruised, effervesce with acids: effects-producible only by a very volatile alkaline principle.

This is that alkali, the lightest of all the principles that can be extracted from bodies, which rises first in our distillation along with the phlegm, and with a degree of heat much inferior to that of boiling water. As the phlegm with which it rises is very copious, it is dissolved thereby; which is the reason it doth not appear in a concrete form. To this water it gives a slight yellowish tinge, because it is impure and oily. The saline alkaline properties of this liquor have procured it the title of a volatile spirit. This volatile alkali, which exists naturally and perfectly formed in mustard-seed, onions, garlick, cresses, and other such vegetables, contitutes a difference between them and animal substances, which contain only the materials requisite to form a volatile alkali, but none ready formed, unless they have undergone the putrid fermentation.

The second volatile alkali, which rises in our distillation, but not without a very strong degree of fire, and at the same time with the last thick oil, seems to be a production of the fire; for, if it were already formed in the mixt, as the other is, it would rise with the same heat, and at the same time, being equally volatile.

OF THE SUBSTANCES OBTAINED FROM VEGETABLES BY COMBUSTION. TO PROCURE A FIXED CAUSTIC ALKALINE SALT, FROM A VEGETABLE SUBSTANCE, BY BURNING IT IN THE OPEN AIR. Take any vegetable matter whatever; set it on fire, and let it burn in the open air till it be wholly reduced to ashes. On these ashes pour a quantity of boiling water sufficient to drench them thoroughly. Filter the liquor, in order to separate the earthy parts; and evaporate your lye to dryness, stirring it incessantly; and you will have a yellowish white salt.

Put this salt in a crucible; set it in a melting furnace, and make a moderate fire, so as not to fuse the salt. It will turn first of a blue-grey colour, afterwards of a blue-green and at last reddish. Put on the dome of the furnace; fill it with coals; make your fire strong enough to melt the salt, and keep it in fusion for an hour, or an hour and half. Then pour it into a heated metal mortar; pound it while it is red-hot; put it as soon as possible into a glass bottle, first made very hot and dry, and shut it up close with a glass stopple rubbed with emery. By this means you will have the pure fixed alkali of the vegetable substance you burnt.

Burning a vegetable substance in the open air is a kind of violent and rapid analysis made by fire, which separates, resolves, and decomposes several of its principles.

When any wood or plant is laid on a quick fire, there ascends from it immediately an aqueous smoke, which consists of little more than phlegm; but this smoke soon becomes thicker and blacker; it is then pungent, draws tears from one's eyes, and excites a cough if drawn into the lungs with the breath. These effects arise from its being replete with the acid, and some of the oil, of the vegetable converted into vapours. Soon after this the smoke grows exceeding black and thick; it is now still more acrid, and the plant turns black. Its strongest acid and last thick oil are now discharged with impetuosity.

This rarefied oil being heated red-hot suddenly takes fire and flames. The vegetable burns and deflagrates rapidly, till all its oil is consumed. Then the flame ceases; and nothing remains but a coal, like that found in a retort after all the principles of a plant have been extracted by the force of fire. But this coal having a free communication with the air, which is absolutely necessary to keep a combustible burning, continues to be red, sparkles, and wastes till all its phlogiston is dissipated and destroyed. After this nothing remains but the earth and fixed salt of the vegetable; which, mixed together, form what we call the ashes. Water, which is the natural solvent of salts, takes up everything of that kind that is contained in the ashes; so that by lixiviating them, as directed, all the salt is extracted, and nothing left but the pure earth of the mixt which is thus decomposed.

The phenomena observed in the burning of a vegetable substance, and the production thereby of a fixed alkali, seem to prove that this salt is the work of the fire; that it did not exist in the plant before it was burnt; that the plant only contained materials adapted to form this salt; and that this salt is no other than a combination of some of the acid, united with a portion of earth, by means of the igneous motion.

The alkali obtained from the ashes of burnt plants is not perfectly pure: it is contaminated with a small mixture of fatty matters, which were probably defended thereby against the action of the fire, and which render it somewhat saponaceous. In order to free it from this extraneous matter, and to render it very caustic, it must be calcined a long time in a crucible, but without melting it at first; because it is with this salt as with most metallic matters, which are sooner and more easily deprived of their phlogiston by being calcined without melting, provided they be comminuted into small particles, than when they are in fusion; all melted matters having but a small surface exposed to the air, by the contact of which the evaporation of any thing whatever is exceedingly promoted.

TO PROCURE THE FIXED SALTS OF A PLANT, BY BURNING IT AFTER THE MANNER OF TACHENIUS. Into an iron pot put the plant whose salt you desire to obtain in the manner of Tachenius, and set it over a fire, strong enough to make its bottom red-hot; at the same time cover your plant with a plate of iron, that may lie immediately upon it in the pot. The plant will grow black, and smoke considerably; but will not flame, because it hath not a sufficient communication with the air. The black smoke only will escape through the interstice left between the side of the pot and the rim of the plate; which for that purpose should be made so as not to fit exactly into the pot. From time to time take up the iron plate, stir the plant, and cover it again immediately, to prevent its taking fire, or to smother it if it should happen to flame; go on thus till the black smoke cease.

Then take off the iron plate: the upper part of the half-burnt plant will take fire as soon as the air is admitted, consume gradually, and be reduced to a white ash. Stir your matter with an iron wire, that the undermost parts, which are still black, may be successively brought uppermost, take fire, and burn to white ashes.

Go on thus as long as you perceive the least blackness remaining. After this, leave your ashes some time longer on the fire; but stir them frequently, to the end that, if any black particles should still be left, they may be entirely consumed.

Your ashes being thus prepared, lixiviate them with seven times their quantity of water, made to simmer over the fire, and keep stirring it with an iron ladle. Then filter the liquor, and evaporate it to dryness in an iron pot, stirring it incessantly towards the end, lest the matter, when it grows stiff, should adhere too closely to the vessel. When all the humidity is evaporated, you will have a salt of a darkish colour and alkaline nature; which you may melt in a crucible, and mould into cakes. This is the fixed salt of plants, prepared in the manner of Tachenius.

TO RENDER FIXED ALKALIS VERY CAUSTIC BY MEANS OF LIME. THE CAUSTIC STONE. Take a lump of newly burnt quick-lime, that hath not yet begun to slake in the air: put it into a stone pan, and cover it with twice its weight of the unwashed ashes of some plant that are full of the salt you design to render caustic. Pour on them a great quantity of hot water; let them steep in it five or six hours, and then boil them gently. Filter the liquor through a thick canvas bag, or through brown filtering paper supported by a linen cloth.

Evaporate the filtered liquor in a copper bason set over the fire; and there will remain a salt, which must be put into a crucible set in the fire. It will melt, and boil for sometime; after which it will be still, and look like an oil, or melted fat. When it comes to this condition, pour it out on a very hot copper plate, and cut it into oblong tapering slips, before it grow hard by cooling. Put these slips, while they are still hot, into a very dry glass bottle, and seal it hermetically. This is the caustic stone, or common caustic.

THE ANALYSIS OF SOOT. Take a wood-soot from a chimney under which no animal matter hath been dressed or burnt; put it into a glass retort set in a reverberating furnace; lute on a receiver and begin to distill with a degree of heat somewhat less than that of boiling water. A considerable quantity of limpid phlegm will come over. Keep the fire in the same degree as long as any of this phlegm rises, but increase it when the drops begin to come slow; and then there will ascend a good deal of a milky water. When this water ceases to run, change the receiver, and increase your fire a little: a yellow volatile salt will rise, and stick to the sides of the receiver. The fire ought now to be very fierce, and if so, will force up at the same time a very thick black oil. Let the vessels cool: you will find a saline matter risen into the neck of the retort, which could not pass over into the receiver: in the bottom of the retort will be a caput mortuum or black charred substance, the upper part of which will be crusted over with a saline matter, like that in the neck of the retort.

As we are at present inquiring into the nature of vegetables, only, it is evidently necessary that we chuse a soot produced by burning vegetables alone. Soot, though dry in appearance, contains nevertheless much humidity, as appears from this analysis; seeing there comes over at first a considerable quantity of phlegm, that doth not seem to be impregnated with any principle, except perhaps an extremely subtile, saline, and oily matter, that communicates to it a disagreeable smell, from which it cannot by any means be entirely freed.

The volatile alkali obtained from soot is, in a double respect, the product of the fire. In the first place, though it derives its origin wholly from wood or other vegetables, which, when distilled in close vessels, yield no volatile alkali at all, yet it produces such a salt when analysed in the present manner: whence it must be inferred, that the principles of those vegetables are metamorphosed into a volatile alkali, by being burnt in the open air, and sublimed in the form of soot. Secondly, though soot, when analysed, yields a great deal of this salt, yet this salt doth not formally pre-exist therein; for it doth not rise till after the phlegm, nor without a very considerable degree of heat; therefore soot contains only the materials necessary to form this salt; therefore the perfect combination of this salt requires that the force of fire be applied a second time; therefore it is, as was said, doubly the product of the fire.

The saline matter which we find sublimed into the neck of the retort, and which also forms the crust that covers the caput mortuum of the soot, appears by all chemical trials to be an ammoniacal salt; that is a neutral salt, consisting of an acid and a volatile alkali. This ammoniacal salt rises only into the neck of the retort, and doth not come over into the receiver; because it is but semi-volatile. We shall treat more at large of the production of a volatile alkali, and of this ammoniacal salt, when we come to the analysis of animals, and the article of sal ammoniac.

THE ANALYSIS OF SOME PARTICULAR SUBSTANCES BELONGING TO THE VEGETABLE KINGDOM. ANALYSIS OF THE NATURAL BALSAMS: INSTANCES IN TURPENTINE. Into a cucurbit put as much rain-water as will fill about a fourth part of its cavity, and pour into it the turpentine you intend to analyse. Cover the cucurbit with its head, and lute it on with slips of sized paper or wet bladder. Set your alembic in a sand-bath; lute on a long-necked receiver; and give a gradual fire till the water in the cucurbit boil. There will come over into the receiver a good deal of phlegm, which, by little and little, will become more and more acid; and at the same time there will rise a great quantity of an aethereal oil, extremely light, fluid, and as limpid and colourless as water.

When you observe that no more oil comes off, unlute your vessels; and in the receiver you will find an acidulated water, and the aethereal oil floating on it. These two liquors may be easily separated from each other, by means of a glass funnel.

In the cucurbit will be left some of the water you put in, together with the remainder of your turpentine; which, when cold, instead of being fluid, as it was before distillation, will be solid, and of the consistence of a resin, and is then called resin.

Put this residuum into a glass retort, and distill it in a reverberatory with a naked fire, gradually increased according to the general rule for all distillations. At first, with a degree of heat a little greater than that of boiling water, you will see two liquors come over into the recipient; one of which will be aqueous and acid, the other will be a transparent, limpid, yellowish oil, floating on the acid liquor.

Continue your distillation, increasing your fire from time to time, by slow degrees. These two liquors will continue to come off together; and the nearer the operation draws to its end, the more acid will the aqueous liquor become, and the thicker and deeper coloured will the oil grow. At last the oil will be very thick, and of a deep reddish-yellow colour. When nothing more ascends, unlute your vessels: in the retort you will find only a very small quantity of a charred, light, friable substance.

All natural balsams, as well as turpentine, are oily, aromatic matters, which flow in great quantities from the trees containing them, either spontaneously, or thro' incisions made on purpose. As these matters have a strong scent, it is not surprising that they should greatly abound with essential oils. They may even be considered as essential oils, that naturally, and of their own accord, separate from the vegetables in which they exist.

Natural balsams, and essential oils grown thick with age, are exactly one and the same thing. Accordingly we see that fire and distillation produce the same effects on both. The rectification of an essential oil, thickened by keeping, is nothing but a decomposition thereof, by separating, with the heat of boiling water, all those parts that are light enough to rise with the degree of heat, from what is so loaded with acid as to remain fixed therein.

The newer natural balsams are, the thinner they are, and the more essential oil do they yield; and this essential oil, like all others, grows thick in time, and at last turns again to an actual balsam.

These balsams, by being long exposed to the heat of the sun, acquire such a consistence as to become solid. They then take another name, and are called resins. Resins yield much less essential oil when distilled, than balsams do. Hence it follows, that resins are to balsams, what balsams are to essential oils.

THE ANALYSIS OF RESINS: INSTANCED IN BENJAMIN. THE FLOWERS AND OIL OF BENJAMIN. Into a pretty deep earthen pot, having a border or rim round its mouth, put the benjamin you intend to analyse. Cover the pot with a large conical cap of very thick white paper, and tie it on under the rim. Set your pot in a sand-bath, and warm it gently till the benjamin melt. Continue the heat in this degree for an hour and half. Then untie the paper cap and take it off, shaking it as little as possible. You will find all the inside of the cap covered with a great quantity of beautiful, white, shining flowers, in the form of little needles. Brush them off gently with a feather, put them into a bottle, and stop it close.

As soon as you take off the first cap, cover your pot immediately with a second like the former. In this manner go on till you perceive the flowers begin to grow yellowish; and then it is proper to desist.

The matter left in the pot will be blackish and friable when cold. Pulverise it; mix it with sand; and distill it in a glass retort with a graduated heat. There will come over a light oil, of a fragrant scent, but in very small quantity; a little of an acid liquor, and a great quantity of a red thick oil. There will be left in the retort a charred, spungy substance.

OF THE NATURE AND PROPERTIES OF CAMPHOR. We do not propose to give an analysis of this singular body; because hitherto there is no process known in chemistry by which it can be decomposed. We shall therefore content ourselves with reciting its principal properties, and making a few reflections on its nature.

Camphor is an oily concrete substance; a kind of resin, brought to us from the island of Borneo, but chiefly from Japan. This substance resembles resins, in being inflammable, and burning much as they do; it is not soluble in water, but dissolves entirely and perfectly in spirit of wine; it is easily separated again from this menstruum, as all other oily matters are, by the addition of water; it dissolves both in expressed and in distilled oils; it hath a very strong aromatic smell. These are the chief properties which camphor possesses in common with resins: but in other respects it differs totally from them; especially in the following particulars.

Camphor takes fire and flames with vastly more ease than any other resin. It is so very volatile, that it vanishes entirely in the air, without any other heat than that of the atmosphere. In distillation it rises entire, without any decomposition, or even the least alteration. It dissolves in concentrated mineral acids; but with circumstances very different from those that attend other oily or resinous substances. The dissolution is accompanied with no effervescence, no sensible heat; and consequently can produce no inflammation. Acids do not burn, blacken, or thicken it, as they do other oily matters; on the contrary, it becomes fluid, and runs with them into a liquor that looks like oil.

Camphor doth not, like other oily matters, acquire a disposition to dissolve in water by the union it contracts with acids; though its union with them seems to be more intimate than that of many oily matters with the same acids. On the contrary, if a combination of camphor and an acid be diluted with water, these two substances instantly separate from each other: the acid unites with the water, and the camphor, being entirely disengaged from it, swims on the surface of the liquor. Neither volatile alkalis, nor the most caustic fixed alkalis, can be brought into union with it; for it always eludes their power.

Notwithstanding these wide differences between camphor and all other oily and resinous substances, the rule, that acids thicken oils, seems to be so universal, and so constantly observed by nature, that we cannot help thinking this substance, like all the rest, is an oil thickened by an acid. But what oil? what acid? and how are they united? This is a subject for very curious inquiries.

With a yellow oil drawn from wine, and an acid vinous spirit, Mr. Hellot made a kind of artificial camphor: a substance having the odour, savour, and inflammability of aether. Can it be a substance of the same nature with aether, a kind of solid aether, an aether in a concrete form?

THE ANALYSIS OF BITUMENS: INSTANCE IN AMBER. THE VOLATILE SALT AND OIL OF AMBER. Into a glass retort put some small bits of amber so as to fill but two thirds of the vessel. Set your retort in a furnace covered with its dome; fit on a large glass receiver; and beginning with a very gentle heat, distill with degrees of fire. Some phlegm will first come off, which will gradually grow more acid, and will be succeeded by a volatile salt, figured like fine needles, that will stick to the sides of the receiver.

Keep the fire up to this degree, in order to drive over all the salt. When you perceive that little or none rises, change the receiver, and increase your fire a little. A light, clear, limpid oil will ascend. As the distillation advances, this oil will grow higher coloured, less limpid, and thicker; till at last it will be opaque, black, and have the consistence of turpentine.

When you perceive that, though the retort be red-hot, nothing more comes off, let the fire go out. You will have in the retort a black, light, spungy coal. If you have taken care to shift the receiver, from time to time, during the distillation of your oil, you will have sundry separate portions thereof, each of which will have a different degree of tenuity or thickness, according as it came over at the beginning, or towards the end of the distillation.

The substance of which we have here given the analysis, together with all others of the same, that is, of the bituminous kind, is, by most chemists and naturalists, classed with minerals: and so far they are right, that we actually get these mixts, like other minerals, out of the bowels of the earth, and never procure them immediately from any vegetable or animal compound. Yet we have our reasons for acting otherwise, and for thinking that we could not, in this work, place them better, than immediately after those vegetable substances which we call resins.

Several motives determine us to proceed in this manner. The analysis of bitumens demonstrates, that, with regard to the principles of which they consist, they are totally different from every other kind of mineral; and that, on the contrary, they greatly resemble vegetable resins in almost every respect. In short, though they are not immediately procured from vegetables there is the greatest reason for believing that they were originally of the vegetable kingdom, and that they are no other than resinous and oily parts of trees or plants, which by lying long in the earth, and there contracting an union with the mineral acids, have acquired the qualities that distinguish them from resins.

Mineralogists know very well that we find, every where in the earth, many vegetable substances, that have lain very long buried under it, and frequently at a considerable depth. It is not uncommon to find, under ground, vast beds of fossile trees, which seem to be the remains of immense forests: and bitumens, particularly amber, are often found among this subterraneous wood.

These considerations, joined to proofs drawn from their analysis, make this opinion more than probable: nor are we singular in maintaining it, as it is adopted by many able modern chemists.

The analysis of amber, above described, may serve as a general specimen of the decomposition of other bitumens: with this single difference, that amber is the only one among them which yields the volatile salt aforesaid; and this determined us to examine it preferably to any other. As for the rest, they all yield a phlegm, an acid liquor, and an oil; which is thin at first, but grows thicker and thicker as the distillation draws towards an end. It must be understood, however, that these acids and these oils may differ, according to the nature of the bitumens from which they are drawn; just as the phlegm, the acid and the oil, resulting from the decomposition of resins, differ in quantity and quality, according to the nature of the resins from which they are procured.

The principal differences observed between resins and bitumens are these: the latter are less soluble in spirit of wine; have a peculiar scent, which cannot be accurately described, and of which the sense of smelling only can judge; and their acid is stronger and more fixed. This last property is one of the motives which induce us to think, that besides the vegetable acid, originally combined with the resinous or oily matter now become a bitumen, a certain quantity of mineral acid hath, in a course of time, been superadded to constitute this mixt. We shall presently see that the fact is certainly so, in the case of amber at least.

THE ANALYSIS OF BEES-WAX. Melt the wax you intend to analyse, and mix with it as much fine sand as will make it into a stiff paste. Put this paste in little bits into a retort, and distil as usual, with a graduated fire, beginning with a very gentle heat. An acid phlegm will come over, and be followed by a liquor which at first will look like an oil, but will soon congeal in the receiver, and have the appearance of a butter or grease. Continue the distillation, increasing the fire by insensible degrees, till nothing more will come off. Then separate the butter from the acid phlegm in the receiver, mix it with fresh sand, and distil it again just as you did the wax before. Some acid phlegm will still come off, and an oil will ascend, which will not fix in the receiver, though it be still thick. Continue the distillation, with a fire so governed that the drops may succeed each other at the distance of six or seven seconds of time. Do not increase it, till you perceive the drops fall more slowly; and then increase it no more than is necessary to make the drops follow each other as above directed. When the distillation is finished, you will find in the receiver the oil come wholly over, and a little acid phlegm. Separate the oil from this liquor; and, if you desire to have it more fluid, redistil it a third time in the same manner.

THE SACCHARINE JUICES OF PLANTS ANALYSED: INSTANCE IN HONEY. Put into a stone cucurbit the honey you intend to distil; set it in a moderate sand-heat, and evaporate the greatest part of its humidity, till you perceive the phlegm to be acid. Then take out the matter remaining in the cucurbit, put it into a retort, leaving a full third thereof empty, and distil in a reverberatory with degrees of fire. An acid amber-coloured liquor will come over. As the operation advances, this liquor will continually become deeper coloured and more acid, and at the same time a little black oil will ascend. When the distillation is over, you will find in the retort a pretty large charred mass, which being burnt in the open air, and lixiviated, affords a fixed alkali.

Sugar, manna, and the saccharine juices of fruits and plants, are of the same nature as honey, yield the same principles, and in the same proportions. All these substances must be considered as native soaps; because they consist of an oil rendered miscible with water, by means of a saline substance. They differ from the common artificial soaps in several respects; but chiefly in this, that their saline part is an acid, whereas that of common soap is an alkali. The natural soaps are not for that reason the less perfect: on the contrary, they dissolve in water without destroying its transparency, and without giving it a milky colour; which proves, that acids are not less proper than alkalis, or rather that they are more proper additaments, for bringing oils into a saponaceous state.

GUMMY SUBSTANCES ANALYSED: INSTANCED IN GUM ARABIC. Distil gum arabic in a retort with degrees of fire. A limpid, scentless, and tasteless phlegm will first come over; and then a russet coloured acid liquor, a little volatile alkali, and an oil, which will first be thin and afterwards grow thick. In the retort will be left a good deal of a charred substance, which being burnt and lixiviated, will give a fixed alkali.

Gums have at first sight some resemblance of resins; which hath occasioned many resinous matters to be called gums, though very improperly: for they are two distinct sorts of substances, of natures absolutely different from each other. It hath been shewn, that resins have an aromatic odour; that they are indissoluble in water, and soluble in spirit of wine; that they are only an essential oil grown thick. Gums, on the contrary, have no odour, are soluble in water, indissoluble in spirit of wine, and, by being analysed as in the process, are converted almost wholly into a phlegm and an acid. The small portion of oil contained in them is so thoroughly united with their acid, that it dissolves perfectly in water, and the solution is clear and limpid. In this respect gums resemble honey, and the other vegetable juices analogous to it. They are all fluid originally; that is, when they begin to ooze out of their trees. At that time they perfectly resemble mucilages, or rather they are actual mucilages, which grow thick and hard in time by the evaporation of a great part of their moisture: just as resins are true oils, which losing their most fluid parts by evaporation at last become solid. Infusions or slight decoctions of mucilaginous plants, when evaporated to dryness, become actual gums.

Some trees abound both in oil and in mucilage: these two substances often mix and flow from the tree blended together. Thus they both grow dry and hard together in one mass, which of course is at the same time both gummy and resinous: and accordingly such mixts are named gum resins.

OF OPERATIONS ON FERMENTED VEGETABLE SUBSTANCES. OF THE PRODUCT OF SPIRITUOUS FERMENTATION. TO MAKE WINE OF VEGETABLE SUBSTANCES THAT ARE SUSCEPTIBLE OF SPIRITUOUS FERMENTATION. Let a liquor susceptible of, and prepared for, the spirituous fermentation, be put into a cask. Set this cask in a temperately warm cellar, and cover the bung hole with a bit of linen cloth only. In more or less time, according to the nature of the liquor to be fermented, and to the degree of heat in the air, the liquor will begin to swell, and be rarefied. There will arise an intestine motion, attended with a small hissing and effervescence, throwing up bubbles to the surface and discharging vapours; while the gross, viscous, and thick parts, being driven up by the fermenting motion, and rendered lighter by little bubbles of air adhering to them, will rise to the top, and there form a kind of soft spungy crust, which will cover the liquor all over. The fermenting motion still continuing, this crust will, from time to time, be lifted up and cracked by vapours making their escape through it; but those fissures will presently close again, till, the fermentation gradually going off, and at last entirely ceasing, the crust will fall in pieces to the bottom of the liquor, which will insensibly grow clear. Then stop the cask close with its bung, and set it in a cooler place.

Matters that are susceptible of the spirituous fermentation are seldom so perfectly prepared for it by nature as they require to be. If we except the juices that flow naturally from certain trees, but oftener from incisions made on purpose in them, all other substances require some previous preparation.

Boerhaave divides the substances that are fit for spirituous fermentation into five classes. In the first he places all the meally seeds, the legumens, and the kernels of almost all fruits. The second class includes the juices of all fruits that do not tend to putrefaction. In the third class stand the juices of all the parts of plants which tend rather to acidity than to putrefaction; and consequently those which yield much volatile alkali are to be excluded. The fourth class comprehends the juices or saps that spontaneously distil from several trees and plants, or flow from them when wounded. He forms his fifth and last class of the saponaceous, saccharine, and concrete or thick juices of vegetables. Resinous or purely gummy matters are excluded, as not being fermentable.

These five classes may be reduced into two; one comprehending all the juices, and another all the meally parts of vegetables that are susceptible of fermentation. The juices want nothing to fit them for fermentation, but to be expressed out of the substances containing them, and to be diluted with a sufficient quantity of water. If they be very thick, the best way is to add so much water as shall render the mixed liquor just capable of bearing a new-laid egg. With respect to farinaceous substances, as they are almost all either oily or mucilaginous, they require a little more management. The method of brewing malt liquors will furnish us with examples of such management. See Brewing.

Besides the preparations relating chiefly to malt-liquors, there are many other things to be observed relating to spirituous fermentation in general, and to all matters susceptible of that fermentation. For example: all grains and fruits designed for that fermentation must be perfectly ripe; for otherwise they will not ferment without difficulty, and will produce little or no inflammable spirit. Such matters as are too austere, too acrid, or astringent, are for the same reason unfit for spirituous fermentation; as well as those which abound too much in oil.

In order to make the fermentation succeed perfectly, so as to produce the best wine that the fermented liquor is capable of affording, it is necessary to let it stand quiet without stirring it, lest the crust that forms on its surface should be broken to little fragments, and mix with the liquor. This crust is a kind of cover, which hinders the spirituous parts from exhaling as fast as they are formed. The free access of the air is another condition necessary to fermentation: and for this reason the vessel that contains the fermenting liquor must not be close stopped; the bung-hole is only to be covered with a linen cloth, to hinder dirt and insects from falling into it. Nor must the bung-hole be too large, lest too much of the spirituous parts should escape and be lost.

Lastly, a just degree of warmth is one of the conditions most necessary for fermentation; for in very cold weather there is no fermentation at all; and too much heat precipitates it in such a manner that the whole liquor becomes turbid, and many fermenting and fermented particles are dissipated.

If notwithstanding the exactest observance of every particular requisite to excite a successful fermentation, the liquor cannot, without difficulty, be brought to effervesce, which scarce ever happens but to malt-liquor, it may be accelerated by mixing therewith some matter that is very susceptible of fermentation, or actually fermenting. Such matters are called ferments. The crust that forms on the surface of fermenting liquors is a most efficacious ferment, and on that account very much used.

It sometimes happens, that there is occasion to check the fermentation excited in the liquor, before it ceases of itself. To effect this, such means must be used as are directly opposite to those mentioned above for promoting fermentation. The same end is obtained by mixing with the liquor a quantity of alkali, sufficient to absorb the acid contained therein: but this method is seldom made use of, because it spoils the liquor: which, after being thus treated, is incapable of any spirituous fermentation, but on the contrary will certainly putrefy.

Spirituour fermentation may also be stopped by mixing with the liquor a great quantity of some mineral acid. But this likewise alters its nature; because these acids, being fixed, always remain confounded therewith, and never separate from it.

The best method yet found out for checking this fermentation, without injury to the fermenting liquor, is to impregnate it with the fumes of burning sulphur. These fumes are known to be acid, and it is that quality in them which suspends the fermentation. But at the same time this acid is extremely volatile; so that it separates spontaneously from the liquor, after some time, and leaves it in a condition to continue its fermentation.

For this reason, when a wine is desired that shall be but half fermented, and shall partly retain the sweet taste it had in the state of must, (the proper name for the unfermented juice of the grape), it is put into casks in which sulphur hath been previously burnt, and the vapours thereof confined by stopping the bung-hole. These are called matched wines. If the same operation be performed on must, its fermentation will be absolutely prevented: it will retain all its saccharine taste, and is then called stum. As the sulphureous acid evaporates spontaneously, in no long space, it is necessary to fumigate matched wines or stums from time to time, when they are intended to be kept long without fermenting.

TO DRAW AN ARDENT SPIRIT FROM SUBSTANCES THAT HAVE UNDERGONE THE SPIRITUOUS FERMENTATION. THE ANALYSIS OF WINE. Fill a large copper cucurbit half full of wine. Fit on its head and refrigeratory. Lute on a receiver with wet bladder, and distill with a gentle fire; yet so that the drops will fall from the nose of the alembic may succeed one another pretty quick, and form a sort of small continued stream. Go on thus till you perceive that the liquor which comes over ceases to be inflammable; and then desist. You will find in the receiver a clear liquor, somewhat inclining to an amber-colour, of a pleasant quick smell, and which being thrown into a fire instantly flames. The quantity thereof will be nearly a fourth part of the wine you put into the alembic; and this is what is called brandy; that is, the ardent spirit of wine loaded with much phlegm.

In order to rectify it, and reduce it to spirit of wine, put it into a long-necked matras, capable of holding double the quantity. Fit a head to the matras, and lute on a receiver: place your matras over a pot half full of water: set this pot over a moderate fire; and with this vapour-bath distil your spirit, which will rise pure. Continue this degree of heat till nothing more will come over. You will find in the receiver a very clear colourless spirit of wine, of a quick but agreeable smell, which will catch fire at once by the bare contact of any flaming substance.

TO DEPHLEGMATE SPIRIT OF WINE BY THE MEANS OF FIXED ALKALIS. Into a glass cucurbit pour the spirit of wine you intend to dephlegmate, and add to it about a third part of its weight of fixed alkali, newly calcined, perfectly dry, heated, and pulverised. Shake the vessel, that the two matters may be mixed and blended together. The salt will gradually grow moist, and, if the spirit of wine be very aqueous, melt into a liquor, that will always lie at the bottom of the vessel, without uniting with the spirit of wine which will swim at top.

When you perceive that the alkali attracts no new moisture, and that no more of it melts, decant your spirit of wine from the liquor beneath it, and add to your spirit fresh salt thoroughly dried as before. This salt also will imbibe a little moisture; but it will not grow liquid, because the alkali, with which it was mixed before, hath left too little phlegm to melt this. Decant it from this salt as at first, and continue to mix and shake it in the same manner with fresh salt, till you observe that the salt remains as dry as it was before mixing it with the spirit of wine. Then distil your spirit in a small alembic with a gentle heat, and you will have it as much dephlegmated as it can be.

SPIRIT OF WINE COMBINED WITH DIFFERENT SUBSTANCES, TO COMBINE SPIRIT OF WINE WITH THE VITRIOLIC ACID. THIS COMBINATION DECOMPOUNDED. AETHER. Into an English glass retort put two pounds of spirit of wine perfectly dephlegmated, and pour on it at once two pounds of highly concentrated oil of vitriol: shake the retort gently several times, in order to mix the two liquors. This will produce an ebullition, and considerable heat; vapours will ascend, with a pretty loud hissing noise, which will diffuse a very aromatic smell, and the mixture will be of a deeper or lighter red colour, according as the spirit of wine was more or less oily. Set the retort on a sand-bath made nearly as hot as the liquor; lute on a tubulated ballon, and distil the mixture with a fire strong enough to keep the liquor always boiling; a very aromatic spirit of wine will first come over into the ballon, after which the aether will rise. When about five or six ounces of it are come off, you will see in the upper concavity of the retort a vast number of little points in a veined form, which will appear fixed, and which are nevertheless so many little drops of aether, rolling over one another, and trickling down into the receiver. These little points continue to appear and succeed each other to the end of the operation. Keep up the same degree of fire, till upon opening the little hole in the ballon you perceive that the vapours, which instantly fill the receiver, have the suffocating smell of volatile spirit of sulphur.

Then unlute the ballon, pour the liquor it contains into a crystal bottle, and stop it close: there will be about eighteen ounces of it. Lute on your receiver again, and continue the distillation with a greater degree of fire. There will come over an aqueous, acid liquor, smelling strong of a sulphureous spirit, which is not inflammable. It will be accompanied with undulating vapours; which being condensed will form an oil, most commonly yellow, one part of which will float on the surface of the liquor, and another will sink to the bottom.

Towards the end of the distillation of this acid liquor, and of the yellow oil of which it is the vehicle, that part of the mixture, which is left in the retort and grown black, will begin to rise in froth. Then suppress your fire at once: stop the distillation, and change your receiver once more. When the vessels are grown pretty cool, finish your distillation with a lamp-heat kept up for twelve or fifteen days, which in all that time will raise but a very little sulphureous spirit. Then break your retort, in which you will find a black, solid mass, like a bitumen. It will have an acid taste, arising from a remainder of the acid imperfectly combined with oil.

This artificial bitumen may be freed from its redundant acid, by washing it in several waters. Then put it into a glass retort, and distil it with a strong reverberated fire. You will obtain a reddish oil that will swim on water, much like the oil obtained by distilling the natural bitumens. This oil also will be accompanied with an aqueous acid liquor. In the retort will be left a charred matter, which, being put into an ignited crucible in the fire, burns for some time, and, when well calcined, leaves a white earth.

The liquors that rise first in this distillation, and which we directed to be kept by themselves, are a mixture consisting, 1. of a highly dephlegmated spirit of wine, of a most fragrant smell; 2. of aether, which the spirit of wine wherewith it is united renders miscible with water; 3. of a portion of oil, which commonly rises with the aether towards the end of the operation; 4. and sometimes of a little sulphureous acid, if the receiver be not changed soon enough.

In order to separate the aether from these other substances, put the whole into an English retort, with a little oil of tartar per deliquium to absorb the sulphureous acid, and distil very slowly in a sand bath heated by a lamp, till near half the liquor be come over. Then cease distilling; put the liquor in the receiver into a phial with some water, and shake it; you will see it rise with rapidity to the upper part of the phial, and float on the surface of the water: this is the aether.

SPIRIT OF WINE COMBINED WITH SPIRIT OF NITRE. SWEET SPIRIT OF NITRE. Into an English retort of crystal glass put some highly rectified spirit of wine; and, by means of a glass funnel with a long pipe let fall into your spirit of wine a few drops of the smoking spirit of nitre. There will arise in the retort an effervescence attended with heat, red vapours, and a hissing noise like that of a live coal quenched in water. Shake the vessel a little, that the liquors may mix thoroughly, and that the heat may be equally communicated to the whole. Then add more spirit of nitre, but in a very small quantity, and with the same precautions as before. Continue thus adding spirit of nitre, by little and little at a time, till you have put into the retort a quantity equal to a third part of your spirit of wine. Let this mixture stand quiet, in a cool place, for ten or twelve hours; then set it to digest in a very gentle warmth for eight or ten days, having first luted on a receiver to the retort.

During this time a small quantity of liquor will come over into the receiver, which must be poured back into the retort. Then distill with a somewhat stronger degree of heat, but still very gently, till nothing be left in the retort but a thick matter. In the receiver you will find a spirituous liquor, of a quick grateful smell which will excite a very smart sensation on the tongue, but without any corrosive acrimony. This is the sweet spirit of wine.

SPIRIT OF WINE COMBINED WITH THE ACID OF SEA SALT. DULCIFIED SPIRIT OF SALT. Mix together, little by little, in a glass retort, two parts of spirit of wine with one part of spirit of salt. Set this mixture to digest for a month in a gentle heat, and distill it, till nothing remain in the retort but a thick matter.

The acid of sea-salt is much less disposed to unite with inflammable matters than the other two mineral acids; and therefore, though it be ever so highly concentrated, when mixed with spirit of wine, it never produces effervescence comparable to that which is produced by the spirit of nitre. Neither the proportion nor strengh of the spirit of salt, requisite to prepare the sweet spirit of salt, are unanimously agreed upon by authors. Some direct equal parts of the two liquors; while others prescribe from two to four or five parts of spirit of wine to one part of spirit of salt. Some use only common spirit of salt; others require the smoking spirit distilled by means of spirit of vitriol. Lastly, some order the mixture to be distilled, after some days digestion; and others content themselves with barely digesting it. The whole depends on the degree of strength which the sweet spirit of salt is intended to have. This composition, as well as the sweet spirit of nitre, is esteemed in medicine to be very apertive and diuretic.

When the mixture of spirit of salt and spirit of wine is distilled, there comes over but one liquor, which appears homogeneous. This is the sweet spirit of salt. The nature of the marine acid is not changed in this combination: the acid is only weakened and rendered more mild: but in other respects it retains its characteristic properties.

OILS, OR OILY MATTERS, THAT ARE SOLUBLE IN SPIRIT OF WINE, SEPARATED FROM VEGETABLES, AND DISSOLVED BY MEANS OF THAT MENSTRUUM. TINCTURES; ELIXIRS: VARNISHES. AROMATIC STRONG WATERS. Put into a matras the substances from which you intend to extract a tincture, having first pounded them, or pulverised them if they are capable of it. Pour upon them spirit of wine to the depth of three fingers breadth. Cover the matras with a piece of wet bladder, and tie it on with packthread. Make a little hole in this bit of bladder with a pin, leaving it in the hole to keep it stopped. Set the matras in a sand-bath very gently heated. If the spirit of wine dissolve any part of the body it will accordingly acquire a deeper or lighter colour. Continue the digestion till you perceive that the spirit of wine gains no more colour. From time to time pull out the pin, to give vent to the vapours, or rarefied air, which otherwise burst the matras. Decant your spirit of wine, and keep it in a bottle well corked. Pour on some fresh spirit in its stead: digest as before; and go on in this manner, pouring on and off fresh spirit of wine, till the last come off colourless.

Spirit of wine impregnated with such parts of any vegetable substance as it is capable of dissolving, is commonly called a tincture. Several tinctures mixed together, or a tincture drawn from sundry vegetable substances at the same time, and in the same vessel, take the name of an elixir. Tinctures of elixirs impregnated with resinous matters only, are true varnishes. All these preparations are made in the same manner: to wit, as directed in our process. We shall only add here, that if the substances from which a tincture or elixir is to be made contain too much moisture, it is proper to free them from it by gentle desiccation; especially if you design that the tincture should be well impregnated with the oily and resinous parts: for their excess of moisture uniting with the spirit of wine would weaken it, and render it unable to act on those matters, which it cannot dissolve when it is aqueous.

If your tinctures or elixirs be not so strong or so saturated as you desire, you may by distillation abstract part of the spirit of wine which they contain, and by that means give them such a degree of thickness as you judge proper. But the spirit of wine thus drawn off constantly carries along with it a good deal of the aromatic principle. It is a truly aromatic strong water. This spirit of wine also carries up with it a portion of thin oil, which is so much the more considerable as the degree of heat employed is greater: and this is the reason why it becomes of a milky colour when mixed with water.

If you intend to make an aromatic strong water only, you need not previously extract a tincture from the vegetable substance with which you mean to prepare your water: you need only put it in a cucurbit, pour spirit of wine upon it, and distil with a gentle heat. By this means you will obtain a spirit of wine impregnated with all the odour of the plant.

OF TARTAR. TARTAR ANALYSED BY DISTILLATION. THE SPIRIT, OIL, AND ALKALINE SALT OF TARTAR. Into a stone retort, or a glass one coated with lute, put some white tartar broken into small bits; observing that one half, or at least a full third, of the vessel be left empty. Set your retort in a reverberating furnace. Fit on a large ballon, having a small hole drilled in it: lute it exactly with fat lute, and secure the joint with a linen cloth smeared with lute made of quick-lime and the white of an egg. Apply at first an exceeding gentle heat, which will raise a limpid, sourish, pungent water, having but little smell, and a bitterish taste.

When this first phlegm ceases to come off, increase your fire a little, and make the degree of heat nearly equal to that of boiling water. A thin, limpid oil will rise, accompanied with white vapours, and with a prodigious quantity of air, which will issue out with such impetuousity, that if you do not open the little hole in the receiver time enough to give it vent, it will burst the vessels with explosion. An acid liquor will rise at the same time. Continue the distillation, increasing the heat by insensible degrees, and frequently unstopping the little hole of the receiver, till the elastic vapours cease to issue, and the oil to distil.

Then raise your fire more boldly. The acid spirit will continue to rise, and will be accompanied with a black, fetid, empyreumatic, ponderous, and very thick oil. Urge the fire to the utmost extremity so that the retort may be of a perfect red heat. This violent fire will raise a little volatile alkali, besides a portion of oil as thick as pitch. When the distillation is finished, you will find in the retort a black, saline, charred matter, which grows hot when wetted, attracts the moisture of the air, runs per deliqium, and hath all the properties of a fixed alkali.

The mass, being exposed to a naked fire in the open air, burns, consumes, and is reduced to a white ash, which is a fiery, caustic, fixed alkali.

The lees of wine resemble tartar, in as much as they contain, and yield when analised, the same principles; but they differ from it in this, that they contain, moreover, a greater quantity of earth, of phlegm, and a little ardent spirit, which are only mixed, but not united, with its tartarous acid.

THE DEPURATION OF TARTAR. CREAM AND CRYSTALS OF TARTAR. Reduce to a fine powder the tartar you intend to purify, and boil it in twenty five or thirty times as much water. Filter the boiling liquor through a flannel bag, and then gently evaporate some part of it: there will soon form on its surface a saline crust, which is the cream of tartar. Let your liquor cool, and there will adhere to the sides of the vessel a great quantity of a crystallized saline matter, which is crystal of tartar.

CRYSTAL OF TARTAR COMBINED WITH SEVERAL SUBSTANCES. CRYSTAL OF TARTAR COMBINED WITH ABSORBENT EARTHS. SOLUBLE TARTARS. Boil an absorbent earth, such as chalk, in a pan with water; and when you perceive the earth thoroughly divided and equally distributed through the water, throw into the pan, from time to time, some pulverised crystal of tartar, which will excite a considerable effervescence. Continue these projections, till you observe no effervescence excited thereby. All the absorbent earth, which obscured the transparency of the water, and gave it an opaque white colour, will gradually disappear as the crystal of tartar combines with it; and when the combination is perfected, the liquor will be clear and limpid. Then filter it, and there will be left on the filter but a very small quantity of earth. Evaporate all the filtered liquor with a gentle heat; and then set it in a cool place to shoot. Crystals will form therein, having the figure of flat quadrangular prisms, with almost always one, sometimes two, of the angles of the prism shaved down, as it were; and then the surfaces at each end are oblique answering to those depressed angles. These crystals are a neutral salt which readily dissolves in water; a true soluble tartar.

CRYSTAL OF TARTAR COMBINED WITH FIXED ALKALIS. THE VEGETABLE SALT. SAIGNETTE'S SALT. THE DECOMPOSITION OF SOLUBLE TARTARS. In eight parts of water dissolve one part of a very pure alkaline salt, perfectly freed from the phlogiston by calcination. Heat this lixivium in a stone pan set on a sand bath, and from time to time throw into it a little powdered cream or crystal of tartar. Each projection will excite a great effervescence, attended with many bubbles which will rise to a considerable height one over the other. Stir the liquor when the effervescence ceases, and you will see it begin again.

When no effervescence appears upon stirring the liquor, add a little more cream of tartar, and the same phenomena will be renewed. Go on thus till you have obtained the point of perfect saturation.

Then filter your liquor. If the alkali you made use of was the salt of Soda, evaporate your liquor quickly to a pellicle, and there will shoot in it crystals of nine sides resembling a coffin; the bottom part thereof being concave, and streaked with a great many parallel lines; and this is Suignette's salt. If you have employed any other alkali but soda, or the basis of sea-salt, evaporate your liquor slowly to the consistence of a syrup: let it stand quiet, and there will form in it crystals having the figure of flatted parallelopipeds; and this is the vegetable salt, or tartarised tartar.

All soluble tartars are easily decompounded, by means of a certain degree of heat. They yield in distillation the same principles as tartar; and the alkali that remains when they are perfectly calcined, consists of that which the tartar naturally afford, and of the alkaline matter with which it was converted into a neutral salt.

CRYSTAL OF TARTAR COMBINED WITH IRON. CHALYBEATED TARTAR. TINCTURE OF STEEL WITH TARTAR. SOLUBLE CHALYBEATED TARTAR. Mix four ounces of iron in filings with one pound of white tartar finely pulverised. Boil the mixture in about twelve times as much water as you took of tartar. When the saline part of the tartar is dissolved, filter the liquor boiling-hot through a flannel bag, and then set it in a cool place. In a very little time crystals of a russet colour will shoot therein. Decant the liquor from these crystals; evaporate it to a pellicle, and set it again to crystallise. Go on in this manner till it will shoot no more. Collect all the salt you have thus obtained, and keep it under the name of chalybeated tartar.

To make the tincture of steel with tartar, mix together six ounces of clean iron filings, and one pound of white tartar in powder. Put this mixture into a large iron kettle, and pour thereon as much rain-water as will moisten it. Make a paste of this matter, and leave it thus in a mass for twenty-four hours. Then pour on it twelve pounds of rain-water, boil the whole for twelve hours at least, stirring the mixture frequently, and adding from time to time some hot water, to supply the place of what evaporates. When you have thus boiled the liquor, let it stand quiet for some time, and then pour it off from the sediment at bottom. Filter, and evaporate to the consistence of a syrup; and you have the tincture of Mars with tartar. The dispensatories generally order an ounce of rectified spirit of wine to be poured on this tincture, in order to preserve it, and to keep it from growing mouldy, as it is very apt to do.

Soluble chalybeated tartar is prepared by mixing four ounces of tartarised tartar with one pound of the tincture of Mars with tartar, and evaporating them together in an iron vessel to dryness; after which it is kept in a well stopped phial to prevent its growing moist in the air.

CRYSTAL OF TARTAR COMBINED WITH THE REGULINE PART OF ANTIMONY. STIBIATED OR EMETIC TARTAR. Pulverise and mix together equal parts of the glass and of the liver of antimony. Put this mixture, with the same quantity of pulverised cream of tartar, into a vessel capable of containing as much water as will dissolve the cream of tartar. Boil the whole for twelve hours, from time to time adding warm water, to replace what is dissipated by evaporation. Having thus boiled your liquor, filter it while boiling hot; evaporate to dryness; and you will have a saline matter, which is emetic tartar.

OF THE PRODUCT OF ACETOUS FERMENTATION. SUBSTANCES SUSCEPTIBLE OF THE ACETOUS FERMENTATION TURNED INTO VINEGAR. The wine, the cyder, or the malt-liquor, you intend to convert into vinegar, being first thoroughly mixed with its lees, and with the tartar it may have deposited, put your liquor into a fat used before either for making or for holding vinegar. This vessel must not be quite full, and the external air must have access to the liquor contained in it. Set it where the air may have a degree of warmth answering nearly to the twentieth degree above zero in Mr. de Reaumur's thermometer. Stir the liquor from time to time. There will arise in it a new fermentative motion, accompanied with heat: its vinous odour will gradually change, and turn to a sour smell, which will become stronger and stronger till the fermentation be finished and cease of itself. Then stop your vessel close; the liquor it contains will be found converted into vinegar.

All substances that have undergone the spirituous fermentation are capable of being changed into an acid by passing through this second fermentation. Spirituous liquors, such as wine, cyder, beer, being exposed to a hot air, grow sour in a very short time. Nay, these liquors, though kept with all possible care, in very close vessels, and in a cool place, degenerate at last, change their natures, and insensibly turn sour. Thus the product of spirituous fermentation naturally and spontaneously degenerates to an acid.

For this reason it is of great importance, in making wine, or any other vinous liquor, to stop the fermentation entirely, if you desire the wine should contain as much spirit as possible. It is even more advantageous to check the fermentation a little before it come to the height than afterwards: because the fermentation, thus slackened and in appearance totally ceased, still continues in the vessels; but in a manner so much the less perceptible as it proceeds more slowly. Thus those liquors, in which the fermentation is not quite finished, but checked, continue for some time to gain more spirit; whereas, on the contrary, they degenerate and gradually turn sour, if you let the spirituous fermentation go on till it be entirely finished.

The production of the second fermentation, which we now to consider, if an acid of so much the greater strength, the stronger and more generous the spirituous liquor in which it is excited originally wins. The strength of this acid, commonly called vinegar, depends likewise in a great measure on the methods used in fermenting the vinous liquor, in order to convert it into vinegar: for if it be fermented in broad, flat vessels, and left to grow sour of itself, the spirituous parts will be dissipated, and the liquor be sour indeed, but vapid and effete.

The vinegar-makers, to increase the strength of their vinegar, use certain methods of which they make a mystery, keeping them very secret. However, Mr. Boerhaave give us, from some authors, the following description of a process for making vinegar:

"Take two large oaken vats or hogsheads, and in each of these place a wooden grate or hurdle, at the distance of a foot from the bottom. Set the vessel upright, and on the grates place a moderately close layer of green twigs, or fresh cuttings of the vine. Then fill up the vessel with the foot-stalks of grapes, commonly called the rape, to within a foot of the top of the vessel; which must be left quite open.

"Having thus prepared the two vessels, pour into them the wine to be converted into vinegar, so as to fill one of them quite up, and the other but half full. Leave them thus for twenty-four hours, and then fill up the half-filled vessel with liquor from that which is quite full, and which will now in its turn be left only half full. Four and twenty hours afterwards repeat the same operation and go on thus, keeping the vessels alternately full and half full during every twenty-four hours, till the vinegar be made. On the second or third day there will arise, in the half-filled vessel, a fermentative motion, accompanied with a sensible heat, which will gradually increase from day to day. On the contrary, the fermentating motion is almost imperceptible in the full vessel; and as the two vessels are alternately full and half full, the fermentation is by that means, in some measure, interrupted, and is only renewed every other day, in each vessel.

"When this motion appears to be entirely ceased, even in the half-filled vessel, it is a sign that the fermentation is finished; and therefore the vinegar is then to be put into common casks close stopped, and kept in a cool place.

"A greater or less degree of warmth accelerates or checks this, as well as the spirituous fermentation. In France it is finished in about fifteen days, during the summer; but if the heat of the air be very great, and exceed the twenty-fifth degree of Mr. de Reaumur's thermometer, the half-filled vessel must be filled up every twelve hours; because if the fermentation be not so checked in that time, it will become so violent, and the liquor will be so heated, that many of the spirituous parts, on which the strength of the vinegar depends, will be dissipated; so that nothing will remain, after the fermentation, but a vapid wash, sour indeed, but effete. The better to prevent the dissipation of the spirituous parts, it is a proper and usual precaution to close the mouth of the half-filled vessel, in which the liquor ferments, with a cover made also of oak wood. As to the full vessel, it is always left open, that the air may act freely on the liquor it contains: for it is not liable to the same inconveniences, because it ferments but very slowly."

The vine-cuttings and grape-stalks, which the vinegar-makers put into their vessels, serve to increase the strength of the liquor. These matters contain a very manifest and perceptible acid. They also serve as a ferment; that is, they dispose the wine to become eager more expeditiously and more vigorously. They are the better and more efficacious for having been once used, because they are thereby thoroughly drenched with the fermented acid: and therefore the vinegar-makers lay them by for preparing other vinegar, after washing them nimbly in running water, in order to free them from a viscid oily matter which settles on them during the fermentation. This matter must by all means be removed; because it is disposed to grow mouldy and rot; so that it cannot be prejudicial to any liquor in which you put it.

As the acetous fermentation differs from the spirituous in its production, so it doth in many circumstances attending it. 1. Motion and agitation are not prejudicial to the acetous fermentation, as they are to the spirituous; on the contrary, moderate stirring, provided it be not continual is of service to it. 2. This fermentation is accompanied with remarkable heat; whereas the warmth of the spirituous fermentation is scarce sensible. 3. We do not believe there ever was an instance of the vapour that rises from a liquor in acetous fermentation proving noxious, and producing either disorders or sudden death, as the vapour of fermenting wine doth. 4. Vinegar deposites a viscid oily matter, as hath just been observed, very different from the lees and tartar of wine. Vinegar never deposites any tartar; even though new wine, that hath not yet deposited its tartar, should be used in making it.

TO CONCENTRATE VINEGAR BY FROST. Expose to the air, in frosty weather, the vinegar you desire to concentrate. Icicles will form in it; but the whole liquor will not freeze. Take out those icicles and if you desire a further conventration of your vinegar by this method, the liquor which did not freeze the first time must be exposed to a stronger frost. More icicles will form therein, which must likewise be separated, and kept by themselves. The liquor which doth not freeze this second time will be a very strong concentrated vinegar.

VINEGAR ANALYSED BY DISTILLATION. Into a glass or stone cucurbit put the vinegar to be distilled; fit to it a glass head; place your alembic in the sand-bath of a distilling furnace, and lute on a receiver. Apply a very gentle heat at first. A clear, limpid, light liquor will rise, and fall in distinct drops, like water, from the nose of the alembic.

Continue distilling this first liquor, till the vinegar contained in the cucurbit be dimished about a fourth part. Then shift your receiver, and increase the fire a little. A clear liquor will still come over, but heavier and more acid than the former. Distil in this manner till you have drawn off into your second receiver two thirds of the liquor that was left in the cucurbit.

A thick matter will now remain at the bottom of the still: put it into a retort; lute on a receiver; set your retort in a reverberating furnace and distil with degrees of fire. There will come over a limpid liquor, very acid and sharp, yet ponderous, and requiring a great degree of fire to raise it; on which account it makes the receiver very hot. It has a strong empyreumatic smell. When the distillation begins to slacken, increase your fire. There will rise an oil of a fetid, quick smell. At last when nothing more will rise with the strongest fire, break the retort, and in it you will find a black charred matter: burn it, and from the ashes lixiviated with water you will obtain a fixed alkali.

THE ACID OF VINEGAR COMBINED WITH DIFFERENT SUBSTANCES. THE ACID OF VINEGAR COMBINED WITH ALKALINE SUBSTANCES. FOLIATED SALT OF TARTAR, OR REGENERATED TARTAR. DECOMPOSITION OF THAT SALT. Into a glass cucurbit put some very pure and well dried salt of tartar; and pour on it some good distilled vinegar, by little and little at a time. An effervescence will arise. Pour on more vinegar, till you attain the point of saturation. Then fit a head to the cucurbit; set it in a sand bath; and, having luted on a receiver, distil with a gentle heat, and very slowly, till nothing remain but a dry matter. On this residuum drop a little of the same vinegar; and if any effervescence appears, add slowly vinegar till you attain the point of saturation, and distil again as before. If you observe no effervescence, the operation was rightly performed.

It is not easy to hit the exact point of saturation in preparing this neutral salt; because the oily parts, with which the acid of vinegar is loaded, hinder it from acting so briskly and readily as it would do, is it were as pure as the mineral acids; and for this reason it often happens that, when we have nearly attained the point of saturation, the addition of an acid makes no sensible effervescence, though the alkali be yet entirely saturated; which deceives the operator, and makes him conclude erroneously that he hath attained the true point of saturation.

But he easily perceives his mistake, when, after having separated from this saline compound all its superfluous moisture by distillation, he drops fresh vinegar upon it; for then the salts being more concentrated, and consequently more active, produce an effervescence, which would not have been sensible if this last portion of acid, instead of coming into immediate contact with the dried alkali, could not have mixed therewith till diffused through, and in a manner suffocated by that phlegm from which the acid of the vinegar before neutralised was gradually separated by its combining with the alkali; that phlegm keeping in solution both the neutral salt already formed, and the alkali not yet saturated. And for this reason it is necessary to try, after the first desiccation of this salt, which is called regenerated tartar, whether or no the just point of saturation hath been attained.

From what hath been said, concerning the desiccation of this neutral salt, it is plain, that the use of it is only to free the salt from the great quantity of superfluous moisture wherein it is dissolved: which proves, that the acid of vinegar, like all other acids dissolved in much water, is separated from most of this redundant phlegm by being combined with a fixed alkali. And hence we must conclude, that the acid of vinegar, contained in regenerated tartar desiccated, is vastly stronger and more concentrated than it was before.

Though the acid of vinegar is freed, by combining with a fixed alkali, from a great quantity of superfluous phlegm, yet the oily parts with which it is entangled still cleave to it: these parts are not separated from it by its conversion into a neutral salt, but, without quitting it, combine also with the fixed alkali; and this gives regenerated tartar a saponaceous quality, and several other peculiar properties.

Regenerated tartar, when dried, is of a brown colour. It is semi-volatile; melts with a very gentle heat, and then resembles an unctuous liquor; which indicates its containing an oil: when cast upon live coals, it flames; and, when distilled with a strong heat, yields an actual oil; all which evidently proves the existence of that oil.

This salt is soluble in spirit of wine; a quality which it probably owes also to its oil. It requires about six parts of spirit of wine to dissolve it; and the dissolution succeeds very well in a matras, with the help of a gentle warmth. If the spirit of wine be abstracted from this solution, by distilling with a small fire, it remains at the bottom of the cucurbit, in the form of a dry substance composed of leaves lying one upon another; which hath procured it the name of terra soliata tartar, or foliated salt of tartar.

It is not absolutely necessary that regenerated tartar be dissolved in spirit of wine to make the foliated salt: for it may be procured in this form only by evaporating the water in which it is dissolved. But the operation succeeds better with spirit of wine; probably because the success thereof depends on using an exceeding gentle warmth: now spirit of wine evaporates with much less heat than water.

Regenerated tartar may also be crystallised. If you desire to have it in this form, combine the acid with the alkali to the point of saturation; evaporate the liquor slowly to the consistence of a syrup, and set it in a cool place; where it will shoot into clusters of crystals lying one upon another like feathers.

Vinegar perfectly dissolves absorbent matters also, and particularly those of the animal kingdom; such as corals, crabs eyes, pearls, etc. In order to a dissolution of such matters, you must pulverize them, put them into a matras, and pour on them spirit of vinegar to the depth of four fingers breadth: an effervescence will arise: when that is over, set the mixture to digest two or three days in a sand-bath; then decant the liquor, filter it, and evaporate it to dryness with a very gentle heat. The matter which remains is called salt of coral, of pearls, of crabs-eyes, etc. according to the substances dissolved. If, instead of evaporating the liquor, a fixed alkali be mixed therewith, the absorbent matter, that was dissolved by the acid, will precipitate in the form of a white powder, which is called the magistery of coral, of pearls, etc.

THE ACID OF VINEGAR COMBINED WITH COPPER. VERDEGRIS. CRYSTALS OF COPPER. THIS COMBINATION DECOMPOUNDED. SPIRIT OF VERDEGRIS. Into a large matras put verdegris in powder. Pour on it distilled vinegar to the depth of four fingers breadth. Set the matras in a moderate sand-heat, and leave the whole in digestion, shaking it from time to time. The vinegar will acquire a very deep blue-green colour. When the liquor is sufficiently coloured, pour it off by inclination. Put some fresh vinegar into the matras; digest as before; and decant the liquor again, when it is sufficiently coloured. Proceed in this manner till the vinegar will extract no more colour. There will remain in the matras a considerable quantity of undissolved matter. The vinegar thus impregnated with verdegris is called tincture of copper.

Mix these several tinctures, and evaporate them with a gentle heat to a pellicle. Then set the liquor in a cool place: in the space of a few days a great many crystals of a most beautiful green colour will shoot therein, and stick to the sides of the vessel. Pour off the liquor from the crystals; evaporate it again to a pellicle, and set it by to crystallise. Continue these evaporations and crystallisations, till no more crystals will shoot in the liquor. These are called crystals of copper, and are used in painting. To this combination of the acid of vinegar with copper the painters and dealers have given them the title of distilled verdegris.

Verdegris is prepared at Montpellier. To make it they take two clean plates of copper which they lay one over another, with husks of grapes between, and after a certain time take them out. Their surfaces are then covered all over with a very beautiful green crust; which is verdegris. This verdegris is nothing but copper corroded by the acid of tartar, analogous to the acid of vinegar, which abounds in the wines of Languedoc, and especially in the rape, husks, and stones of grapes that have a very austere taste. Verdegris is a sort of rust of copper, or copper corroded and opened by the acid of wine, but not yet converted entirely into a neutral salt: for it is not soluble in water, nor does it crystallise. This arises from its not being united with a sufficient quantity of acid. The design of the operation here described is to furnish the verdegris with the quantity of acid requisite to make it a true metallic salt; for which purpose distilled vinegar is very fit.

Crystals of copper may be obtained, without employing verdegris, by making use of copper itself dissolved by the acid of vinegar, according to the method practised with respect to lead, as shall be shewn hereafter. But verdegris is generally used, because it dissolves soonest; it being a copper already half dissolved by an acid correspondent to that of vinegar.

Crystals of copper are decompounded by the action of fire alone, without any additament; because the acid of vinegar adheres but loosely to copper. In order to decompound this salt, and extract its acid, it must be put into a retort, and distilled in a reverbatory furnace with degrees of fire. An insipid phlegm rises first, which is the water retained by the salt in crystallising. This phlegm is succeeded by an acid liquor, which rises in the form of white vapours that fill the receiver. Towards the end of the distillation the fire must be violently urged, in order to raise the strongest and most fixed acid. At last there remains in the retort a black matter, which is nothing but copper, that may be reduced by melting it in a crucible with one part of saltpetre and two parts of tartar. A similar acid, but more oily, and in a much smaller quantity, may be obtained from verdegris by distillation.

The acid, which in this distillation comes over after the first phlegm, is an exceeding strong and concentrated vinegar. It is known by the title of spirit of verdegris.

THE ACID OF VINEGAR COMBINED WITH LEAD. CERUSE. SALT OR SUGAR OF LEAD. THIS COMBINATION DECOMPOUNDED. Into the glass head of a cucurbit put thin plates of lead; and secure them so that they may not fall out when the head is put upon the cucurbit. Fit on this head to a wide-mouthed cucurbit containing some vinegar. Set it in a sand-bath; lute on a receiver, and distil with a gentle heat for ten or twelve hours. Then take off the head; in it you will find the leaden plates covered, and, in a manner, crusted over with a white matter. This being brushed off with a hare's foot is what we call ceruse. The leaden plates thus cleansed may be employed again for the same purpose, till they be wholly converted into ceruse by repeated distillations. During the operation there will come over into the receiver a liquor somewhat turbid and whitish. This is a distilled vinegar in which some lead is dissolved.

Reduce a quantity of ceruse into powder; put it into a matras; pour on it twelve or fifteen times as much distilled vinegar; set the matras in a sand-bath; leave the matter in digestion for a day, shaking it from time to time: then decant your liquor, and keep it apart. Pour fresh vinegar on what is left in the matras, and digest as before. Proceed thus till you have dissolved one half or two thirds of the ceruse.

Evaporate to a pellicle the liquors you poured off from the ceruse, and set them in a cool place. Greyish crystals will shoot therein. Decant the liquor from the crystals; evaporate it again to a pellicle, and set it by to crystallise. Proceed thus evaporating and crystallising, as long as any crystals will shoot. Dissolve your crystals in distilled vinegar, and evaporate the solution, which will then shoot into whiter and purer crystals. This is the salt, or sugar of lead.

Lead is easily dissolved by the acid of vinegar. If it be barely exposed to the vapour of that acid, its surface is corroded, and converted into a kind of calx or white rust, much used in painting, and known by the name of ceruse, or white lead. But this preparation of lead is not combined with a sufficient quantity of acid to convert it into a salt: it is no more than lead divided and opened by the acid of vinegar; a matter which is to lead what verdegris is to copper. And therefore if you desire to combine ceruse with the quantity of acid necessary to convert it into a true neutral salt, you must treat it in the same manner as we did verdegris in order to procure crystals of copper; that is, you must dissolve it in distilled vinegar, as the process directs.

The salt of lead is not very white when it first shoots; and for this reason it is dissolved again in distilled vinegar, and crystallised a second time. If salt of lead be repeatedly dissolved in distilled vinegar, and the liquor evaporated, it will grow thick; but still cannot be desiccated without great difficulty. If the same operation be oftener repeated, this quality will thereby more and more increase; till at last it will remain on the fire like an oil or melted wax: it coagulates as it cools, and then looks, at first sight, like a metallic mass, somewhat resembling silver. This matter runs with a very gentle heat, almost as easily as wax.

The salt of lead hath a saccharine taste, which hath procured it the name also of sugar of lead. For this reason, when wine begins to turn sour, the sure way to cure it of that disagreeable taste, is to substitute a sweet one which is not disagreeable to the taste, by mixing therewith ceruse, litharge, or some such preparation of lead; for the acid of the wine dissolves the lead, and therewith forms a sugar of lead, which remains mixed with the wine, and hath a taste which, joined with that of the wine is not unpleasant. But, as lead is one of the most dangerous poisons we know, this method ought never to be practised; and whoever uses such a pernicious drug deserves to be most severly punished. Yet some thing very like this happens every day, and must needs have very bad consequences; while there is nobody to blame, and those to whom the thing may prove fatal can have no mistrust of it.

Salt of lead may be decompounded by distillation without additament. In order to perform this, you must put the salt of lead into a glass or stone retort, leaving a full third thereof empty, and distil in a reverberating furnace with degrees of fire. A spirit rises, which fills the receiver with clouds. When nothing more will come over with a fire that makes the retort red-hot, let the vessels cool, and then unlute them. You will find in the receiver an austere liquor, which is inflammable; or, at least, an inflammable spirit may be obtained from it, if about one half thereof be drawn off by distillation in a glass alembic. The retort in which the salt of lead was decompounded contains, at the end of the operation, a blackish matter: this is lead, which will resume its metallic form on being melted in a crucible; because the acid by which it was dissolved and from which it hath been separated, being of a very oily nature, hath left in it a sufficient quantity of phlogiston.

What is most remarkable in this decomposition of salt of lead is the inflammable spirit which it yields, though the vinegar which entered into the composition of the salt seemed to contain none at all.

OF THE PUTRID FERMENTATION OF VEGETABLE SUBSTANCES. THE PUTREFACTION OF VEGETABLES. Fill a hogshead with green plants, and tread them down a little; or, if the vegetables be hard and dry substances, divide them into minute parts, and steep them a little in water to moisten them: then leave them, or the green plants, in the vessel, uncovered and exposed to the open air. By degrees a heat will arise in the center of the vessel, which will continue increasing daily, at last grow very strong, and be communicated to the whole mass. As long as the heat is moderate, the plants will retain their natural smell and taste. As the heat increases, both these will gradually alter, and at last become very disagreeable, much like those of putrid animal substances. The plants will then be tender as if they had been boiled; or even be reduced to a kind of pap, more or less liquid according to the quantity of moisture they contained before.

Almost all vegetable matters are susceptible of putrefaction; but some of them rot sooner, and others more slowly. As putrefaction is only a species of fermentation, the effect whereof is to change entirely the state of the acid, by combining it with a portion of the earth and oil of the mixt, which are so attenuated that from this union there results a new saline substance in which no acid is discernible; which on the contrary hath the properties of an alkali, but rendered volatile; it is plain that, the nearer the acid of a plant set to putrefy is to this state the sooner will the putrefaction of that plant be completed. Accordingly all plants that contain a volatile alkali ready formed, or from which it can be obtained by distillation, are the most disposed to putrefaction.

Those plants, in which the acid, is very manifest and sensible, are less apt to putrefy; because all their acid must undergo the change above specified. But vegetable matters, whose acid is entangled and clogged by several of their other principles, must be still longer elaborated before they can be reduced to the condition into which complete putrefaction brings all vegetables. The earthy and oily parts, in which the acids of these substances are sheathed, must be attenuated and divided by a previous fermentation, which, of those parts subtilised and united with the acid, forms an ardent spirit, wherein the acid is more perceptible than in the almost insipid of saccharine juices out of which it is produced. The acid contained in the ardent spirit must be still further disengaged, before it can enter into the combination of a volatile alkali: consequently the ardent spirit must undergo a sort of decomposition; its acid must be rendered more sensible, and be brought to the same condition as the acid of plants in which it manifests all its properties.

Hence it appears that the spirituous and acetous fermentations are only preparatives which nature makes use of for bringing certain vegetable matters to putrefaction. These fermentations therefore must be considered as advances towards that putrefaction in which they terminate, or rather as the first stages of putrefaction itself.

PUTREFIED VEGETABLE SUBSTANCES ANALYSED. Put the putrefied plants you mean to analyse into a glass cucurbit, and set it in a sand bath. Fit to it a head; lute on a receiver; distil with a gentle fire, and a limpid fetid liquor will come over. Continue the distillation till the matter contained in the retort be almost dry.

Then unlute your vessels, and keep the liquor you find in the receiver by itself. Put the matter remaining in the cucurbit into a retort, and distil with a graduated heat. There will rise white vapours; a pretty considerable quantity of liquor nearly like that of the former distillation; a volatile salt in a concrete form; and a black oil, which towards the end will be very thick. In the retort there will remain a black charred matter, which being burnt in the open air will fall into ashes, from which no fixed alkali can be extracted.

By means of a funnel separate your oil from the aqueous liquor. Distil this liquor with a gentle heat. You will by this means obtain a volatile salt like that of animals; of which you may also get some, by the same means, from the liquor which came over in the first distillation.

This analysis shews the changes which putrefaction produces in vegetable matters. Scarce any of their principles are now to be discerned. They now yield no aromatic liquor; no essential oil; no acid; and consequently no essential salt, ardent spirit, or fixed alkali: in a word, whatever their natures were before putrefaction, they are all alike when they have once undergone this fermentative motion in its full extent. Nothing can then be obtained from them but phlegm, a volatile alkali, a fetid oil, and an insipid earth.

Almost all these changes are owing to the transmutation of the acid, which is depraved by putrefaction, and combined with a portion of the oil and subtilised earth of the mixt; so that the result of their union is a volatile alkali. Now, as the fixed alkali, found in the ashes of unputrefied plants, is only the most fixed part of their earth and of their acid, closely united together by the igneous motion, it is not surprising, that, when all the acid, with a part of the earth, is subtilised and volatilised by putrefaction, no fixed alkali can be found in the ashes of putrefied vegetables. The alteration which the acid suffers by the putrefactive motion is, in our opinion, the greatest it can undergo, without being entirely destroyed and decomposed, so as to be no longer a salt.

OF OPERATIONS ON ANIMAL SUBSTANCES. OF MILK. MILK SEPARATED INTO BUTTER, CURD, AND WHEY: INSTANCED IN COW'S MILK. Put new cow's milk into a flat earthen pan, and set it in a temperate heat. In ten or twelve hours time there will gather on its surface a thick matter, of a somewhat yellowish white: this is called cream. Gently skim off this cream with a spoon, letting the milk you take up with it run off. Put all this cream into another vessel, and keep it. The milk thus skimmed will not be quite so thick as before; nor will it be of such a dead white, but have a little blueish cast. If all the cream be not separated from it, more will gather on its surface after some time, which must be taken off as the former. In two or three days the skimmed milk will coagulate into a soft mass called curd, and then it tastes and smells sour.

Cut this curd across in several places. It will immediately discharge a large quantity of serum. Put the whole into a clean linen cloth; hang it up, and underneath it set a vessel to receive the serum as it drops. When the aqueous part hath done dripping, there will remain in the filter a white substance somewhat harder than the curdled milk. This substance is called cheese, and the serum separated from it is known by the name of whey.

The milk of animals that feed only on vegetables is, of all animal matters, the least removed from the vegetable nature. The truth of this will be demonstrated by the experiments we shall produce by and by, for the further analysis of milk.

Most chemists justly consider milk as of the same nature with chyle. Indeed there is great reason to think, that, except some small differences to be afterwards taken notice of, these two matters are nearly the same. They are both of a dead white colour, like that of an emulsion; which proves that, like emulsions, they consist of an oily matter divided, diffused and suspended, but not perfectly dissolved, in an aqueous liquor.

It is not surprising that these liquors should resemble emulsions; for they are produced in the same manner, and may very justly be called animal emulsions. For how are vegetable substances converted into chyle and milk in an animal body? They are bruised, divided and triturated by mastication and digestion, as perfectly, at least, as the matters pounded in a mortar to make an emulsion; and must thereby undergo the same changes as those matters; that is, their oily parts, being attenuated by those motions, must be mixed with and lodged between the aqueous parts, but not dissolved therein; because they do not, in the bodies of animals, meet with saline matters, sufficiently disentangled and active, to unite intimately with them, and by that means render them soluble in water.

Nevertheless, chyle and milk, though produced in the same manner as emulsions, and very much resembling them, differ greatly from them in some respects; owing chiefly to the time they remain in the bodies of animals, their being heated while there, the elaborations they undergo therein, and the animal juices commixed with them.

New milk hath a mild agreeable taste, without any saline pungency; nor hath any chemical trial discovered in it either an acid or an alkali. Yet it is certain, that the juices of plants, out of which milk is formed, contain many saline matters, and especially acids: accordingly milk also contains the same; but the acids are so sheathed and combined, that they are not perceptible. The case is the same with all the other liquors intended to constitute part of an animal body: there is no perceptible acid in any of them.

Hence it may be inferred, that one of the principal changes which vegetables undergo, in order to their being converted into an animal substance, consists in this, that their acids are combined, entangled, and sheathed in such a manner, that they become imperceptible, and exert none of their properties.

Milk left to itself, without the help of distillation, or any additament whatever, undergoes a sort of decomposition. It runs into a kind of spontaneous analysis; which doth not indeed reduce it to its first principles, yet separates it into three distinct substances, as the process shews; namely, into cream, or the buttery fat part, into curd or cheese, and into serum or whey: which shews, that those three substances of which milk consists, are only mixed and blended together, but not intimately united.

The first parts, being the lightest rise gradually to the surface of the liquor as they separate from the rest: and this forms the cream

Cream, as skimmed from the surface of milk, is not however the pure buttery or fat part: it is still mixed with many particles of cheese and whey, which must be separated in order to reduce it into butter. The most simple, and at the same time the best method of effecting this, is daily practised by the country people. It consists in beating or churning the cream, in a vessel contrived for that purpose, with the flat side of a circular piece of wood, in the centre of which a staff is fixed. One would think that the motion, impressed on the cream by this instrument, should rather serve to blend more intimately the particles of butter, cheese, and whey, of which it consists, than to separate them from each other; as this motion seems perfectly adapted to divide and attenuate those particles. But, if we consider what passes on this occasion, we shall soon perceive that the motion by which butter is churned is nothing like triture: for churning is no other, properly speaking, than a continually repeated compression, the effect whereof is to squeeze out from amongst the buttery particles those of cheese and whey mixed therewith; by which means the particles of butter are brought into contact with each other, unite and adhere together.

Milk, whether skimmed or no, grows sour of itself and curdles in a few days. When is is newly curdled, the cheese and whey seem to be united, and to make but one mass: but these two matters separate spontaneously from each other, with the greatest ease, and in a very short time.

The acidity, which milk naturally contracts in the space of a few days, must be considered as the effect of a fermenting motion, which discovers in that liquor an acid that was not perceptible before. This, properly speaking, is an acetous fermentation, which milk passes through in its way to putrefaction; and it soon follows, especially if the milk be exposed to a hot air.

If, instead of leaving milk to grow sour and curdle of itself, an acid be mixed therewith, while it is yet sweet and newly milked, it immediately coagulates; which gives reason to think, that its curdling naturally is the effect of the acid, which discovers itself therein as it grows stale.

The coagulation of milk may also be considerably accelerated, by setting it in a sand-bath gently heated; or by mixing therewith a little of what, in the language of the dairy, is called runnet; which is nothing but some curdled and half-digested milk taken from the stomach of a calf: or both these methods may be employed at once, which will produce the effect still more expeditiously.

It is not difficult to find out the cause of these effects. The runnet, which is milk already curdled and grown sour, is an actual ferment to sweet milk, disposing it to turn sour much more readily: for though milk, when thus hastily curdled by the runnet, hath not a manifestly acid taste, yet it is certain that the acid begins to exert itself. The proof thereof is, that, being exposed to the same degree of heat with milk equally new, that is not mixed with this ferment, it turns sour much sooner. As to the effect of heat in coagulating milk, there is nothing extraordinary in it: we know how much it promotes and accelerates all fermentative motions. The whole of this perfectly agrees with what we said before concerning fermentation.

Fixed alkalis also coagulate milk; but at the same time they separate the whey from the cheese, which floats on the liquor in cloats. They give the milk a russet colour inclining to red; which may arise from their attacking the fat part.

The separation of milk into butter, cheese, and whey, is a kind of imperfect analysis thereof, or rather the beginning of one. In order to render it complete, we must examine each of these substances separately, and find the principles of which they consist. This we shall endeavour to do in the following process.

BUTTER ANALYSED BY DISTILLATION. Into a glass retort put the quantity of fresh butter you intend to distil. Set the retort in a reverberatory; apply a receiver; and let your fire be very gentle at first. The butter will melt, and there will come over some drops of clear water, which will have the peculiar smell of fresh butter, and shew some tokens of acidity. If the fire be increased a little, the butter will seem to boil: a froth will gather on its surface, and the phlegm, still continuing to run, will gradually come to smell just like butter clarefied in order to be preserved. Its acidity will be stronger and more manifest than that of the first drops that came over.

Soon after this, by encreasing the fire a little more, there will rise an oil, having nearly the same degree of fluidity as fat oils; but it will grow thicker as the distillation advances, and at last will fix in the receiver when it cools. It will be accompanied with some drops of liquor, the acidity whereof will always increase, while its quantity decreases, as the distillation advances.

While this thick oil is distilling, the butter contained in the retort, which at first seemed to boil, will be calm and smooth, without the least appearance of ebullition; though the heat be then much greater than when it boiled. Continue the distillation, constantly increasing the fire by degrees as you find it necessary for the elevation of the thick oil. This oil, or rather this kind of butter, will be at last of a russet colour. There will rise along with it some white vapours exceeding sharp and pungent.

When you observe that nothing more comes over, though the retort be quite red-hot, let the vessels cool, and unlute them. You will find in the receiver an aqueous acid liquor, a fluid oil, and a kind of fixed brown butter. Break the retort, and you will find therein a kind of charred matter; the surface of which, where it touched the glass, will be of a thining black, and have a fine polish.

The analysis of butter proves, that this substance, which is an oily matter in a concrete form, owes its consistence to the acid only, with which the oily part is combined: that is, it follows the general rule frequently mentioned above in treating of other oily compounds; the consistence whereof we shewed to be so much the firmer, the more acid they contain. The first portions of oil that come over in the distillation of butter are fluid, because a pretty considerable quantity of acid rose before them, which being mixed with the phlegm, gives it the acidity we took notice of.

This oil, being freed from its acid, and by that means rendered fluid, rises first; because it is by the same means rendered lighter. The kind of butter that comes over afterwards, though it be fixed, is nevertheless far from having the same consistence as it had before distillation; because it loses much of its acid in the operation. This acid is what rises in the form of white vapours. These vapours are at least as pungent and irritating as the sulphureous acid or volatile alkalis: but their smell is different: it hath a resemblance, or rather is the same, with that which rises from butter when it is burnt and browned in an open vessel. But when concentrated and collected in close vessels, as in the distillation of butter, they are vastly stronger: they irritate the throat so as to inflame it; they are exceeding sharp and pungent to the smell, and are so hurtful to the eyes that they quickly inflame them, as in an ophthalmy, and make them shed abundance of tear. The great volatility of this acid is entirely owing to a portion of the phlogiston of the butter with which it is still combined.

We took notice in the process, that butter seems to boil with a very moderate heat at the beginning of the distillation, and that in the course of the operation the ebullition ceases entirely, though the heat be then greatly increased; which is contrary to the general rule. The reason is, that butter, though a seemingly homogeneous mass, contains nevertheless some particles of cheese and whey. The particles of whey, being much the lightest, endeavour, on the first application of heat, to extricate themselves from amongst the particles of butter, and to rise in distillation. Thus they form the drops of acidulated phlegm which come over at first, and, in struggling to get free, lift up the buttery parts, or actually boil, which occasions the ebullition observable at the beginning of the process. When they are once separated, the melted butter remains calm and smooth, without boiling. If you want to make it boil, you must apply a much greater degree of heat; which you cannot do in close vessels, without spoiling the whole operation; because the degree of heat necessary for that purpose would force up the butter in substance, which would rush over into the receiver, without any decomposition. Indeed if the vessels were luted, they would be in danger of bursting,

As to the caseous parts, which are mixed with fresh butter, they also separate at the beginning of the distillation when the butter is melted, and gather on its surface in a scum. These particles of cheese and whey, which are heterogeneous to butter, help to make it spoil the sooner. And for this reason, those who want to keep butter a long time, without the use of salt, melt it, and thereby evaporate the aqueous parts. The lightest portion of the particles of cheese rises to the surface, and is skimmed off; the rest remains at the bottom of the vessel, from which the butter is easily separated, by decanting it while it is yet fluid.

Butter may also be distilled, by incorporating it with some additament which will yield no principle itself, nor retain any of those of the butter. It may be distilled in this manner with the additament of fine sand: the operation succeeds very well, is sooner finished, and more easily conducted.

If you desire to convert the butter wholly into oil, you must take the fixed matter you find in the receiver, and distil it once more or oftener, according to the degree of fluidity you want to give it. The case is the same with this matter as with all other thick oils, which, the oftener they are distilled, grow always the more fluid, because in every distillation they are separated from part of the acid, to which alone they owe their consistence.

THE CURD OF MILK ANALYSED BY DISTILLATION. Into a glass retort put some new curd having first drained it thoroughly of all its whey, and even squeezed it in a linen cloth to express all its moisture. Distil it as you did butter. There will come over at first an acidulated phlegm, smelling like cheese or whey. As the distillation advances, the acidity of this phlegm will increase.

When it begins to run but very slowly, raise your fire, There will come over a yellow oil, somewhat empyreumatic. Continue the distillation, still increasing the fire by degrees as occasion requires. The oil and acid phlegm will continue to rise; the phlegm growing gradually more acid, and the oil deeper coloured and more empyreumatic. At last, when the retort is almost red-hot, there comes off a second black oil, of the consistence of turpentine, very empyreumatic, and so heavy as to sink in water. In the retort will be left a considerable quantity of charred matter.

Cheese curd barely drained, till no more whey will drip from it, is not entirely freed thereof; and for this reason we directed it to be pressed in a linen cloth, before it be put into the retort to be distilled. Without this precaution, the remaining whey would rise in a considerable quantity on the first application of heat; and, instead of analysing the curd only, we should at the same time analyse the whey also. This is to be understood of green curd and new-made cheese; for, if it be suffered to grow old, it will at length dry of itself: but then we should not obtain from it the same principles by dis tillation; as it corrupts and begins to grow putrid after some time, especially if it be not mixed with some seasoning to preserve it.

The first-phlegm that rises in this distillation, as in that of butter, is a portion of the whey that was left in the cheese, notwithstanding its being well pressed: This phlegm grows gradually more acid, being the vehicle of the acids of the cheese, which are forced up along with it by the fire.

The acid obtained from this matter is less in quantity, and weaker, than that of butter: and accordingly the oil distilled from cheese is not fixed like that of butter. Yet it is remarkable that the last empyreumatic oil, which is as thick as turpentine, is heavier than water: a property which it probably derives from the quantity of acid it retains.

The quantity of charred matter, which remains in the retort after the distillation of cheese, is much greater than that left by butter; which proves that the former contains a much greater quantity of earth.

WHEY ANALYSED. Evaporate two or three quarts of whey almost to dryness in a balneum marine; and distil the extract or residuum in a retort set in a reverberating furnace, with degrees of fire, according to the general rule. At first some phlegm will come over then a lemon coloured acid spirit; and afterwards a pretty thick oil. There will remain in the retort a charred matter, which being exposed to the air grows moist. Lixiviate it with rain water, and evaporate the lixivium; it will yield you crystals of sea-salt. Dry the charred matter, and burn it in the open air with a strong fire, till it be reduced into ashes. A lixivium of these ashes will shew some tokens of a fixed alkali.

It will appear, on examining the three analyses of the substances whereof milk consists, that none of them yields a volatile alkali which is worthy of notice; as it is the only animal matter from which such a salt cannot be obtained. It is true, the milk of animals that feed on vegetables may be considered as an intermediate liquor between vegetables and animal substances; as an imperfect animal-juice, which still retains much of the vegetable nature: and we actually find, that milk almost always hath, at least in part, the properties of those plants with which the animals that yield it are fed. Yet, as it cannot be formed in the body of the animal, without mixing with several of its juices that are entirely perfected, and become purely animal, it must appear strange that the analysis thereof should not afford the least vestige of that principle which all other animal-matters yield in the greatest plenty.

The reason of this may be found in the use to which milk is destined. It is intended for the nourishment of animals of the same species with those in whose bodies it is produced. Consequently it ought as much as possible to resemble the juices of the food which is proper for those animals. Now, as animals that live only on vegetables could not be properly nourished by animal matters, for which nature itself hath even given them an aversion, it is not surprising that the milk of such animals should be free from any mixture of such things as are unsuitable to the young ones whom it is designed to nourish. There is reason therefore to think, that nature hath disposed the organs in which the secretion of milk is performed, so as to separate it entirely from all the animal juices first mixed with it; and this is the principal difference between milk and chyle; the latter being necessarily blended with the saliva, the gastric and pancreatic juices, the bile and lymph, of the animals in which it is formed. Hence it may be concluded, that, if a quantity of chyle could be collected sufficient to enable us to analyse it, the analysis thereof would differ from that of milk, in this chiefly, that it would yield a great deal of volatile alkali, of which milk, as hath been said, yields none at all.

The same thing probably takes place in carnivorous animals. It is certain, that those animals chuse to eat the flesh of such others only as feed upon vegetables; and that nothing but extreme hunger, and the absolute want of more agreeable food, will force them to eat the flesh of other carnivorous animals. Wolves, which greedily devour sheep, goats, etc. seldom eat foxes, cats, polecats, etc. though these animals are not strong enough to resist them. Foxes, cats, birds of prey, that make such havock among wild-fowl, and other sorts of game, do not devour one another. This being laid down, there is reason to think, that the milk of carnivorous animals is something of the nature of the flesh of those animals that feed on vegetables, and which they chuse to eat, and not of the nature of their own flesh; as the milk of animals that feed on vegetables is analo-gous to the juices of vegetables, and when analysed yields no volatile alkali though every other part of their body does.

But whatever be the nature of milk, and of whatever ingredients it be formed, it al-ways contains the three several substances above mentioned; namely, the fat, or buttery part, properly so called, the cheesy, and the serous part, the last of which we are now to examine. It is, properly speaking, the phlegm of the milk, and consists almost en-tirely of water. For this reason it is proper to lessen the quantity thereof consider-ably by evaporation, so that its other principles, being concentrated and brought nearer together, may become much more sensible. There is no danger of losing any essential part of the whey in the evaporation, if it be performed in the balneum mariae with such a gentle heat as may carry off the aqueous parts only: this greatly shortens the analy-sis, which will be exceeding long and tedious if all the water be distilled off in close vessels.

As whey is chiefly the aqueous part of milk, as said above, it must contain all the principles thereof that are soluble in water; that is, its saline and saponaceous parts. And accordingly the analysis thereof shews that it contains an oil, rendered perfectly saponaceous by an acid; that is, made perfectly miscible with water. This quality of the oil contained in whey appears from the perfect transparency of that liquor, which we know is the mark of a complete dissolution. In the distillation of whey, the saponaceous mat-ter contained therein is decomposed; the saline part rises first, as being the lightest; this is the acid taken notice of in the process; after which the oil, now separated from the principle which rendered it miscible with water, comes over in its natural form, and doth not afterwards mix with the aqueous part.

Besides the saponaceous matter, whey contains also another saline substance; namely, sea-salt: this is obtained by lixiviating the caput mortuum left in the retort, which, because of its fixedness, cannot rise with the other principles in distillation. To this salt it is owing that what remains in the retort after distillation grows moist in the air; for we know that sea-salt thoroughly dried hath this property.

The fixed alkaline salt, obtained from the caput mortuum burnt to ashes, proves that milk still retains something of the vegetable nature: for the following analysis will shew us that matters purely animal yield none at all.

OF THE SUBSTANCES WHICH COMPOSE AN ANIMAL BODY. BLOOD ANALYSED. INSTANCED IN BULL-OCK' BLOOD. In a balneum mariae evaporate all the moisture of the blood that the heat of boiling water will carry off. There will remain an almost dry matter. Put this dried blood into a glass retort, and distil with degrees of heat, till nothing more will come over, even when the retort is quite red-hot, and ready to melt. A brownish phlegm will rise at first: this will soon be impregnated with a little volatile alkali, and then will come over a yellow oil, a very pungent volatile spirit, a volatile salt in a concrete form, which will adhere to the sides of the receiver; and, at last, a black oil, as thick as pitch. There will be left in the retort a charred matter, which being burnt yields no fixed alkali.

Blood, which is carried by the circulation into all the parts of the animal body, and furnishes the matter of all the secretions, must be considered as a liquor consisting of almost all the fluids necessary to the animal machine: so that the analysis thereof is a sort of general though imperfect analysis of an animal.

Blood drawn from the body of an animal, and set by in a vessel, coagulates as it grows cold; and sometimes afterwards the coagulum discharges a yellowish serum of lymph;

and in the midst thereof swims the red part, which continues curdled. These two substances, when analysed, yield nearly the same principles; and in that respect seem to differ little from each other. Though the serum of blood be naturally in a fluid form, yet it hath also a great tendency to coagulate; and a certain degree of heat applied to it, either by water or by a naked fire, will curdle it. Spirit of wine mixed with this liquor produces on it the same effect as heat.

Blood, while circulating in the body of a healthy animal, and when newly taken from it, hath a mild taste, which discovers nothing like either an acid, or an alkali; nor doth it shew any sign of either the one or the other in chemical trials. When tasted with attention, it betrays something like a savour of sea-salt; because it actually contains a little thereof, which is found in the charred matter left in the retort after the distillation, when carefully examined.

We shewed that milk also contains a little of this salt. It enters the bodies of animals with the food they eat which contains more or less thereof according to its nature. It plainly suffers no alteration by undergoing the digestions, and passing through the strainers, of the animal body. The case is the same with the other neutral salts which have a fixed alkali for their basis: we find them unchanged in the juices of animals into whose bodies they have been introduced. They are incapable of combining, as acids do, with the oily parts; and so are dissolved by the aqueous fluids, of which nature makes use to free herself from those salts, and discharge them out of the body.

Blood, like all animal-matters, is, properly speaking, susceptible of no fermentation but that of putrefaction. Yet it turns somewhat sour before it putrefies. This small degree of acetous fermentation is most sensible in flesh; and especially in the flesh of young animals, such as calves, lambs, chickens, etc.

The quantity of pure water, which blood, in its natural state contains, is very considerable, and makes almost seven eighths thereof. If it be distilled, without being first dried, the operation will be much longer; because it will be necessary to draw off all this insipid phlegm with a gentle fire. There is no reason to apprehend that, by drying blood in open vessels as directed, any of its other principles will be carried off with its phlegm: for it contains no other substance that is volatile enough to rise with the warmth of a balneum mariae. This may be proved by putting some undried blood into a glass cucurbit, fitting thereto a head and receiver, and distilling, in a balneum mariae, all that the heat of the bath, not exceeding the heat of boiling water, will raise: for, when nothing more will come over, you will find in the receiver an insipid phlegm only, scarce differing from pure water, except in having a faint smell like that of blood; wherein it resembles all the phlegms that rise first in distillation, which always retain something of the smell of the matters from which they were drawn. That part of the blood, which remains in the cucurbit after this first distillation, being put into a retort, and distilled with a stronger fire, yields exactly the same principles, and in the same proportion, as blood dried in open vessels in the balneum mariae: so that, if this phlegm of blood contains any principles, the quantity thereof is so small as to be scarce perceptible.

The volatile alkali that rises with the oil, when blood is distilled in a retort with a degree of heat greater than that of boiling water, is either the production of the fire, or arises from the decomposition of an ammoniacal salt of which it made a part. For we shall see, when we come to treat of this saline substance, that it is so extremely volatile as to exceed, in that respect, almost all other bodies that we know: and therefore, if this volatile alkali pre-existed formerly in the blood, uncombined with any other matter capable, in some measure, of fixing it, it would rise at first almost spontaneously, or at least on the first application of the gentlest heat. We have an instance of this in blood, or any other animal matter, that is perfectly putrefied; which containing a volatile alkali, either formed or extricated by putrefaction, lets go this principle when distilled, even before the first phlegm: and, for this reason, when putrefied blood is to be analysed, it must by no means be dried, like fresh blood, before distillation; for all the volatile alkali would by that means be dissipated and lost at once.

Though blood and other animal matters afford no fixed alkali, but, on the contrary, yield much volatile alkali, it doth not therefore follow that all the acid, which those substances contained before they were analysed, is employed in the production of a volatile alkali.

FLESH ANALYSED. INSTANCED IN BEEF. Into an alembic or retort, placed in a sand-bath, put some lean beaf from which you have carefully separated all of the fat. Distil till nothing more will rise. In this first distillation a phlegm will come over, weighing at least half the mass of the distilled flesh. In the retort you will find a matter almost dry, which you must afterwards distil with a naked fire in a reverberating furnace, taking the usual precautions. There will come over at first a little phlegm replete with volatile alkali; then a volatile alkali in a dry form, which will stick to the sides of the vessel; and also a thick oil. After the distillation there will be left in the retort a black, shining light coal. Burn it to ashes in the open air, and lixiviate those ashes: the water of the lixivium will have not alkaline property, but will shew some tokens of its containing a little sea-salt.

The flesh of an animal, as appears from the process, yields much of the same principles with its blood: and it cannot be otherwise; because it is formed altogether of materials furnished by the blood.

BONES ANALYSED. INSTANCED IN OX-BONES. Cut into pieces the bones of a leg of beef, carefully separating all the marrow. Put them into a retort, and distil them in a reverberating furnace as usual. A phlegm will come over first; then a volatile spirit, which will become stronger and stronger; afterwards a volatile salt in a dry form, with some oil; and, lastly, a black oil, with a little more volatile salt. There will be left in the retort a charred matter, from which a little sea-salt may be extracted. Reduce this charred matter to ashes, by burning it in the open air. These ashes will give some slight tokens of a fixed alkali.

The analysis of bones proves, that they consist of the same principles with flesh and blood; and the same may be said in general of all matters that are truly animal, that actually constitute any part of an animal.

ANIMAL FAT ANALYSED. INSTANCED IN MUTTON-SUET. Put as much mutton-suet as you please into a glass retort, only taking care that the vessel be but half full; and distil with degrees of fire as usual. A phlegm smelling of the suet will rise first, and soon grow very acid. After this some drops of oil will come over, and be followed by a matter like oil, in appearance, when it comes over; but it will fix in the receiver, and acquire a consistence somewhat softer than the suet. This kind of butter of suet will continue to rise to the end of the distillation; and there will be left in the retort a small quantity of charred matter.

EGGS ANALYSED. INSTANCED IN PULLET'S EGGS. Put some hens eggs in water, and boil them till they be hard. Then separate the yolks from the whites. Cut the whites into little bits; put them into a glass cucurbit; fit on a head and receiver; distil in a balneum mariae with degrees of fire, raising it towards the end to the strongest heat which that bath can give; that is, to the heat of boiling water. There will come over an aqueous liquor, or insipid phlegm; the quantity whereof will be very considerable seeing it will make about nine tenths of the whole mass of the whites of the eggs. Continue your distillation, and keep the water in the bath constantly boiling, till not a drop more of liquor will ascend from the alembic. Then unlute your vessels. In the cucurbit you will find your whites of eggs considerably shrunk in their bulk. They will look like little bits of brown glass, and be hard and brittle.

Put this residuum into a glass retort, and distil, as usual, in a reverberating furnace with degrees of heat. There will come over a volatile oily spirit, a yellow oil, a volatile salt in a dry form, and, at last, a black thick oil. There will be left in the retort a charred matter.

Reduce also into the smallest pieces you can the hard yolks of the eggs which you separated from the whites. Set them in a pan over a gentle fire: stir them with a stick till they turn a little brown; and discharge a substance like melted marrow. Then put them into a new, strong, canvass bag, and press them between two iron plates well heated; whereby you will obtain a considerable quantity of yellow oil.

Let what remains in the bag be distilled in a retort set in a reverberating furnace: and it will give you the same principles as you got from the whites.

Of the two perfectly distinct substances that constitute the egg, the yolk contains the embryo of the chick, and is destined to hatch it: the white is to serve for the nourishment of the chick when it is formed.

These two matters, though they contain the very same principles, yet differ considerably from each other; and chiefly in this, that their principles are not in the same proportions.

The white of an egg contains so much phlegm, that it seems to consist almost totally thereof. All the aqueous liquor, obtained by distilling it in the balneum mariae, is, properly speaking, nothing but pure water; for no chemical trial can discover in it either an acid or a volatile alkali; or any very perceptible oily part. And yet it must contain some oil, because the liquor that rises last is a little bitterish to the taste, and smells somewhat of empyreuma. But the principles from which it derives these properties are in too small quantities to be distinctly perceived.

If, instead of distilling the hard white of an egg, with a view to draw off the great quantity of water it contains, you leave it some time in an air that is not too dry, the greatest part of its moisture separates spontaneously, and becomes very sensible. In all probability this is the effect of a beginning putrefaction, which attenuates this substance, and breaks its contexture. The liquor thus discharged by the white of an egg thoroughly dissolves the gum-resins, and particularly myrrh. If you desire to dissolve myrrh in this manner, cut a hard-boiled egg in halves; take out the yolk; put the powdered gum-resin into the cavity left by the yolk; join the two halves of the white; fasten them together with a thread, and hang them up in the cellar. In a few days time the myrrh will be dissolved by the moisture that issues from the white of the egg, and will drop into the vessel placed underneath to receive it. This liquor is improperly called oil of myrrh per deliquim.

All the properties of the whites of eggs, as well as the principles obtained by analysing them, are the same with those of the lymphatic part of the blood; so that there is a great resemblance between these two substances.

As to the yolk, it is plain from its analysis, that oil is the predominant principle thereof. If the yolk of an egg be mixed with water, the oil with which it is replete, and which is by nature very minutely divided, diffuses easily through the whole liquor, and remains suspended therein by means of its viscosity. The liquor at the same time becomes milk-white like an emulsion, and is in fact a true animal emulsion.

In order to obtain the oil of eggs by expression with the more ease, care must be taken to chuse eggs that are seven or eight days old; because they are then a little less viscous. Nevertheless their viscosity is still so great, that they will not easily yield their oil by expression; and therefore, in order to attenuate and destroy entirely this viscosity, they must be torrefied before they are put to be pressed.

The oil of eggs, like all other oily animal matters, seems analogous to the fat oils of vegetables. It hath all the properties that characterise those oils. Its colour is yellow, and it smells and tastes a little of the empyreuma, occasioned by torrefying the yolks. It is rendered somewhat less disagreeable by being exposed to the dew for thirty or forty nights, if care be taken to stir it often in the meantime.

To conclude all the principles both in the yolk and the white of an egg are the same as those found in blood, flesh, and all other matters that are perfectly animal.

OF THE EXCREMENTS OF ANIMALS. DUNG ANALYSED. INSTANCED IN HUMAN EXCREMENTS. MR. HOMBERG'S PHOSPHORUS. Take any quantity you please of human excrement and distil it in a glass alembic set in the balneum mariae. You will obtain an aqueous, clear, insipid liquor; which will nevertheless have a disagreeable odour. Having urged the distillation as far as is possible with the heat of this bath, unlute your vessels, and you will find at the bottom of the cucurbit a dry matter, making about an eighth part only of what you put into it. Put this residuum into a glass retort, and distil in a reverberating furnace, with degrees of heat. You will obtain a volatile spirit, and a volatile salt, with a fetid oil; and a charred matter will be left in the retort.

This substance, consisting of matters subject to putrefaction, hath constantly a fetid smell, like that of all putrid matters; having been for some time confined in a warm, moist place, which we know promotes putrefaction, and even quickly produces it. Yet the analysis thereof proves that it is not putrefied, or at least not entirely so: for all putrefied matters contain a volatile alkali perfectly formed and extricated; and, as this principle rises with less heat than that of boiling water, it always comes over first in distillation. Now we have seen that, with the heat of boiling water, it parts with nothing but an insipid phlegm, containing no volatile alkali: a sure proof that the fecal matter is not completely putrefied.

One of the methods by which Mr. Homberg endeavoured to obtain from excrement a clear oil, without any bad smell, was to separate its earthy and gross parts, by filtering it before he distilled it. "For this purpose he diluted excrement newly discharged with hot water, using a quart of water to an ounce of feces. Then he let the mixture stand to cool, and the gross parts falling to the bottom, he poured off the water by inclination. This liquor he filtered through brown paper, and evaporated to a pellicle over a gentle fire. There shot in it long crystals of four, five and six sides, which Mr. Homberg thinks may be called the essential salt of excrement. They resemble salt-petre, in some measure, and deflagrate in the fire much like it; with this difference, that their flame is red, and they burn slowly; whereas the flame of salt-petre is white and very vivid: probably, says Mr. Homberg, because there is too much of an oily matter in the one, and less in the other.

"Mr. Homberg distilled this salt in a glass retort with degrees of fire, and at last with a very violent one. At first there came over an aqueous liquor, sharp and acid, which was followed by a brown fetid oil, smelling very strong of empyreuma. This distillation he attempted four several times; and each time the matter in the retort took fire, just when the oil began to come off."

The salt which Mr. Homberg obtained from excrement is very remarkable. Its nitrous character is by no means ambiguous: its deflagrating on live coals convinced Mr. Homberg of its being a true nitre. But its constantly taking fire in the retort, as oft as distilled, is a sure proof that it is a nitrous salt; for nitre only hath the property of thus taking fire in close vessels, and making other combustible matters burn along with it.

The process, by which Mr. Homberg at last obtained from excrement a clear oil without any bad smell, is curious, and worthy of a place here, on account of the views and occasions of reflection which it may open.

"Mr. Homberg having tried in vain, by distilling excrement a great many different ways, to obtain from it such an oil as he wanted, resolved to employ fermentation, the effect whereof is to change the disposition of the principles of mixts. With this view he dried some excrement in the water-bath, and, having pulverised it, poured thereon six times its weight of phlegm that had been separated from it by distillation, and put the whole into a large glass cucurbit, covered with an inverted vessel that fitted exactly into it and was close luted. This vessel he set in a balneum mariae for six weeks keeping up such a gentle heat as would not burn one's hand. After which he uncovered the cucurbit, and having fitted thereto a head and a receiver, distilled off all the aqueous moisture in the balneum mariae with a very gentle heat. It had now lost almost all its bad smell, which was changed into a faint one. It came over somewhat turbid, whereas it was very clear when put into the cucurbit. Mr. Homberg found this water to have a cosmetic virtue: he gave some of it to persons whose complexion, neck, and arms, were quite spoiled, being turned brown, dry, rough, and like a goose skin: they washed with it once a day, and, by continuing the use of this water, yheir skin became very soft and white.

"The dry matter left in the cucurbit after the first distillation, had not the least smell of feces: on the contrary, it had an agreeable aromatic odour; and the vessel in which Mr. Homberg had digested it, being left open in a corner of his laboratory, acquired in time a strong smell of ambergris. It is surprising, as Mr. Homberg justly observes, that digestion alone should change the abominable smell of excrement into an odour as agreeable as that of ambergris.

"This dry matter he powdered coarsely, and put two ounces thereof at once into a glass retort that would hold about a pound or a pound and a half of water. This he distilled in a sand-bath with a very gentle heat. A small quantity of an aqueous liquor came over first, and then an oil as colourless as spring-water. Mr. Homberg continued the same gentle degree of heat till the drops began to come off a little redish; and then he changed the receiver, stopping that which contained the clear oil very close with a cork. Having carried on the distillation with a fire gradually augmented, there came over a considerable quantity of red oil; and there remained in the retort a charred matter which burnt very readily."

The clear oil, without any ill smell, which Mr. Homberg obtained from the fecal matter by this process, was the very thing he was in search of, and which he had been assured would convert mercury into fine fixed silver; yet he ingenuously owns, that, whatever way he applied it he could never produce any change in that metallic substance. We shall now proceed to the other discoveries made by Mr. Homberg on this occasion.

In his attempt to obtain a clear oil from excrement, he distilled it with different additaments, and amongst the rest with vitriol and alum. He found that the matters left in the retort, when he made use of these salts, being exposed to the open air, took fire of themselves; that they kindled combustible matter; in a word, that they were a true phosphorus, of a species different from all then known. Pursuing these first hints, he sought and found the means of preparing this phosphorus by a way much more expeditious, certain, and easy. His process is this.

"Take four ounces of feces newly excreted: mix therewith an equal weight of rock alum coarsely powdered; put the whole into a little iron pan that will hold about a quart of water, and set it over a gentle fire under a chimney. The mixture will melt, and become as liquid as water. Let it boil with a gentle fire, constantly stirring it, breaking it into little crumbs, and scraping off with a spatula whatever sticks to the bottom or sides of the pan, till it be perfectly dry. The pan must from time to time be removed from the fire, that it may not grow red hot: and the matter must be stirred, even while it is off the fire, to prevent too much of it from sticking to the pan. When the matter is perfectly dried, and in little clots, let it cool, and powder it in a metal mortar. Then put it again into the pan, set it over the fire and stir it continually. It will again grow a little moist, and adhere together in clots, which must be continually roasted and bruised till they be perfectly dry; after which they must be suffered to cool, and then be pulverised. This powder must be returned a third time to the pan, set on the fire, roasted, and perfectly dried: after which it must be reduced to a fine powder, and kept in a paper in a dry place. This is the first or preparatory operation.

"Take two or three drams of this powder. Put it into a little matras, the belly of which will hold an ounce, or an ounce and a half of water, and having a neck about six or seven inches long. Order it so that your powder shall take up no more than about a third part of the matras. Stop the neck of the matras slightly with paper: then take a crucible four or five inches deep: in the bottom of the crucible put three or four spoonfulls of sand: set the matras on this sand, and in the middle of the crucible so as not to touch its sides. Then fill up the crucible with sand, so that the belly of the matras may be quite buried therein. This done, place your crucible with the matras in the midst of a little earthen furnace, commonly called a stove, about eight or ten inches wide above, and six inches deep from the mouth to the grate. Round the crucible put lighted coals about half way up, and when it hath stood thus half an hour, fill up with coals to the very top of the crucible. Keep up this fire a full half hour longer, or till you see the inside of the matras begin to be red. Then increase your fire, by raising your coals above the crucible. Continue this strong heat for a full hour, and then let the fire go out.

"At the beginning of this operation dense fumes will rise out of the matras, through the stopple of paper. These fumes issue sometimes in such abundance as to push out the stopple; which you must then replace, and slacken the fire. The fumes cease when the inside of the matras begins to grow red: and then you may increase the fire without any fear of spoiling your operation.

"When the crucible is so cold that it may be safely taken out of the furnace with one's hand, you must gradually draw the matras out of the sand, that it may cool slowly, and then stop it close with a cork.

"If the matter at the bottom of the matras appear to be in powder when shaken, it is a sign the operation hath succeeded: but if it be in a cake, and doth not fall into powder on shaking the matras, it shews that your matter was not sufficiently roasted and dried in the iron pan during the preparatory operation."

Mr. Lemeri hath shewn, that excrement is not the only matter capable of producing this phosphorus with alum; but that, on the contrary, almost all animal and even vegetable matters are fit for this combination; that though Mr. Homberg mixed alum in equal quantities only with the fecal matter, it may be used in a much greater proportion, and, in certain cases, will succeed the better; that according to the nature of the substances to be worked on, the quantity of that salt may be more or less increased; and that whatever is added, more than the dose requisite for each matter, serves only to lessen the virtue of the phosphorus, or even destroys it entirely; that the degree of fire applied must be different according to the nature of those matters; and, lastly, that salts containing exactly the same acid with that of alum, or the acid of those salts separated from its basis and reduced into spirit, do not answer in the present operation: which shews, says Mr. Lemeri, that many sulphureous matters may be substituted for excrement in this operation: but that there are no salts, or very few, if any, that will succeed in the place of alum.

This phosphorus made either by Mr. Homberg's or by Mr. Lemeri's method, shines both by day and by night. Besides emitting light, it takes fire soon after it is exposed to the air, and kindles all combustible matters with which it comes in contact; and this without being rubbed or heated.

Mess. Homberg and Lemeri have given the most probable and the most natural explanation of the cause of the accension and other phenomena of this phosphorus. What they say amounts in short to what follows.

Alum is known to be a neutral salt, consisting of the vitriolic acid and a calcareous earth. When this salt is calcined with the fecal matter, or other substances abounding in oil, the volatile principles of these substances, such as their phlegm, their salts, and their oils, exhale in the same manner as if they were distilled; and there is nothing left in the matras, when those principles are dissipated, but a charred matter, like that which is found in retorts wherein such mixts have been decomposed by distillation.

This remainder therefore is nothing but a mixture of alum and charcoal. No as the acid of this salt, which is the vitriolic, hath a greater affinity with the phlogiston than with any other substance, it will quit its basis to unite with the phlogiston of the coal, and be converted by that union into a sulphur. And this is the very case, of which we have certain proofs in the operation for preparing this phosphorus; for when, after the volatile principles of the oily matter are drawn off, the fire is increased, in order to combine closely together the fixed parts that remain in the matras, that is, the alum and the charred matter, we perceive at the mouth of the matras a small blue sulphureous flame, and a pungent smell of burning sulphur. Nay, when the operation is finished, we find a real sulphur sticking in the neck of the matras; and, while the phosphorus is burning, it hath plainly a strong sulphureous smell. It is therefore certain, that this phosphorus contains an actual sulphur, that is, a matter disposed to take fire with the greatest ease. But though sulphur be very inflammable, it never takes fire of itself, without being either in contact with some matter that is actually ignited, or else being exposed to a considerable degree of heat. Let us see then what may be the cause of its accension, when it is a constituent part of this phosphorus.

We mentioned just now, that the acid of the alum quits its basis, in order to form a sulphur by combining with the phlogiston of the coal. This basis we know to be an earth capable of being converted into lime; and that it is actually converted into quick-lime by the calcination necessary to produce the phosphorus. We know that new made lime hath the property of uniting with water so readily, that it thereby contracts a very great degree of heat. Now when this phosphorus, which is partly constituted of the basis of the alum converted into quick-lime, is exposed to the air, the lime instantly attracts the moisture of which the air is always full, and by this means, probably grows so hot as to fire the sulphur with which it is mixed. Perhaps also the acid of the alum is not totally changed into sulphur: some part thereof may be only half disengaged from its basis, and in that condition be capable of attracting strongly the humidity of the air, of growing very hot likewise by imbibing the moisture, and so of contributing to the accension of the phosphorus.

There is also room to think that all the phlogiston of the charred matter is not employed in the production of sulphur in this phosphorus, but that some part of it remains in the state of a true coal. The black colour of the unkindled phosphorus, and the red sparkles it emits while burning, sufficiently prove this.

HUMAN URINE ANALYSED. Put some human urine into a glass alembic; set it in a water bath, and distil till there remain only about a fortieth part of what you put in; or else evaporate the urine in a pan set in the balneum mariae till it be reduced to the same quantity. With this heat nothing will exhale but an insipid phlegm, smelling however like urine. The residuum will, as the evaporation advances, become of a darker and darker russet and at last acquire an almost black colour. Mingle this residuum with thrice its weight of sand, and distil it in a retort set in a reverberating furnace, with the usual precautions. At first there will come over a little more insipid phlegm like the former. When the matter is almost dry, a volatile spirit will rise. After this spirit, white vapours will appear on increasing the fire; a yellow oily liquor will come off, trickling down in veins; and together with this liquor a concrete volatile salt, which will stick to the sides of the receiver. At last there will come over a deep-coloured fetid oil. In the retort there will remain a saline earthy residuum, which being lixiviated will yield some sea-salt.

OF THE VOLATILE ALKALI. VOLATILE ALKALIS RECTIFIED AND DEPURATED. Mix together the spirit, the volatile salt, the phlegm, and the oil, obtained from any substance whatever. Put the whole into a large wide-mouthed glass body, and thereto fit a head with a large beak. Set this alembic in a water-bath, lute on a receiver, and distil with a very gentle heat. There will ascend a spirit strongly impregnated with volatile alkali, and a volatile salt in a concrete form, which must be kept by itself. Then increase your heat to the degree of boiling water; whereupon there will rise a second volatile spirit, somewhat more ponderous than the former, with a light oil that will swim on its surface, and a little concrete volatile salt. Proceed till nothing more will rise with this degree of heat. Keep by itself what came over into the receiver. At the bottom of the cucurbit you will find a thick fetid oil.

Into such another distilling vessel put the spirit and salt that rose first in this distillation, and distil them in the balneum mariae with a heat still gentler than before. A whiter, purer, volatile salt will sublime. Continue the distillation till an aqueous moisture rise, which will begin to dissolve the salt. At the bottom of the vessel will be left a phlegm, with a little oil floating on it. Keep your salt in a bottle well stopped.

VOLATILE ALKALIS COMBINED WITH ACIDS. SUNDRY AMMONIACAL SALTS. SAL AMMONIAC. On a volatile spirit or salt pour gradually any acid whatever. An effervescence will arise, and be more or less violent according to the nature of the acid. Go on adding more acid in the same manner, till no effervescence be thereby excited, or at least till it be very small. The liquor will now contain a semi-volatile neutral salt, called an ammoniacal salt; which may be obtained in a dry form by crystallising as usual, or by subliming it in close vessels, after the superfluous moisture hath been drawn off.

Volatile alkalis have the same properties with fixed alkalis, fixity only excepted: so that a volatile alkali must produce an effervescence when mixed with acids, and form therewith neutral salts, differing from each other in nothing but the nature of the acid in their composition.

It must be observed, that the point of saturation is very difficult to hit on this occasion; owing probably to the volatility of the alkali, which, being much lighter than the acid, tends always to possess the uppermost part of the mixture, while the acid sinks to the bottom: whence it comes to pass, that the lower part of the liquor is sometimes overcharged with acid, while the upper part is still very alkaline. But it is most eligible that the alkali should predominate in the mixture; because the excess of this principle easily flies off while the moisture is evaporating in order to crystallisation or sublimation of the ammoniacal salt; which being only semi-volatile, resists the heat longer, and remains perfectly neutral.

If the vitriolic acid be combined with a volatile alkali, and the mixture distilled in a retort to draw of the superfluous moisture, a liquor comes over into the receiver which smells strong of a sulphureous acid. Now, as the acid of vitriol never becomes sulphureous, but when it is combined with an inflammable matter, this experiment is one of those which demonstrate that volatile alkalis contain a very sensible quantity of inflammable matter. This same liquor tastes of an ammoniacal salt; which proves that it carries up with it some of the neutral salt contined in the mixture. The rest of this salt, which is called Glauber's secret sal ammoniac, or vitriolic sal ammoniac, sublimes into the neck of the retort. It is very pungent on the tongue; it crackles a little when thrown on a red-hot shovel, and then flies off in vapours.

The ammoniacal salt formed by the acid of nitre exhibits much the same phenomena; but it requires greater care in drying and subliming it, because it hath the property of detonating all alone, without the addition of any other inflammable matter: and it will infallibly do so, if too strong a fire be applied towards the end of the operation, when it begins to be very dry. This property of detonating by itself it derives from the inflammable matter contained in the volatile alkali which serves for its basis: and this is another demonstrative proof of the existence of such an inflammable matter in the volatile alkali. This salt is called nitrous ammoniacal salt.

With the vegetable acids, that of vinegar for instance, is formed an ammoniacal salt of a singular nature, and which can scarce be brought to a dry form.

A volatile alkali, combined to the point of saturation with the acid of sea-salt, forms another neutral salt, which takes a concrete form either by sublimation or crystallisation. The crystals of this salt are so very soft and fine, that a parcel of it looks like cotton or wool. This is the salt properly called sal ammoniac. It is of great use in chemistry and in manufactures, but that which is daily consumed in great quantities is not made in the manner above mentioned. It would come extremely dear, if we had no other way of procuring it, but by forming it thus with the acid of sea-salt and a volatile alkali. This salt, or at least the materials of which it is formed, may be found in the fuliginosities and soots of most animal, and of some vegetable substances. The greatest part of what we use comes from Egypt, where vast quantities thereof are made.

The method of preparing sal ammoniac in Egypt was not known among us till Mess. Lemaire and Granger. Their memoirs inform us, that chimney-soot alone, without any addiment, is the matter from which they obtain their sal ammoniac; that those chimneys under which nothing is burnt but cow's-dung, furnish the best soot. Six and twenty pounds of that soot yield usually six pounds of sal ammoniac.

"The operation takes up about fifty, or two and fifty hours. The vessels in which they put the soot are ballons of very thin glass, terminating in a neck of fifteen or sixteen lines long, and an inch in diameter: but they are not all of the same size. The least contain twelve pounds of soot, and the greatest fifty; but they fill them only three quarters full, in order to leave room for the sublimation of the salt.

"The furnace, in which they place these ballons, consists of four walls built in a quadrangular form. The two front walls are ten, and the sides nine foot long: but they are all five foot high, and ten inches thick. Within the quadrangle formed by these walls, three arches run lengthwise from end to end thereof, at the distance of ten inches asunder. The mouth of this furnace is in the middle of one of its fronts, and of an oval form; two foot four inches high, and sixteen inches wide.

"The ballons lie in the spaces between the arches of the furnace, which serve instead of a grate to support them. Four of them are usually placed in each interval; which makes sixteen for one furnace. They are secured in their places with brick and earth. But they leave about four inches on the upper part of the ballon uncovered, with a view to promote the sublimation, as they also do six inches of the inferior part, that the heat may the better act on the matters to be sublimed. Things being thus prepared, they first make a fire with straw, which they continue for an hour. Afterwards they throw in cow's dung made up in square cakes like bricks. (The want of wood in this country is the reason that they generally make use of this fuel.) These cakes of dung add to the violence of the fire, which they continue in this manner for nineteen hours; after which they increase it considerably for fifteen hours more; and then they slacken it by little and little.

"When the matter contained in the vessels begins to grow hot, that is, after six or seven hours baking, it emits a very thick and ill-scented smoke, which continues for fifteen hours. Four hours after that, the sal ammoniac is observed to rise in white flowers, which adhere to the inside of the neck of the vessel; and those who have the direction of the operation take care from time to time to pass an iron rod into the neck of the ballon, in order to preserve a passage through the saline vault, for giving vent to some bluish vapours, which constantly issue out of the vessel during the whole operation."

From this history of the preparation of sal ammoniac it appears that soot, and particularly the soot of animal matters, either contains abundance of this salt perfectly formed, and waiting only for sublimation to separate it therefrom, or at least that it contains the proper materials for forming it; and that during the operation, which is a kind of distillation of soot, these materials combine together and sublime.

We shewed, in our analysis of soot, that this substance yields by distillation a great deal of volatile alkali; and this is an ingredient which makes at least one half of sal ammoniac. As to the other principle of this salt, the marine acid, this also must need exist in soot: but it is not so easy to conceive how it should come there.

It is very true that vegetable and animal substances, the only ones that produce soot in burning, contain some portion of sea-salt: but then this salt is very fixed, and seems unfit to rise with the acid, the oil, and the subtile earth, of which the volatile alkali is formed. Therefore we must suppose either that its elevation is procured by the force of the fire, aided by the volatility of the matters that exhale in burning; or that, being decomposed by the violence of the combination, its acid alone rises with the other principles above mentioned. The latter seems probable enough: for though in the common operations of chemistry the bare force of fire doth not seem sufficient to decompose sea-salt; yet the example of sea-plants, which, before burning, contains this salt

salt in abundance, and whose ashes contain scarce any at all, but are replete with its fixed part, that is, with its alkaline basis, seems to prove, that, when this salt is intimately mixed with inflammable matters, it may be destroyed by burning; so that its acid shall desert its basis, and fly off with the soot.

Before the exact method of procuring sal ammoniac was known, it was generally imagined that the manufacturers mixed sea-salt, and even urine, with the soot; because these two substances contain the principles of which this salt consists. But, besides that the contrary now certainly appears from the above mentioned memoirs, it hath been shewn by Mr. Duhamel, who hath published several memoirs and experiments concerning the composition and decomposition of sal ammoniac, from which we have partly taken what we have already said on this subject; it hath been shewn, in the first of these memoirs, that the addition of sea-salt to the soot, from which sal ammoniac is to be extracted, contributes nothing to its production, and cannot increase its quantity. That alone, therefore, which was originally contained in the matters that produced the soot, enters as a principle into the composition of sal ammoniac.

Sal ammoniac is sometimes found perfectly formed in the neighborhood of volcanos. This salt is probably produced from the fuligionosities of vegetable or animal matter consumed by the fire of the volcano.

Sal ammoniac is often impure, because it carries up with it, in sublimation, some of the black charred matter which ought to be left at the bottom of the vessel: but it is easily purified. For this purpose you need only dissolve it in water, filter the solution, then evaporate and crystallize; by which means you will have a very white and very pure sal ammoniac. You may if you please, sublime it again in a cucurbit and blind head, with a fire not too brisk. Some of it will rise in the form of a light white powder, called flowers of sal ammoniac. These flowers are no other than true sal ammoniac, which hath suffered no decomposition; because the bare action of fire is not capable of separating the acid and the volatile alkali, of which this neutral salt consists. When you intend to decompose it, you must use the means to be mentioned hereafter.

Though sal Ammoniac be only semi-volatile, and requires a considerable heat to sublime it, yet it hath the property of carrying up with it matters that are very fixed and ponderous; such as metallic substances, and some kinds of earths. For medicinal uses we sublime therewith iron, lapis haematites, the copper in blue vitriol, etc. and then it takes different names as martial flowers of sal ammoniac, ens veneris, and other such denominations, which it borrows from the matters sublimed with it.

SAL AMMONIAC DECOMPOUNDED BY ACIDS. Into a large tabulated retort put a small quantity of sal ammoniac in powder; set your retort in a furnace, and lute on a large ballon, as in the distillation of the smoking acids of nitre amd sea-salt. Through the hole in your retort pour a quantity of oil of vitriol or spirit of nitre equal in weight to your sal ammoniac. An efervescence will instantly follow. The mixture will swell, and discharge white vapours which will come over into the receiver. Stop the whole in the retort immediately, and let the first vapours pass over, together with some drops of liquor, which will distil without fire. Then put a few coals into the furnace, and continue the distillation with a very gentle heat; which however must be increased little by little till nothing more will come over. When the operation is finished, you will find in the receiver a spirit of salt if you made use of oil of vitriol or an aqua regis, if the spirit of nitre was employed: and in the retort will be left a saline mass, which will be either a glauber's secret sal ammoniac, or a nitrous sal ammoniac, according to the nature of the acid used to decompound the sal ammoniac.

SAL AMMONIAC DECOMPOUNDED BY FIXED ALKALIS. VOLATILE SALT. THE FEBRIFUGE OF SYLVIUS. Into a glass alembic or retort put sal ammoniac and salt of tartar pulverised and mixed together in equal quantities. Set your vessel in a proper furnace, and immediately lute on a large receiver. A little volatile spirit will ascend; and a volatile alkali, in a concrete form, very white and beautiful will sublime into the head, and come over into the receiver, in quantity near two thirds or three fourths of the sal ammoniac used. Continue the distillation, increasing the fire by degrees till nothing more will sublime. Then unlute the vessels. Put up your volatile salt immediately into a wide mouthed bottle and stop it close with a crystal stopple. At the bottom of the retort or cucurbit you will find a saline mass, which, being dissolved and crystallised, will form a salt nearly cubical having the taste and other properties of sea-salt. This is the sal febrifugum silvii.

SAL AMMONIAC DECOMPOUNDED BY ABSORBENT EARTHS AND LIME. FIXED SAL AMMONIAC. Let one part of sal ammoniac and three parts of lime slaked in the air be pulverised separately. and expeditiously mixed together. Put this mixture immediately into a glass retort, so, large that half of it may remain empty. Apply thereto a capacious receiver, with a small hole in it to give vent to the vapours, if needed. Let your retort stand in the furnace about a quarter of an hour, without any fire under it. While it stands thus, a great quantity of invisible vapours will rise, condense into drops, and form liquor in the receiver. Then put two or three live coals in your furnace, and gradually increase the fire till no more liquor will rise. Now unlute your vessles, taking all possible care to avoid the vapours, and quickly pour the liquor out of the receiver into a bottle, which you must stop with a crystal stopple, rubbed with emery. There will remain, at the bottom of the retort, a white mass, consisting of the lime employed in the distillation, together with the acid of the sal ammoniac: this is called fixed sal ammoniac.

VOLATILE ALKALIS COMBINED WITH OILY MATTERS. A VOLATILE OILY AROMATIC SALT. Pulverise and mix together equal parts of sal ammoniac and salt of tartar: put the mixture into a glass or stone cucurbit: pour on it good spirit of wine till it rise half an inch above the matter. Mix the whole with a wooden spatula; apply a head and a receiver, and distil in a sand-bath, gently heated, for two or three hours. A volatile salt will rise into the head; and then the spirit of wine will distil into the receiver, carrying with it a portion of the volatile salt.

When nothing more will come over, let your vessels cool; then unlute them, separate the volatile salt, and weigh it directly. Return it into a glass cucurbit, and for every ounce thereof add a dram and a half of essential oil, drawn from one or more sorts of aromatic plants. Stir the whole with a wooden spatula, that the essence may incorporate thoroughly with the volatile salt. Cover the cucurbit with a head, fit on a receiver, and, having luted it exactly, distil in a sand-bath, as before with a very gentle heat. All the volatile salt will rise, and stick to the head. Let the fire go out, and when the vessels are cooled take your salt out of the head. It will have an odour compounded of its own proper smell, and the smell of the essence with which it is combined. This is an aromatic oily salt. Put it into a bottle stopped close with a crystal stopple.

CPSIA information can be obtained
at www.ICGtesting.com
Printed in the USA
BVHW010939110419
545261BV00012B/56/P